European Banking

European Banking

Efficiency, Technology and Growth

John A. Goddard, Philip Molyneux and John O.S. Wilson

JOHN WILEY & SONS, LTD

Chichester • New York • Weinheim • Brisbane • Singapore • Toronto

Copyright © 2001 by John Wiley & Sons, Ltd,
Baffins Lane, Chichester,
West Sussex PO19 1UD, England

National   01243 779777
International   (+44) 1243 779777
e-mail (for orders and customer service enquiries):
cs-books@wiley.co.uk
Visit our Home Page on http://www.wiley.co.uk

Other Wiley Editorial Offices

John Wiley & Sons, Inc., 605 Third Avenue,
New York, NY 10158-0012, USA

Wiley-VCH Verlag GmbH, Pappelallee 3,
D-69469 Weinheim, Germany

John Wiley & Sons Australia, Ltd, 33 Park Road, Milton,
Queensland 4064, Australia

John Wiley & Sons (Asia) Pte Ltd, 2 Clementi Loop #02-01,
Jin Xing Distripark, Singapore 129809

John Wiley & Sons (Canada) Ltd, 22 Worcester Road,
Rexdale, Ontario M9W 1L1, Canada

Library of Congress Cataloging in Publication Data

Goddard, John A.
    European banking : efficiency, technology, and growth / by John A. Goddard, Philip Molyneux, and John O.S. Wilson.
        p. cm.
    Includes bibliographical references and index.
    ISBN 0-471-49449-6 (cloth)
    1. Banks and banking—Europe.   2. Banks and banking—Europe—Cost effectiveness.
I. Molyneux, Philip.   II. Wilson, John O.S.   III. Title.

HG2974 .G63 2001
332.1'094—dc21

                                                                  00–068631

British Library Cataloguing in Publication Data

A catalogue record for this book is available from the British Library

ISBN 0-471-49449-6

Typeset in 11/13pt TimesTen by Dorwyn Ltd, Rowlands Castle, Hants
Printed and bound in Great Britain by Biddles Ltd, Guildford and King's Lynn

This book is printed on acid-free paper responsibly manufactured from sustainable forestry, in which at least two trees are planted for each one used for paper production.

For Les and Chris   JAG

For Delyth, Lois, Rhiannon, Gethin and Gareth   PM

For Alison and Jean   JOSW

Contents

Acknowledgements

A number of acknowledgements are in order. Thanks are due to staff at the Institute of European Finance, University of Wales, Bangor for their excellent library support and other information services. Thanks are also due to IBCA for access to the Bank-Scope database, without which the empirical work reported in this book could not have been completed. Thanks are due to a number of staff at John Wiley and Sons, who have provided support and encouragement at all stages as the project has progressed. We are particularly indebted to Sally Smith (Commissioning Editor), Juliet Booker (Production Controller), Ben Earl (Editorial Assistant) and Colette Holden (Copy Editor). Thanks are also due to Jackie Butterly for indexing. Finally, we are indebted to a number of colleagues at Bangor and elsewhere for invaluable discussions on methodological and other issues. Particular thanks are due to Yener Altunbas, Barbara Casu, Shanti Chakravarty, Ted Gardener, John Lipczynski, Donal McKillop and Jonathan Williams. The usual disclaimer applies.

Tables

Figures

Chapter 1

Introduction

European banking has experienced fundamental changes over the last decade. As a result of structural deregulation and conduct re-regulation, banks now compete in previously inaccessible domestic and foreign markets. The erosion of lines of demarcation between the various types of financial services has caused the distinctions between different types of banks (and other financial sector institutions) to become blurred, creating greater homogeneity between the services and products offered. In addition, technological developments have transformed the possibilities for economies of scale and scope. A trend towards internationalisation means that there has been greater involvement of foreign banks than ever before, leading to intensified competition and reduced profit margins in many European national banking sectors.

In response to these pressures, banks have attempted to adopt strategies aimed at improving efficiency, in order to expand output and increase the range of services offered. The trend towards consolidation through merger and acquisition activity can be interpreted as a response of this kind (Morgan Stanley Dean Witter, 1997). A major motivation has been to realise potential scale and scope economies, and also to reduce labour and other costs in an attempt to eliminate inefficiencies. Many banks have also pursued strategies of diversification and financial innovation. The outcome is that banks now offer a wider range of products and services, and conduct much of their business off balance sheet. The pursuit of financial innovation has also led to the introduction of sophisticated financial instruments, including swaps and options.

The outcome of these changes has been increasing competition, accompanied by increases in concentration through a process of consolidation. Many banks have been forced to increase in size, either through mergers or through internally generated growth, in order to compete on a Europe-wide basis. This process has been encouraged by the existence of excess capacity in many banking sectors, and can be viewed as an unforeseen result of deregulation. Growth for its own sake, however, is certainly not the sole objective for banks. According to Llewellyn (1995, p. 18), 'Overall, the rate of return on equity rather than balance sheet size growth is likely to become the dominant business objective, and this could significantly affect the internal culture of banks.'

The academic literature on banking acknowledges the importance of concentration in determining bank performance (Berger, 1995; Rhoades, 1997). Waterson (1993) notes that there has been a revival of interest in analysing the determinants of concentration, as researchers have sought to explain why industries dominated by a few large firms tend to evolve. Traditional industrial organisation literature suggests that factors including economies of scale, entry and exit barriers, merger and acquisition activity, changes in technology, government regulation, and various kinds of price and non-price strategies adopted by incumbents can all create advantages for larger firms, allowing them to become increasingly dominant over time. Applied specifically to banking, this view suggests that large banks are likely to gain a competitive advantage as a result of superior efficiency, or by exercising market power. An alternative view suggests that size does not necessarily affect a bank's growth prospects. High levels of concentration and skewed firm size distributions may still tend to emerge over time, purely as the cumulative effect of a series of 'shocks' that act on individual bank sizes in an essentially random manner. Stochastic models of random growth processes are capable of generating theoretical firm size distributions that include a few large banks and a long tail of smaller banks, and that seem to correspond closely to the structures observed empirically in many 'real world' banking sectors. Following the seminal contribution of Gibrat (1931), this view of the growth process has become known as the law of proportionate effect (LPE).

Given the limited attention that has been paid to the determinants of concentration in banking, and to the relationship between the size and growth of banks, this book attempts to contribute towards filling the void. The objective is to study both systematic and nonsystematic influences on bank growth, and thus structural change, in the European banking industry. In particular, even if growth is nonsystematic and the LPE provides an appropriate description of the pattern of growth in the European banking sector, banking will naturally tend to become more highly concentrated over time. Factors such as technological change, economies of scale and scope and other efficiency advantages for large banks, the integration of national financial markets within Europe, and the trend towards consolidation appear likely to accelerate this tendency towards increased concentration.

We provide below a brief overview of the structure of this book, by summarising the scope and contents of each chapter. Chapter 2 describes a number of recent trends affecting the structure and performance of the banking industry in Europe. Evidence is presented highlighting trends in the number of banks and branches, changes in average interest margins and the composition of banking business, and trends in costs, profitability and efficiency. Three specific and related aspects of structural change in European banking are also discussed: the intensification of competition in financial services; the trend towards consolidation throughout banking and financial services; and the impact of European Monetary Union (EMU) on the banking and financial sectors.

Market structure is important in determining the conduct and performance of firms, which in turn are instrumental in shaping the future evolution of the industry concerned. Chapter 3 provides a selective review of topics in the field of industrial organisation that are most relevant to the economic analyses of the banking industry contained elsewhere in this book. The chapter begins by outlining the early development of the neoclassical theory of the firm. The usefulness of the structure–conduct–performance (SCP) paradigm, which dominated early empirical research in industrial organisation, is then discussed. The role of factors such as economies of scale, barriers to entry and exit, internally generated growth, innovation, merger and acquisition, and strategic decisions by incumbent firms in determining market structure and the size distribution of firms are also considered.

Chapter 4 provides a general review of the economic analysis of the banking sector, drawing on many of the ideas and techniques developed by industrial organisation researchers. A topic that received particular attention from early banking researchers was the question of the most appropriate explanation for any positive relationship between concentration and profitability observed in banking markets. A related theme involves investigation of the sources of efficiency and inefficiencies within the banking firm. The chapter also considers the nature of barriers to entry and exit in banking, and the extent to which banking markets are contestable. Following a structure similar to that of the previous chapter, determinants of market structure and concentration in banking are then considered. These include economies of scale, technological change over the long term, merger and acquisition activity, the strategic behaviour of incumbent banks, and government regulation.

The main objective of Chapter 5 is to provide a more detailed analysis of efficiency issues in the banking sector. Academic studies of efficiency in banking have tended to proliferate during the 1990s. This chapter provides an introduction and guide to the banking efficiency literature. In the process, it evaluates the available evidence on the sources of economies of scale and scope, and the presence of x-inefficiencies in banking. The implications for the performance of banks and the evolution of the banking industry are considered, along with some limitations that may affect the interpretation of previous empirical research in this area.

Chapter 6 investigates the impact of technological change on the structure, operations and economics of European banking markets. Naturally, developments in information collection, storage, processing, transmission and distribution technologies have a major impact on many aspects of banking activity. In general, developments in information technology affect banking by reducing the costs associated with the collection, storage, processing and transmission of information, and by transforming the ways in which customers can gain access to banks' services and products. Technological developments in delivery systems, such as the growth in use of automated teller machines (ATMs), electronic funds transfer at the point of sale (EFTPOS), telephone banking, Internet banking and e-money are discussed. In addition, the substantial changes to banks' own internal systems, such as in the development of customer relationship management systems, business management technologies, core processing technologies and various support and integration technologies, are also covered. The chapter concludes by reviewing a number of academic studies that investigate the long-term impact of technological change on the cost structure of the banking industry.

Chapter 7 reviews previous empirical literature on the firm size–growth relationship in manufacturing and banking. This topic is covered in some detail, as it provides the background to the investigation of the suitability of the LPE as a descriptor of the firm growth process in European banking that is the subject of subsequent chapters. Previous empirical evidence across a range of different industries and countries suggests that many observed firm size distributions are consistent with the type of growth pattern described by the LPE. The empirical evidence is not entirely consistent, however, suggesting that sample selection criteria or the choice of time period may have affected the results in some cases. In contrast to the situation with manufacturing, the quantity of evidence relating specifically to banking, especially outside the USA, is rather limited. The subsequent chapters of this volume represent an attempt to address this situation.

Chapter 8 uses simulation methods to investigate the properties of a stochastic growth model of the evolution over time of the size distribution of a group of banks. Stochastic simulation uses randomly generated numbers to explore a model's underlying properties. The construction of a simulation model for a constant population of banks is described, and the implications for the size distributions of banks of various combinations of parameter values are explored. The exercise is carried out for a 'closed' population of banks, and for an 'open' model in which the population of incumbents can be supplemented or depleted by entry, exit or merger. The technical analysis is entirely theoretical: all

simulations refer to a hypothetical population of banks. Some
empirical content is provided in the following chapter.

Chapter 9 presents some new empirical results of tests of the
LPE, using data on seven European banking sectors (Belgium,
Denmark, France, Germany, Italy, Spain and the UK) covering
the period 1990–96. Various methodological approaches to testing
the LPE, and their relationship to the tests for convergence and
divergence in the sizes of a cohort of economic units employed
elsewhere in the economics literature, are considered. The data
set for the empirical tests of the LPE is obtained from the International Bank Credit Agency's (IBCA) BankScope database, and
comprises 551 banks. As well as evaluating the LPE using conventional (assets and equity) size measures, tests are also applied to
growth in off-balance-sheet business, one of the most dynamic
and rapidly expanding forms of banking business in the 1990s. On
the whole, the results suggest that there is little reason to reject
the LPE for conventional assets and equity size measures. There
is rather stronger evidence against the LPE for off-balance-sheet
business, however. Chapter 9 finishes by drawing some overall
conclusions from the analysis in this book.

Chapter 2

Current developments in European banking

INTRODUCTION

Chapter 2 describes a number of recent trends affecting the structure and performance of the banking industry in Europe. In the first section, the analysis is mainly quantitative. A number of tabulations of banking sector data are presented, which highlight the impact of several of the most important developments on the number of banks and branches, trends in interest margins and the composition of banking business, and trends in costs, profitability and efficiency. Subsequent sections then go on to describe three specific and related aspects of structural change in European banking: intensification of competition in financial services; the trend towards consolidation in banking and financial services; and the impact of EMU on the banking and financial sector. Chapter 2 provides the background to the more detailed economic analyses of various aspects of European banking presented in subsequent chapters of this volume.

TRENDS IN THE STRUCTURE AND PERFORMANCE OF EUROPEAN BANKING

A trend common to many European banking markets over the last decade or so has been the fall in bank numbers. This trend is apparent across different types of banks, including mutual savings and co-operative banks, as well as domestic commercial banks. Nevertheless, there still remains a large number of banks operating in Europe as illustrated in Table 2.1. All countries (apart from Portugal) have experienced a decline in the number of banks since 1989. What Table 2.1 does not reveal, however, is that the number of foreign banks has increased in every banking market over the same period, reflecting the internationalisation trend and the opportunities afforded by the European Union's (EU) Single Market Programme (see European Commission, 1997; and De Bandt, 1999). Foreign banks constitute a significant proportion of banking sector assets in the UK (254 foreign banks with a 57% assets share in 1998), Belgium (eight banks with 48% of banking sector assets), France (280 banks with around 15% of banking sector assets), and Portugal (16 banks with 35% of banking sector assets). In all other European countries (except for Luxembourg), foreign banks generally account for less than 10% of total banking sector assets.

Table 2.1 Number of banks by country, 1984–97

Country	1984	1989	1992	1994	1996	1997
Austria	1257	1240	1104	1053	1019	995
Belgium	165	157	157	147	141	134
Denmark	231	233	210	202	197	197
Finland	644	552	365	356	350	350
France	358	418	617	607	570	519
Germany	3025	4089	4200	3872	3674	3578
Italy	1137	1127	1073	1002	937	935
Netherlands	2079	1058	921	744	658	628
Norway	248	179	158	153	153	154
Portugal	18	29	35	44	51	62
Spain	369	333	319	316	313	307
Sweden	176	144	119	125	124	120
Switzerland	581	631	569	494	403	398
UK	598	551	518	486	478	466

Source: Central bank reports (various)

Typically, the nationality of foreign banks operating in different countries varies enormously. In London, for example, continental European banks predominate, followed by US and Japanese banks. These are primarily investment banking/asset management/wholesale subsidiaries doing eurocurrency business, and under 10% of their business is sterling based. They play only a marginal role in domestic retail and corporate banking. The majority of foreign banks tend to perform similar functions in Europe's other main financial centres: Frankfurt, Paris, Amsterdam and Zurich. Typically, the top US investment and commercial banks have a presence in every European country, but only Citibank is involved to any significant degree in retail banking, targeted mainly at high-net-worth clients. UK banks have an almost nonexistent presence in continental banking markets, significantly reducing their minor operations in the early 1990s because of poor performance. The only places where foreign banks are involved strongly in domestic banking activities are Belgium, the Netherlands, Portugal and Scandinavia. Recent cross-border deals reflect the fact that within Europe, big banks in small, highly concentrated systems are increasingly viewing expansion in contiguous geographical markets, especially as domestic alternatives are very limited. Recent cross-border deals include the Dutch bank ING's acquisition of the Belgian Banque Bruxelles Lambert (BBL), and the merger between Finland's Merita and Nordbanken from Sweden. The ING/BBL deal reflects the ability of a much larger, well-capitalised bank to acquire banks operating in markets that are familiar to them. The Nordbanken/Merita deal, between medium-sized operators, is generally regarded as defensive: affording protection from unfriendly foreign or domestic acquirers.

Despite the recent merger wave, however, Table 2.1 still indicates that in most European banking markets, there is a large number of domestic and foreign banks serving the needs of domestic clients.

The widespread decline during the 1990s in the number of banks operating in Europe, however, has not been mirrored by a similar trend in branch numbers, as shown in Table 2.2. In fact, in many of the larger banking sectors (Germany, Italy and Spain), branch numbers proliferated during the 1990s. In the latter two cases, this has mainly been the result of the removal of branching/ territorial restrictions that were in place up to the late 1980s or early 1990s. In Germany, the increase in branch numbers has mainly been a result of unification, as well as the expansion of the savings bank sector, reflecting increased non-price competition. In Belgium, Finland, Norway, Sweden, Switzerland and the UK, there has been a decline in branch numbers. The fall in branches in Scandinavian countries is mainly a consequence of the consolidation and restructuring of their systems resulting from the banking crises of 1991–92. Only in the cases of Belgium, Switzerland and the UK can it be attributed mainly to the domestic consolidation processes. In the case of Switzerland, the 1998 merger between Union Bank of Switzerland and Swiss Bank Corporation created a bank with 555 domestic branches; this number, however, is expected to shrink by up to 20% by 2001.

Table 2.2   Number of bank branches, 1984–97

Country	1984	1989	1992	1994	1996	1997
Austria	4005	4378	4667	4683	4694	4691
Belgium	23 502	19 211	16 405	17 040	10 441	7358
Denmark	3515	3182	2358	2245	2138	2480
Finland	2886	3528	3087	2151	1785	1745
France	25 490	25 634	25 479	25 389	25 434	25 464
Germany	35 752	39 651	39 295	48 721	47 741	48 136
Italy	13 045	15 683	20 914	23 120	24 406	25 250
Netherlands	5475	8006	7518	7269	7219	7071
Norway	1940	1796	1593	1552	1503	1500
Portugal	1469	1741	2852	3401	3842	4645
Spain	31 876	34 511	35 476	35 591	37 079	37 634
Sweden	3083	3302	2910	2998	2527	2505
Switzerland	3874	4245	4169	3821	3543	3487
UK	21 853	20 419	18 218	17 362	16 192	15 253

Source: Central bank reports (various).

In general terms, Table 2.2 indicates that European banking markets are characterised by a relatively large number of domestic banks, which, in some cases, expanded their branching presence during the 1990s. So, while consolidation has undoubtedly been taking place in each banking sector, the trend in branch numbers suggests that access to banking services in a range of countries, notwithstanding the introduction of new delivery systems such as telephone- and Internet-based operations, has not been dramatically reduced. While access to bank branches in most countries does not appear to have been significantly adversely affected by consolidation and market restructuring during the 1990s, the fall in the number of banks and increased market concentration may have adversely affected customer choice, De Bandt (1999), for example, shows that in every EU country between 1985 and 1997, apart from France, Greece and Luxembourg, the five-firm assets concentration ratio increased.

Overall, European banking markets are (in most cases) characterised by a declining number of banks. Most banking sectors have a large number of small local and regional banks, however, with substantial branch operations serving, together with the main commercial banks and specialist lenders, a wide range of banking customers. Market concentration is increasing, and in the smaller banking sectors the five-firm assets ratio typically exceeds 60%. While the decline in the number of banks and increased market concentration may suggest that banking service choice is declining, the growth in branch numbers in many countries may, in fact, counter this trend. In addition, increasing foreign bank presence, as well as the growth of nontraditional banking service providers, such as retailers, asset-backed financing firms (leasing and factoring companies), consumer finance companies and so on, make it difficult to state categorically that overall customer choice is declining.

A stronger indication that consolidation and the overall fall in the number of banks has not adversely affected competitive conditions in European banking is reflected perhaps in the decline in net interest margins in virtually every banking sector, as shown in Table 2.3.

While margins obviously vary with the interest cycle, and there has been a convergence of money market rates to a lower level during the 1990s (especially in countries aiming to achieve the criteria for membership of the EMU), the overall trend is downward. As net interest margins have been subjected to increasing competitive pressures, resulting, generally, in a depression of earnings streams relative to cost, banks have focused increasingly on achieving growth from other non-interest income sources of

Table 2.3   Net interest margins (%), 1984–97

Country	1984	1989	1992	1994	1996	1997
Austria	–	1.73	1.85	1.90	1.43	1.35
Belgium	–	1.57	1.51	1.33	1.32	1.46
Denmark	3.01	2.55	3.56	3.83	1.79	1.75
Finland	2.42	1.84	1.55	2.05	1.90	2.73
France	–	1.91	1.63	1.27	1.20	1.39
Germany	2.50	2.01	2.07	2.18	1.46	1.60
Italy	–	3.28	3.17	2.63	2.42	2.57
Netherlands	2.23	2.08	1.83	1.89	1.67	1.09
Norway	3.71	3.45	3.51	3.44	2.41	2.46
Portugal	1.86	4.12	4.11	2.78	1.95	2.14
Spain	4.15	4.05	3.59	3.00	2.54	2.66
Sweden	2.55	2.53	2.55	2.77	1.81	1.98
Switzerland	–	–	1.56	1.79	1.98	1.86
UK	3.00	3.10	2.60	2.40	2.10	2.20

Source: Calculated from BankScope (1998); central bank reports (various).

earnings. Fees and commissions are one example of an income stream arising from banks diversifying their activities. The growth of bancassurance and off-balance-sheet operations has further fuelled the potential of non-interest income in generating profitability. This has been an important motivation for mergers intended to enhance revenue and/or expand product ranges. Table 2.4 shows the trend towards an increase in non-interest income as a proportion of total income in every European banking sector.

The leading commercial banks have been generating an increasing amount of their gross income from non-interest income-earning activities. In the UK, nearly 44% of gross income in banking was derived from non-interest income sources in 1997. In other European banking sectors, the ratio is either above or approaching 40% (Austria, 38.7%; Finland, 43.6%; France, 39.4%; and Sweden, 42%). The Swiss banking sector has the highest ratio at 64%, reflecting the focus on private banking and asset-management services. In contrast, both Germany and Norway have a more powerful tradition of banks advancing credit to industry and customers: in these countries between 20% and 25% of gross income comes from sources of non-interest income. In Denmark (17.7%) and Spain (24.3%), there would appear to be

Table 2.4 Non-interest income/gross income (%), 1984–97

Country	1984	1989	1992	1994	1996	1997
Austria	–	27.9	33.4	28.7	38.7	32.6
Belgium	–	22.7	21.6	23.9	35.2	35.0
Denmark	15.5	21.8	13.1	16.7	17.7	34.5
Finland	43.2	48.5	59.6	46.9	47.7	40.2
France	–	19.7	31.3	35.7	39.4	38.4
Germany	18.0	25.6	23.9	19.4	21.5	26.7
Italy	–	22.3	18.3	23.7	30.4	34.1
Netherlands	24.7	29.4	28.6	29.0	35.0	40.6
Norway	24.2	26.1	21.1	17.9	24.7	25.7
Portugal	39.4	16.3	24.8	27.3	34.2	36.3
Spain	14.0	17.6	20.3	21.6	24.3	25.8
Sweden	46.2	45.0	39.6	35.7	42.0	27.5
Switzerland	–	–	61.3	60.8	63.8	64.2
UK	35.6	37.6	42.2	43.2	44.4	43.7

Source: Calculated from BankScope (1998).

opportunities for banks to generate other forms of non-interest income through diversification. Overall, given the increasingly varied and sophisticated demands of banks' customers, non-interest income is likely to account for an increasing proportion of total income, at the expense of traditional interest earnings, on most banks' income statements.

Tables 2.3 and 2.4 also suggest that variations in the product mix, reflected in different margins and fee income, also influence the income-generating capacity of different banking sectors. In countries where bancassurance is well established, such as France, non-interest income tends to be higher (Genetay and Molyneux, 1998). In addition, the largest Swiss banks depended for the bulk of their income and profit in 1998 on private banking, investment banking and asset-management services. The major Dutch banks also derive significant income from insurance business (half of ING's balance sheet is an insurance company) as well as international operations. Note that the data cited in Table 2.4 relate to the entire banking sector in each country. Given the large number of small local and regional banks in most markets, it is likely that Table 2.4 understates the proportion of non-interest income earned by the largest banks, since these are usually much more involved in activities such as off-balance-sheet business, trading and so on.

The trend in the sources of bank income is clear: a fall in interest margins compensated by an increase in non-interest income. The picture for changes in costs, however, is less obvious. The usual measure for bank efficiency is the cost : income ratio. It must be remembered that bank efficiency levels can be affected both by endogenous and exogenous factors. Adverse economic conditions affect the cost : income ratio in the sense that banks do not have total control over their income streams, while restrictive labour laws in many continental European countries hinder staff reductions and productivity improvements on the cost side. In addition, merger and acquisition activity can add to costs in the short term, before all the efficiency savings and/or increased revenue streams have been realised. Several income sources, such as those from trading activities, are also notoriously volatile. Recent increases in the cost : income ratio are therefore as likely to reflect trends in earnings as they are trends in costs. The overall trend in cost : income ratios, however, is expected to be downwards because *inter alia* banks are seeking quality business against a background of improving risk controls and enhanced efficiency. The trend towards consolidation could inflate costs in the short term. The medium-term outlook, however, is much more optimistic, given that increased consolidation is expected to alleviate overcapacity, and put more pressure on managers to improve efficiency and realise cost savings.

Table 2.5 shows that recently, the trend in cost/income ratios has been varied. Between 1992 and 1997, Austria, Denmark, Finland, Germany, Sweden, Switzerland and the UK all witnessed efficiency gains, but in other countries the trend was in the reverse direction. According to McCauley and White (1997) and White (1998), the UK experienced more merger and acquisition activity in its banking sector (in value terms) between 1991 and 1996 than any other European country. The cost improvements shown in Table 2.5 could in part be a consequence of this trend. All the main UK banks have also embarked on aggressive cost-cutting strategies, including branch closures and staff reductions. The improved cost performance of the Scandinavian banks is (again) mainly a consequence of the enforced reorganisation following the banking crises of the early 1990s. Many continental banks, as noted earlier, are unable to generate rapid cost savings through staff reductions because of restrictive employment laws.

Table 2.5 Cost : income ratios (%), 1984–97

Country	1984	1989	1992	1994	1996	1997
Austria	–	65.5	64.0	65.1	61.4	57.6
Belgium	–	66.8	66.9	71.3	61.1	67.8
Denmark	75.6	64.9	81.4	72.5	53.5	58.1
Finland	84.0	84.8	190.4	139.9	69.3	63.6
France	–	64.6	62.5	73.5	72.8	71.2
Germany	59.3	64.6	64.5	60.7	61.2	56.2
Italy	–	61.7	63.8	65.0	69.6	72.0
Netherlands	62.3	66.0	67.7	66.7	69.5	66.1
Norway	68.5	69.9	60.3	63.4	66.5	67.6
Portugal	67.0	46.8	53.0	58.2	56.5	63.2
Spain	64.0	60.9	60.3	59.7	63.8	63.7
Sweden	67.6	62.7	122.2	80.0	49.3	47.0
Switzerland	–	–	93.9	84.9	71.1	69.8
UK	66.9	64.8	65.9	64.1	60.3	60.9

Source: Calculated from BankScope (1998).

Naturally, the trends in income and costs that are described above are reflected in the data for profitability, which are shown in Table 2.6. The results for return on equity (ROE) present a mixed picture, although in the majority of cases, returns improved between 1994 and 1997. Given that there is no obvious downward trend in bank performance across all countries, some would argue that this is clear evidence that competition has not increased. This viewpoint, however, is too simplistic. It neglects the fact that traditional margin-based business is probably more competitive than ever before. In addition, banks are increasingly building on non-interest income in areas such as investment banking, brokerage, insurance, pensions, mutual funds and other collective investment product areas (to name but a few) where there are strong established operators. So, competition is likely to be intense in many of these areas. The simplistic argument also neglects the important roles of technology and new competitors. For instance, advances in technology allow banks to outsource non-core processing and other activities to scale efficient third-party service providers. Customer databases also make the cross-selling and delivery of new types of financial products and services more effective and profitable. Technology has promoted the development of direct banking services. Non-bank financial intermediaries, retailers and other brand-name firms also compete against banks in the financial services area. These are all important factors leading to changes in the economics of European banking business. Consequently, it is inappropriate to infer that competition is 'obviously' falling if the number of banks declines and there is no systematic decline in industry profitability.

Table 2.6 Return on equity (%), 1984–97

Country	1984	1989	1992	1994	1996	1997
Austria	–	10.0	6.9	7.9	9.4	5.1
Belgium	–	6.0	6.4	8.8	20.3	14.8
Denmark	1.0	3.0	–18.3	–0.9	16.4	11.8
Finland	5.1	4.0	–49.5	–25.7	11.9	19.8
France	–	9.4	4.3	–1.4	5.8	8.5
Germany	21.1	12.4	13.2	11.9	11.9	15.8
Italy	–	14.0	9.8	4.4	6.8	5.7
Netherlands	14.0	13.6	12.8	14.1	13.7	4.2
Norway	14.1	5.5	–5.8	19.3	18.0	10.1
Portugal	5.5	9.2	8.5	6.1	9.3	11.3
Spain	8.9	14.6	10.6	8.2	14.6	14.5
Sweden	4.6	5.9	18.5	19.1	23.9	8.7
Switzerland	–	–	8.2	7.8	9.6	9.8
UK	20.8	3.4	10.7	19.6	21.0	25.9

Source: Calculated from BankScope (1998).

COMPETITION IN FINANCIAL SERVICES IN EUROPE

Traditionally, the business domain of commercial banking has been defined relatively clearly. Its scope was broader or narrower according to different national regulations and historical inheritance. As a typical feature, the production and distribution of banking products and services has traditionally been vertically integrated. Nowadays, however, the picture is more blurred, as regulatory barriers do not establish a clear border between banking and other financial service providers. Financial innovations and new technologies are reshaping the process of production and distribution of all financial services according to the comparative advantages of different institutions and markets. As a logical outcome, banks tend to seek new opportunities to diversify or to refocus their supply of financial services according to their relative competitiveness.

In all major industrial countries, the distinction between traditional banking activities, such as supplying deposits and making loans, and other capital market activities, has become eroded. An ever increasing array of negotiable assets, fed by a sustained innovation process, has combined with the use of new technologies to support the emergence and rapid growth of money and financial markets. Banks have experienced widespread disintermediation, losing significant market share in deposit taking and lending, especially to large corporate clients and institutional investors. The substantial growth of the retail mutual fund sector, as well as sectors specialising in other collective savings and investment vehicles, such as life insurance and pensions, is also promoting disintermediation in consumer banking business. These changes, which have also tended to benefit other capital market institutions, such as investment banks, brokerage firms and institutional investors, have forced many commercial banks also to diversify in order to benefit from the disintermediation trend. Fee and commission income, as we noted earlier, now accounts for a much larger proportion of commercial banks' net income than it did a decade ago.

The traditional separation between commercial banking, insurance, investment banking, brokerage and asset management that characterised many national financial markets no longer exists in Europe, and is gradually being eroded in the USA, Japan and many other jurisdictions. The desire to seek profitable opportunities in an ever widening range of financial service areas and markets is a reflection of the heightened competitive environment brought about by deregulation, new technology and changing customer demands, as well as limited growth opportunities in traditional business areas. Many of these forces are reflected in the proliferation of new financial service providers. Consequently, competition in financial services has intensified. Such competition may initially impact on the domestic banking market, as domestic banks acquire and/or develop a wider array of fee-earning business to compete with other financial market institutions. As margins and fees tighten in the domestic financial services arena, so firms seek to diversify and expand overseas in order to maintain or improve their profitability.

[In such an environment, the costs of entry into many banking areas have fallen significantly. The rapid growth of direct banking and insurance services, as well as the increase in new asset-financing firms (factoring and leasing), credit card operators, consumer finance firms, venture capitalists and so on, provides a clear indication of these trends. Increasingly, it seems that any large firm with a significant brand image can enter the retail financial services industry (at least). The rapid growth of Internet-based financial services is further opening up the market to high-technology firms, and significantly reducing transaction and processing costs. The sunk costs associated with Internet banking are, of course, negligible in comparison with traditional branch banking.]

Overall, there is reasonably strong (albeit anecdotal) evidence that deregulation and technological advances are breaking down both internal and external barriers to competition in banking and financial services in Europe (and throughout the rest of the developed world). While formal research in this area is in its infancy, investigations undertaken by Molyneux et al. (1994) and De Bandt and Davis (1998) find evidence of monopolistic competition in a variety of European banking sectors. Although De Bandt and Davis (1998) note that competitive conditions in the French, German and Italian banking markets still lag behind those in the USA, the empirical evidence that is available does seem consistent with the notion that European banking markets are becoming increasingly competitive.

THE ROLE OF CORE BANKS AND THE RATIONALE FOR CONSOLIDATION

Reason.

An argument for having large banks of similar size is that it reduces the chance of one leader exerting undue influence in a wide range of areas, especially if there is always the chance of credible competitive threats from similar-sized rivals. This view is, to a certain extent, based on the notion that it is in the interests of government to promote and preserve a small number of core banks. Revell (1987) identifies 'core banks' as the group of any country's largest banks that, by dint of their size, have certain privileges (i.e. are considered to be too important or too big to be allowed to fail), are balanced, and can often be outweighed by their duties. Gardener and Molyneux (1997) note that core banks:

- are entrusted with the bulk of industry financing, and form a pivotal role in the domestic economy;
- traditionally occupy a key position in central bank control of the financial system, bearing the brunt of monetary policy measures and being critical in the transmission mechanism for monetary policy;
- have been expected to play their part in dealing with bank failures by acquiring troubled banks or providing extra liquidity at certain critical times;
- are used as a conduit for various government financing initiatives, such as subsidised trade credit, preferential lending to certain sectors, student loans and so on.

It has also been stated that it is in the national interest to encourage mergers between large banks, especially if there is the threat of foreign acquisition of a market leader. This view was recently trumpeted widely in France (by the Minister of Finance in early 1998), and in Italy and Spain in the early 1990s, especially given the expected competitive threats posed by the EMU. Various commentators argue that core banks or national leaders have to achieve a critical size in order to be competitive. Typically, an asset size of at least $150–200 billion might be sufficient to create a reasonable European presence, and to afford a reasonable degree of protection from hostile takeover. (The proposed merger between Deutsche Bank and Dresdner Bank announced on 9 March 2000 would have created a bank with assets of more than $700 billion, but the deal fell through.)

These factors, along with the more obvious economic ones (economies of scale and scope, product and geographical diversification, and so on) have probably also contributed towards the recent trend for consolidation in European banking. The failed Deutsche Bank–Dresdner Bank merger, Royal Bank of Scotland's acquisition of NatWest in February 2000, and several other large bank deals in France, Italy and Spain during 1999 reflect this trend. If a merger occurs to create a bank substantially larger than the current second bank, experience suggests that mergers between other large banks will soon take place to preserve the status quo.

The European financial services sector has experienced substantial consolidation over the last decade or so. Most mergers between banks, however, have been between partners from the same parent country. The defensive nature of the bank consolidation process is based on the conviction of the necessity of a strong home market before moving abroad, and perhaps a certain reluctance in some cases to see the control of domestic banks pass into the hands of foreigners (Boot, 1999). Figures 2.1 and 2.2 summarise the levels of domestic and cross-border merger and acquisition activity in European financial services between 1985 and 1998. They show that there has clearly been a much stronger preference for domestic mergers in the banking sector than in insurance. In addition, mergers between two financial institutions

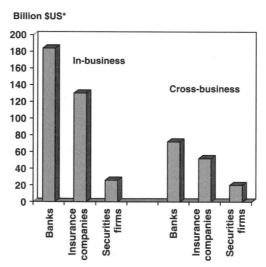

Figure 2.1 European domestic mergers and acquisitions, 1985–98.
Source: Van Dijcke (2000) p. 2 from Walter (1999).
* Sum of the equity values of the target institutions.

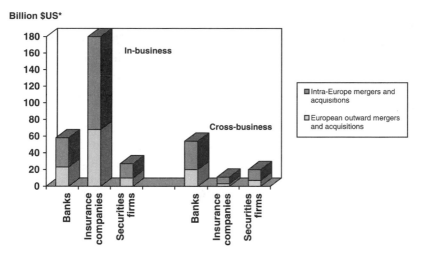

Figure 2.2   European cross-border mergers and acquisitions, 1985–98.
Source: Van Dijcke (2000) p. 2 from Walter (1999).
* Sum of the equity values of the target institutions.

of the same type (in-business) have been more common than mergers between different types of institution (cross-business)

Mergers and acquisitions will be considered in greater detail from both a theoretical and an empirical perspective in the next two chapters. Theoretical explanations for merger activity are discussed in Chapter 3. The empirical evidence on the motives for mergers in the banking sector, and on outcomes of mergers in terms of efficiency and profitability, is then described in Chapter 4

IMPACT OF EUROPEAN MONETARY UNION

EMU is tending to accelerate many of the trends outlined above, mainly because it eliminates two sources of market segmentation or competitive advantage for local banks: currency risk and expertise on national monetary policy (Vives, 1998). The credible commitment to liberalise European banking markets will continue to make banking practices more uniform, and pricing more transparent. Radecki (1998) argues that the presence of banks that operate state-wide in the USA undermines the position of local banks. As branching restrictions have been relaxed, the link between local concentration and interest rates has eroded. Even if a bank is a leader in local market share, its ability to wield market power is increasingly constrained. Following EMU, European banking sectors are likely to experience similar effects. National banks will increasingly have to compete with foreign banks and other service providers, hindering their ability to exert market power despite increasing consolidation. It should also be noted that while concentration in individual national European banking sectors is mostly higher than in the USA, across the euro-zone as a whole concentration is significantly lower (CEPR 1999).

For the forseeable future, European financial markets seem likely to continue to deepen and become more integrated, providing further impetus to European capital market and money market activity. Many commentators believe the moves towards a fully integrated European capital market will boost corporate bond issuance and the securitisation trend. EMU also provides substantial opportunities in the asset-management business, which was previously not well diversified across national boundaries within Europe. In addition, the prospect that the state will withdraw from the provision of adequate pensions is expected to lead to increasing numbers of households turning to private-sector institutions in order to save for retirement. This will lead to an increased demand for suitable investment products, which will further boost capital market, asset management and private banking business. In fact, this was one of the major motives for the recent UBS–SBC and (failed) Deutsche–Dresdner bank mergers. (CEPS 1998a).

Both increased financial market integration and the trend towards consolidation in banking raise concerns about the possible implications of a major bank failure. According to Vives (1998, p. 32), 'The prospect of a liquidity crisis or a domino effect because of a failure of interbank commitments is not remote . . . This means that Europe will need a lender of last resort . . . and coordinated supervision of financial institutions.' This is likely to become a necessity if a variety of major pan-European banking or financial service groups emerge. At present, supervisory responsibility rests with national authorities, but this may become inappropriate if national regulators do not take into account the possible external effects of a bank failure (CEPS 1998b)

Over time, EMU is likely to lead to a more competitive and integrated European financial and banking sector. Prices will become more transparent, and the industry will continue to consolidate at a rapid pace. De Bandt (1999) suggests that the emergence of a handful of major pan-European banking firms is likely, together with a host of national champions and smaller regional and local operators. Restructuring of the banking system should help to reduce excess capacity and improve efficiency in the system. Greater banking and financial sector integration will put more pressure on the authorities to develop an effective pan-European supervisory structure, encompassing banking, insurance and other financial services.

CONCLUSION

This chapter has examined recent trends and developments in European banking. It has been shown that since the mid-1980s, there have been substantial reductions in the number of banks, while the number of branches in most countries has actually risen. The representation of foreign-owned banks has grown considerably, as the European market as a whole has become more integrated. Trends in interest margins suggest that the fall in the number of banks has not dampened competition, which has extended considerably into non-traditional, non-interest-bearing areas of banking activity. Cost and returns data, however, provide rather mixed evidence concerning general trends in efficiency and profitability among European banks.

Given the large number of banks and branches that still operate in many countries, it seems likely that despite major rationalisation in the recent past, some excess capacity still remains. Meanwhile, the level of competition, both between banks and between banks and other financial sector institutions, continues to intensify relentlessly. Important strategic drivers, such as deregulation and technological change, are transforming the economics of the banking industry, lowering entry barriers and making markets more competitive. The increasingly wide range of financial service providers, the larger 'domestic' market created by EMU, and the consolidation trend means that the structure of European banking continues to experience marked changes. Further banking and financial sector integration is, however, likely to put more pressure on the authorities to develop a more effective pan-European supervisory structure, encompassing banking, insurance and other financial service product areas. The next chapter continues on the theme of industry structure, and reviews various economic approaches to evaluating market structure issues relevant to European banking.

Chapter 3

The economics of industry structure

INTRODUCTION

Chapter 3 provides an overview of the theoretical and empirical industrial organisation literature most relevant to the economic analysis of the European banking industry that forms the content of the remaining chapters of this book. The review does not pretend to be comprehensive; rather, it is highly selective, focusing primarily on topics within industrial organisation that have received most attention in the banking literature. The discussion in Chapter 3 is at a general level, however. Our review of the applications of the theoretical ideas and empirical techniques of industrial organisation to the field of banking takes place in Chapter 4.

This chapter begins with a brief description of the early development of the neoclassical theory of the firm, beginning with Cournot's pioneering analysis of competition, which first appeared in the 1830s. It continues through to the synthesis of the theories of perfect competition and monopoly that was achieved by theorists such as Chamberlin and Robinson during the 1930s. One crucial defining characteristic of the spectrum of market structures considered by the neoclassical theory of the firm is the number and size distribution of sellers in the market. Empirical researchers have found it convenient to summarise this characteristic using various numerical measures of concentration, which are discussed.

The immediate post-war period witnessed the early development of the field now known as industrial organisation, originally pioneered by Bain and Mason. In contrast to the deductive approach of standard microeconomic theory, research in industrial organisation analyses empirical data, and, by a process of induction, develops theories that purport to explain the real-world behaviour of firms and industries. Most early work was based around the structure–conduct–performance (SCP) paradigm, which we describe. While concentration was probably the most important structural characteristic of industries for early industrial organisation researchers, the threat of (actual or potential) competition from entrants has been the focus of increasing attention in the more recent literature. Barriers to entry and exit and the notion of contestability are discussed.

In its simplest form, the SCP paradigm views market structure as exogenous, in the sense that it is the structural characteristics of markets that tend to influence or dictate both the conduct and, ultimately, the performance of firms. During the last 50 years, however, theoretical and empirical research that has relied, either explicitly or implicitly, on this ordering of SCP variables has been increasingly open to criticism and attack. Ultimately, structure, as well as conduct and performance, must surely require explanation, and therefore be regarded as endogenous. More specifically, it is easy to envisage numerous ways in which conduct and performance variables create feedback effects that impact on market structure, either in the present or in future periods. The final section of this chapter discusses a number of specific examples of this kind of effect, and provides a selective review of some of the most important literature.

THE NEOCLASSICAL THEORY OF THE FIRM

Four basic theoretical market structures are described by neoclassical microeconomic theory: perfect competition, monopolistic competition, oligopoly and monopoly. The defining characteristics of market structure include the number and the size distribution of the firms, the type of product produced (homogeneous or differentiated), the extent of control over prices by incumbents, and the ease with which firms can enter or exit markets.

The neoclassical theory of the firm originates from the static framework first developed by Cournot in 1838 (Cournot, 1927), who described the nature of competitive equilibrium, an ideal state in which the effects of the forces of competition have reached their ultimate limit. Cournot also developed a theory of oligopoly, which suggests that as the number of sellers in an industry increases, price falls towards marginal cost. Emphasis is placed on the condition of equilibrium, rather than the processes by which equilibrium is achieved. Subsequent work by Jevons in 1871 (Jevons, 1970), Edgeworth in 1881 (Edgeworth, 1932), Clark (1899) and Knight (1921) contributed to the development of the present-day model of perfect competition. Paradoxically, long-run equilibrium under perfect competition implies an absence of rivalry. If the individual firm can do nothing to influence price, and if all individual participants in the market (buyers and sellers) are perfectly informed about all relevant characteristics of products and their prices, then the competitive process has run its course.

A perfectly competitive market has the following characteristics:

- There are many buyers and sellers. Consequently, the action of any individual buyer or seller has negligible influence on the market price.
- Producers and consumers have perfect knowledge and act upon this knowledge.
- The product is homogeneous, so consumers are indifferent between specific producers' products.
- Firms seek to maximise their own individual profit, and act independently of each other in pursuit of this objective.
- There are no geographical (or other) barriers to the mobility of resources, or to entry to and exit from the market.

If these conditions are satisfied, then there exists a competitive equilibrium in which all firms earn normal profit, the minimum necessary to enable the firm to remain in business. In the short run, it is possible for firms to earn abnormal profit, defined simply as any profit over and above normal profit. In the long run, however, new firms will be attracted into the industry by the existence of abnormal profit. Entry causes the market price to fall, until the point is reached at which all firms earn only the normal profit. If any firm is unable to earn the normal profit because it is operating inefficiently, then in the long run productive resources leave the firm for other firms, or the firm withdraws from the industry.

The assumptions of the theoretical model of perfect competition ensure that each firm has no control over price, and that in the long run all firms earn no more than normal profit. In reality, however, many industries seem to be dominated by a few large firms, which may have considerable discretion over the prices they charge, and which may be able to earn abnormal profits without necessarily attracting entry. Drawing on earlier insights of Marshall in 1890 (Marshall, 1961), Sraffa (1926) formulated a theory of monopoly. As firms grow in size, their average costs tend to fall as a result of economies of scale. Consequently, larger firms are able to undercut their smaller counterparts or potential entrants on price. Smaller competitors are forced out of business, and a highly concentrated industry structure evolves, consisting of a small number of large firms. In the extreme, if average costs decline over the entire range of output that the market can absorb, a natural monopoly may emerge, in which a single firm supplies the entire market and charges a price at which abnormal profit is earned in the long run.

Influenced by Sraffa, Chamberlin in 1933 (Chamberlin, 1962) and Robinson (1933) synthesised the previously separate theories of monopoly and perfect competition to develop new theories of oligopoly and monopolistic competition. Under the theory of monopolistic competition, markets contain elements of both monopoly and competition. Chamberlin emphasises non-price as well as price competition. Non-price competition can take the form of product differentiation or the creation of trademarks and brand names. Although a large number of sellers may supply a single market (the 'competitive' part of monopolistic competition), each firm's product has some unique characteristics, which give the firm some discretion over price (the 'monopolistic' part of monopolistic competition). In contrast to the situation in perfect competition, each firm's product is slightly different from that of its nearest competitors. An individual firm has discretion to raise its price slightly, without running the risk that it will lose all of its business, because there is brand loyalty among consumers. As in perfect competition, there is free entry and exit. In the short run, individual firms may be able to earn abnormal profit. The competitive discipline enforced by free entry conditions, however, ensures that only normal profit is earned in the long run.

Chamberlin's contribution to the theory of oligopoly builds on the insights of Cournot in 1838 (1927), Bertrand (1883) and von Stackelberg (1934), among others. In Cournot's model, each firm makes decisions about its own output on the assumption that the output levels of others will remain fixed at their present levels. In Bertrand's model, there is a similar pattern of behaviour with respect to price. In both models, firms sell homogeneous products. Von Stackelberg developed a model in which one firm assumes a leadership role and decides its own output on the assumption that other firms will respond passively to this decision. The leader exploits its capacity to anticipate the reactions of its rivals to earn abnormal profit at their expense.

Chamberlin in 1933 (1962) emphasised competition amongst firms selling differentiated products. Under oligopoly, firms realise that their actions are interdependent. A change in output by one firm will alter the profits of rival firms, and cause them to adjust their output. The nature of competition under oligopoly ranges from vigorous price competition, which can lead to substantial losses, to implicit or explicit forms of collusion. Implicit collusion includes models of dominant firm or barometric price leadership. Explicit collusion may take the form of a cartel agreement, which in the most extreme case might enable the firms to operate at the point of joint profit maximisation. In this case, the firms collectively produce and set prices as would a single monopolist, enabling the industry profit to be maximised. The maximised profit is then divided among the participants (Machlup, 1952; Bain, 1956).

MEASURES OF CONCENTRATION

As seen earlier, theoretical market structures have a multidimensional array of defining characteristics, including the number and size distribution of firms, the extent of product differentiation, and the size of entry barriers. Nevertheless, much empirical research into the link between market structure and the behaviour and performance of firms tends to rely heavily on a number of alternative measures of the first of these characteristics: the number and size distribution of firms. No doubt the emphasis on this aspect of structure is influenced strongly by the relative ease with which firm size distributions can be observed and quantified, in comparison with some of the other structural characteristics. This section reviews the most commonly used measures of industry or market concentration.

Hannah and Kay (1977) argue that if a measure is to capture the structure of an industry adequately, it must satisfy a number of key criteria. A concentration measure should rank industry A as more concentrated than industry B if the cumulative share of output when the firms in industry A are ranked in descending order is greater in all areas than the cumulative share of the firms in industry B. A transfer of sales from a smaller to a larger firm should always increase concentration. The entry of firms below a certain size threshold should always reduce concentration, while the exit of firms below the threshold should increase concentration. A merger between two existing firms should always increase concentration. As will be seen, not all of the measures of concentration defined below satisfy all of these criteria, and there is no perfect measure. Nevertheless, while all measures are subject to their own idiosyncracies and limitations, they do usually tend to correlate highly with one another (Curry and George, 1983; Scherer and Ross, 1990).

The *n-firm concentration ratio*, CR_n, measures the market share of the top n firms in the industry:

$$CR_n = \sum_{i=1}^{n} S_i \qquad [3.1]$$

where S_i is the market share of the ith firm when firms are ranked in descending order of market share.

Typically, market share is measured in terms of sales, assets or number of employees. Commonly used values of n include 3, 4 and 8. Unsurprisingly, researchers have found that there is high correlation between concentration ratios defined using alternative values of n (Bailey and Boyle, 1971). The n-firm concentration ratio has the advantage of being easily measurable; one needs to know only the total size of the industry and the individual sizes of the top n firms. By focusing only on the share of the top n firms, however, it takes no account of the size distribution of remaining firms. It therefore fails to satisfy several of Hannah and Kay's criteria. For example, a merger between two firms outside the top n does not affect CR_n.

In contrast, the much more data-intensive *Herfindahl–Hirschman index*, H-H (Hirschman, 1945; Herfindahl, 1950) uses information about all points in the firm size distribution. It is defined as the sum of the squares of the market shares of all firms:

$$H\text{-}H = \sum_{i=1}^{N} S_i^2 \qquad [3.2]$$

where S_i is market share of firm i as before, and N is the total number of firms in the industry. In the calculation of H-H, the larger firms receive a heavier weighting than their smaller counterparts, reflecting their relative importance. The numbers equivalent of the H-H index, calculated as 1/H-H, takes values between 1 and N, and shows how close the industry structure is to one of N equal-sized firms.

Hannah and Kay (1977) argue in favour of a generalised version of the H-H index, which allows the user to decide the relative weights that should be attached to the larger and smaller firms in the calculation. The *Hannah–Kay index*, H-K, is:

$$H\text{-}K = \sum_{i=1}^{N} S_i^{\alpha} \qquad [3.3]$$

where S_i is market share of firm i, and N is the total number of firms in the industry, as before. The researcher chooses α. The higher the value of α, the greater the weight attached to the larger firms in the calculation of the index. Values within the range $1.5 \le \alpha \le 2.5$ are typical; $\alpha = 2$ reproduces the H-H index.

The *gini coefficient*, G, is based on the Lorenz curve, which is also used widely in other areas of economics, for example in the measurement of inequalities in the distribution of incomes. The horizontal axis of Figure 3.1 represents the population of firms, ranked in ascending order of their market shares. The Lorenz curve shows for each firm the cumulative value of the market shares of all firms up to and including the firm concerned. If all firms were of equal size, the Lorenz curve would be a 45-degree line; the greater the curvature of the Lorenz curve below the 45-degree line, the greater the degree of inequality in the firm size distribution. The gini coefficient is the ratio of the shaded area between the 45-degree line and the Lorenz curve to the entire area beneath the 45-degree line, or OCAD/OAB, that is:

$$G = 1 - \left(\frac{\sum_{i=1}^{N} \sum_{j=1}^{i} S_j}{0.5N \sum_{i=1}^{N} S_i} \right) \qquad [3.4]$$

where S_i is the market share of the ith firm when firms are ranked in ascending order of market share, and N is the total number of firms in the industry.

A G value of zero would indicate that all firms are equal in size, while values of G approaching one indicate that a single firm dominates increasingly a fringe of small competitors. One obvious limitation of the gini coefficient is that an industry with two equal-sized firms would have the same value as one with 100 equal-sized firms, even though from an industrial organisation perspective, the two cases might be regarded as very different in terms of market structure.

As will be seen in Chapter 7, many empirical firm size distributions appear to correspond quite closely to members of a family of skewed distributions, which includes the lognormal distribution. Aitchison and Brown (1966) suggest that the *variance of the logarithms of market shares*, VL, is therefore a natural measure of the inequality in firm sizes:

$$VL = \frac{\sum_{i=1}^{N} (s_i - \bar{s})^2}{N} \qquad [3.5]$$

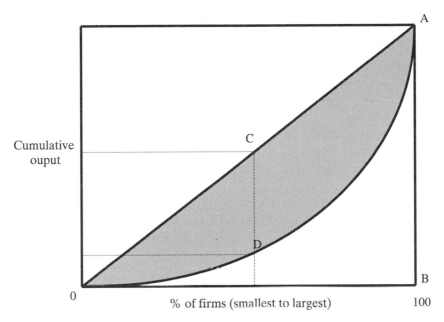

Figure 3.1   The Lorenz curve.

where s_i is the natural logarithm of the market share of firm i, and

$$\bar{s} = \sum_{i=1}^{N} s_i / N .$$

This measure suffers from the same limitations as the gini coefficient.

The *entropy coefficient*, E, is calculated as the weighted sum of the market shares of all firms in the industry, using weights equal to the natural logarithm of the reciprocal of market share, as follows:

$$E = \sum_{i=1}^{N} S_i \ln \left(\frac{1}{S_i} \right) \qquad [3.6]$$

where S_i is the market share of firm i and N is the total number of firms in the industry, as before. The entropy coefficient is inversely related to the level of concentration: $E = 0$ would represent a single-firm industry, for which $N = 1$ and $S_i = 1$. The entropy coefficient is sensitive to the number of firms in the industry, but it can be standardised for $N > 1$ by dividing by the maximum value that E can attain, given that the number of firms is N. The maximum attainable value of E (if all N firms were equal in size) is ln(N), so the *relative entropy coefficient*, Ẽ is:

$$\tilde{E} = \frac{E}{\ln(N)} \qquad [3.7]$$

Ẽ is constrained to lie between zero (for a high-concentration industry) and one (for a low-concentration industry), and can therefore be compared directly across industries with different values of N.

Finally, based on textbook models of profit-maximising behaviour under perfect competition and monopoly, the *Lerner index*, L, is more accurately described as a measure of monopoly power rather than a measure of concentration:

$$L = \frac{(P - MC)}{P} \qquad [3.8]$$

where P is the price and MC is the marginal cost. In the extreme theoretical cases, L = 0 indicates a perfectly competitive industry in which price equals marginal cost, while values of L above zero indicate that there is some element of monopoly power, allowing firms to set prices higher than marginal cost. L is subject to a maximum value of one.

THE STRUCTURE–CONDUCT–PERFORMANCE PARADIGM

Since the Second World War, Chamberlin's pre-war work on monopolistic competition and oligopoly has had a profound influence on the development of the field now known as industrial organisation. Among the early pioneers of research in this field were Edward Mason and Joe Bain, both of whom adopted a methodology that was primarily empirical rather than theoretical. In contrast to the deductive approach of standard microeconomic theory, the field of industrial organisation analyses empirical data, and by a process of induction develops theories that attempt to explain the real-world behaviour of firms and industries (Schmalensee, 1988).

Mason (1939, 1949) and Bain (1951, 1956, 1959) were the origin-ators of what has become known as the structure–conduct–performance (SCP) paradigm. The SCP paradigm seeks to ex-plain aspects of the conduct and performance of firms in terms of structural characteristics of the industries or markets in which they operate. As before, structural characteristics of industries include the number of firms and their absolute and relative sizes, the extent of product differentiation, and the nature of entry conditions.

According to the SCP approach, market structure is expected to influence the conduct of the firms that comprise the industry. Conduct variables include price setting, collusion and other forms of strategic behaviour, expenditure on advertising, research and development and innovation. Conduct, dictated or influenced by structure, in turn determines performance. Relevant performance measures may include profit, growth, market share, technological progress and efficiency. In many respects, the SCP paradigm de-velops seamlessly from the insights of the early neoclassical theory of the firm described earlier. For example, it is quite con-sistent with the SCP approach to argue that the smaller the num-ber of firms in an industry, the easier it is for these firms to exploit their market power in order to charge prices above marginal costs, and so the greater will be the profitability of incumbent firms. An overview of the SCP approach is reproduced sche-matically in Figure 3.2, in which the solid arrows indicate the direction of SCP linkage.

Most early empirical research based on the SCP paradigm focused on the relationship between concentration and perfor-mance measured by profitability. A positive correlation between concentration and profit was typically interpreted as evidence that

Figure 3.2 The structure–conduct–performance paradigm.

firms act collusively in order to achieve high profits. Bain (1951) tests the concentration hypothesis using data for US manufacturing industries covering the period 1936–40, and finds that in industries with eight-firm concentration ratios (CR_8) above 70%, profits were significantly higher than in those with CR_8 below 70%. These results have been interpreted as supporting the hypothesis that concentration facilitates collusion and limits rivalry. Bain's findings were confirmed by numerous other studies, which at the time were interpreted as providing empirical justification for government intervention aimed at increasing competition. Weiss (1974) reviews a large number of early concentration–profits studies, most of which report a significant positive relationship between the two variables. Bain's findings went largely unchallenged for more than 20 years, until the early 1970s.

Proponents of the SCP paradigm therefore tend to view most existing markets as imperfect in terms of their competitive structure, and in need of some form of regulation in order to check the abuse of market power. The Chicago school, however, represented by academics including Stigler (1968) and Demsetz (1973, 1974), argues that government interference tends to lead to less competition rather than more. A positive relationship between concentration and profits does not necessarily imply collusive behaviour on the part of firms. It may simply reflect the fact that the larger firms tend to operate more efficiently, and tend to make higher profits as a result. Demsetz argues that market structure affects profitability not through concentration but by the association between market share and profitability. Because by definition concentrated industries contain firms with high market shares, the average level of profit also tends to be higher than in less highly concentrated industries. A positive relationship between market share and profitability at the firm level therefore suggests a relationship between profit and concentration, even if concentration has no effect on conduct. If the positive relationship between market concentration and profitability reflects the exercise of market power, then it should affect all firms equally. If large firms in concentrated industries have higher profits than small firms, however, the correlation between profit and concentration is the result of the underlying relationship between profit and efficiency that has allowed these firms to become large.

If some firms have an efficiency advantage, they tend to attain large market shares, and consequently the industry becomes concentrated. If all firms operate at similar levels of efficiency, concentration and average profitability tend to remain low. This implies that regulation or intervention aimed at achieving deconcentration is not an appropriate policy prescription, since it penalises the largest and most efficient firms.

The Chicago school is instinctively suspicious of any suggestion that government intervention may be at all helpful in enabling markets to reach competitive outcomes. Usually, the best option for governments is to stand back and allow market forces to run their course (Posner, 1979; Reder, 1982). For example, there is no point in having laws against collusive agreements if such agreements are inherently unstable. When agreements break down, there is an automatic tendency for reversion towards competitive equilibrium, without any need for government or other regulatory intervention.

The 'efficiency hypothesis' proposed by the Chicago school presented a challenge to the earlier findings of Bain and others, which became known as the 'collusion hypothesis'. The debate between the two camps stimulated a large volume of empirical research, which attempted to resolve the matter using empirical criteria. A small number of representative contributions to this literature are now considered. Demsetz (1973) tests the efficiency hypothesis using data from the US Internal Revenue Service for 95 industries. The data are classified by industry concentration and firm sizes. The profit rates of firms in the three smallest of four size classes do not rise with concentration. No association between collusion and concentration is evident in the profits data of firms in these three size classes. In the largest size class, however, profits do increase with concentration, lending support to the efficiency hypothesis.

Subsequently, Smirlock et al. (1984) test the efficiency hypothesis using Fortune data on 132 US manufacturing firms covering the period 1961–69. The estimated equation is:

$$q^* = \alpha_0 + \beta_1 MS + \beta_2 CR_4 + \beta_3 HBTE + \beta_4 MBTE + \beta_5 MSG + u$$
[3.9]

where q^* is the average value over the sample period of Tobin's q (the ratio of the market valuation of the firm to replacement cost of its assets); MS is the market share; CR_4 is the four-firm concentration ratio; HBTE and MBTE are dummy variables measuring high and medium entry barriers, respectively; and MSG is a measure of growth. $\beta_1 > 0$ and $\beta_2 = 0$ would support the efficiency hypothesis, while $\beta_1 = 0$ and $\beta_2 > 0$ would support the traditional concentration hypothesis. Overall, Smirlock et al. found that $\hat{\beta}_3$ and $\hat{\beta}_4$ are insignificant. $\hat{\beta}_5$ is significant, perhaps because past growth influences investors' expectations as to whether market share will increase in the future. More importantly, however, $\hat{\beta}_1$ is significantly greater than one, while $\hat{\beta}_2$ is also positive but insignificant. These findings lend support to the efficiency hypothesis.

Schmalensee (1985) uses US Federal Trade Commission line-of-business data for 456 firms in 261 industries for 1975 to investigate the relative importance of firm-specific and industry-specific determinants of profitability. The estimated equation is:

$$\Pi_{ij} = \mu + \alpha_i + \beta_j + \gamma S_{ij} + \varepsilon_{ij} \qquad [3.10]$$

where Π_{ij} is the accounting rate of return on firm i's production in industry j; S_{ij} is firm i's market share in industry j; α_i is the component of Π_{ij} that is specific to firm i; β_j is the component of Π_{ij} that is specific to industry j; and ε_{ij} is the error term. The data set includes multiproduct firms. If firm i is a multiproduct firm, then the same value of Π_{ij} is included for each industry j in which firm i operates. $\alpha_i = 0$ and $\beta_j \neq 0$ would support the SCP hypothesis: industry effects (such as competitive structure) determine profitability, while firm effects (such as efficiency) are irrelevant. $\alpha_i \neq 0$ and $\beta_j = 0$ would support the efficiency hypothesis, as it would imply that firm effects are relevant and industry effects irrelevant. Schmalensee finds that industry effects are very important, explaining 75% of the variations in profits, while firm effects are less important. This seems to lend credence to the traditional SCP hypothesis. Schmalensee's estimations can, however, be criticised for omitting relevant firm- and industry-level explanatory variables, possibly biasing the empirical results.

Finally, Eckard (1995) uses US data for five cohorts of firms (based on size) to examine the relationship between changes in profits (measured by the price–cost margin), arising from changes in market share between 1967–72 and 1972–77. If the efficiency hypothesis is valid, a positive relationship should hold between changes in profit and changes in market share. This is confirmed in the empirical results, suggesting 'a market process in which firms become large and profitable through superior efficiency . . .' (Eckard, 1995, p. 223). As a general concusion, however, the empirical evidence for and against the concentration and efficiency hypotheses is somewhat mixed and inconclusive.

Another challenge to the SCP approach begins from the realisation that conduct and performance variables can have feedback effects that influence the evolution of industry structure (Phillips, 1976). Heavy advertising expenditure, for example, is a conduct variable that, by creating brand loyalties, may help to differentiate products in the minds of consumers (perhaps spuriously); the extent of product differentiation is a structure variable. A successful research and development programme may lead to a product innovation that creates a position as monopoly supplier for the firm concerned, or a process innovation that changes the structure of costs, perhaps with implications for the ability of competitors or potential entrants to compete with the firm on price or in terms of product quality. In either case, the industry's structural characteristics are modified by both the conduct variable (the decision to invest in research and development) and the performance variable (the technological improvement that the research brings about).

Returning to Figure 3.2, the dotted arrows show feedback effects from firm conduct and performance variables to industry structure. Discussion of such effects created a tendency to challenge the presumption that structure was the most important variable in driving the competitive process. Instead, some researchers argued that the strategies (conduct) of individual firms were important in determining industry structure (Scherer and Ross, 1990). Research based on this view was subsumed under the general heading of 'the new industrial organisation' (Schmalensee, 1982). Under this approach, firms are not seen as passive entities alike in all respects bar size. Game theoretic models are often applied, in which firms are seen as active entities that can choose from a plethora of strategies over finite and infinite time horizons. We return to this topic later.

ENTRY AND EXIT

Entry barriers play a crucial role in defining industry structure. If established firms are able to prevent entry, the extent to which competitive pressure imposes restraints on their pricing decisions and other aspects of conduct may be severely curtailed. This is likely to have far-reaching consequences for performance indicators as well. Bain (1956) defines entry as the establishment of a new firm that introduces new capacity that did not previously exist, or the conversion of existing plant and machinery already used by an established firm in another industry for use in the new venture. Bain's broad definition of barriers to entry includes any factors that allow established firms to earn abnormal profits without attracting entry. Stigler defines entry barriers as 'a cost of producing (at some or every rate of output) which must be borne by a firm which seeks to enter an industry but is not borne by firms already in the industry . . .' (Stigler, 1968, p. 67). Entry barriers can be created by incumbents' favoured access to high-quality inputs that are in short supply, cheaper long-term finance, or from learning economies of scale. According to Caves and Porter (1977), such barriers may not only separate incumbents from potential entrants, but also separate groups of existing firms. Such groups may emerge due to product differentiation, vertical integration or differences in ownership.

Shepherd (1997) distinguishes between exogenous and endogenous entry barriers. *Exogenous* barriers derive from structural characteristics of the industry, such as product characteristics and production technology. *Endogenous* barriers derive from conscious decisions taken by incumbent firms to seek to impede entry, through their own price or non-price decisions. Shepherd provides a convenient classification of exogenous and endogenous entry barriers, which is reproduced in Table 3.1.

Exogenous barriers to entry

Shepherd's classification of exogenous entry barriers begins with the four types of exogenous barrier discussed by Bain (1956):

capital requirements, economies of scale, absolute cost advantage and product differentiation. A capital requirements barrier exists if there are substantial set-up costs. Potential entrants may find it difficult or impossible to raise the finance to meet these costs. An economies-of-scale advantage can arise from the use of more efficient large-scale technology, opportunities for greater specialisation, the availability of cheaper sources of finance to large-scale producers, and spreading the cost of indivisibilities over a larger quantity of output. If the incumbent firm has an economies-of-scale advantage, there are two possibilities. Either the potential entrant can enter at a lower output level than the incumbent, in which case it will incur higher average costs; or the entrant can produce at the same level of output, in which case it may need to spend heavily in order to create capacity and capture market share.

An incumbent firm may obtain an absolute cost advantage from control of the supply of key raw materials or other factors of production, superior production techniques, exclusive deals with suppliers or discounts for bulk buying. For example, a new firm may experience difficulty in hiring skilled labour. If the latter is in finite supply, the entrant may find itself paying above the odds to attract skilled labour away from incumbent firms. Product differentiation also represents a barrier to entry if an established firm benefits from customer brand loyalties and goodwill. The entrant then has to spend heavily on advertising or on other methods of creating its own brand identity in order to overcome this barrier and establish its product.

Baumol et al. (1982) and Sutton (1991) emphasise the role of sunk costs in general as an entry barrier. Sunk costs are any costs that once incurred are unrecoverable. Sunk costs are important for incumbents and entrants because in both cases they demonstrate commitment to a chosen course of action. The recognition of sunk costs as a barrier to exit therefore acts in itself as a barrier to entry. A heavy advertising campaign required to establish a new brand is one example of a sunk cost. In high-technology industries, such as pharmaceuticals and electronics, substantial initial investment in research and development may be required to establish the capability to produce some products. If the assets required to supply a certain good or service are highly specific to that product, then

Table 3.1 Sources of entry barriers

I. Exogenous causes: external sources of barriers

1. **Capital requirements:** related to minimum efficient scale of plants and firms, capital intensity, and capital market imperfections.
2. **Economies of scale:** both technical and pecuniary, which require large-scale entry, with greater costs, risks and intensity of retaliation.
3. **Absolute cost advantages:** many possible causes, including lower wage rates and lower-cost technology.
4. **Product differentiation:** may be extensive.
5. **Sunk costs:** any cost incurred by an entrant that cannot be recovered upon exit.
6. **Research and development intensity:** requires entrants to spend heavily on new technology and products.
7. **High durability of firm-specific capital (asset specificity):** imposes costs for creating narrow-use assets for entry, and losses if entry fails.
8. **Vertical integration:** may require entry at two or more stages of production for survival; raises costs and risks.
9. **Diversification by incumbents:** mass resources deployed among diverse branches may defeat entrants.
10. **Switching costs:** complex systems may entail costs of commitment and training, which impede switching to other systems.
11. **Special risks and uncertainties:** entrants' higher risks may raise their costs of capital.
12. **Gaps and asymmetries of information:** incumbents' superior information helps them bar entrants and may raise entrants' cost of capital.
13. **Formal, official barriers set by government agencies or industry-wide groups:** examples are utility franchises, bank entry limits, and foreign trade duties and barriers.

II. Endogenous causes: voluntary and strategic sources of barriers

1. **Pre-emptive and retaliatory actions by incumbents:** including selective price discounts to deter or punish entry.
2. **Excess capacity:** the incumbent's excess capacity lets it retaliate sharply and threaten retaliation credibly.
3. **Selling expenses, including advertising:** increases the degree of product differentiation.
4. **Segmenting the market:** segregates customer groups by demand elasticities, and makes broad entry more difficult.
5. **Patents:** may provide exclusive control over critical or lower-cost technology and products.
6. **Exclusive controls over other strategic resources:** such as superior ores, favourable locations, and unique talents of personnel.
7. **Raising rivals' costs:** actions that require entrants to incur extra costs.
8. **Packing the product space:** may occur in industries with high product differentiation.

Source: Shepherd (1997, p. 210).

according to Williamson (1975) this in itself may act as a barrier to entry. Expenditure on such assets is essentially a sunk cost, which cannot be recovered by employing the same assets elsewhere to produce alternative goods and services.

The extent to which incumbent firms are integrated vertically also has implications for ease of entry into markets (Davies, 1987). Vertical integration occurs when a firm operating at one stage of a production process moves into production at another stage. Movement into an earlier part of the production process is backward integration, and movement into a later stage is forward integration. A vertically integrated incumbent can make it difficult for non-integrated firms to enter, for example by charging the entrant a prohibitive price for an essential input. The entrant could attempt to overcome this barrier by integrating into an earlier stage of the production process, but this increases the cost of entry.

If an incumbent is diversified, its capacity to fight a price war may be greater than that of a potential entrant, as losses in the market threatened by entry can be cross-subsidised by profits elsewhere. Of course, the same may apply in reverse if the incumbent is a single-product firm and the entrant is an established producer in another market seeking to diversify.

Entry may be costly if capturing market share requires customers to bear switching costs. In order to persuade customers to switch, the entrant may have to provide subsidies, thus raising the costs of entry (Klemperer, 1987). Special risks and uncertainties associated with production may also act as an entry barrier. Due to inexperience, new entrants may be more likely than incumbents to make mistakes, again raising the expected or potential costs of entry. Information gaps and asymmetries can also create advantages for incumbents. The more experienced the incumbent firm is, the more likely it is to have specialised knowledge of the market, enabling it to keep costs down (Spence, 1981). If this makes the incumbent competitive on price, its demand is likely to remain high. This may create further opportunities for learning by doing, enabling the incumbent's cost advantage to be maintained.

Finally, legal barriers to entry are often a potent force in preventing competition in certain industries. Such barriers include restrictions on the numbers of firms permitted to operate, or various types of registration and licensing requirement. Governments can also create barriers indirectly, for example through employment legislation or unfriendly fiscal regimes (Demsetz, 1982).

Endogenous barriers to entry

It is also possible for incumbent firms to act strategically in order to raise entry barriers. Endogenous barriers include pre-emptive and retaliatory pricing actions by established firms, the creation of excess capacity, the imposition of extra selling costs on entrants by excessive advertising, market segmentation, pre-emptive patenting activity, raising entrants' costs through control over key resources, and brand proliferation.

Firms can implement certain pre-emptive and retaliatory pricing strategies that make new entry unprofitable, and thus act as a deterrent to potential entrants. If an incumbent has either an absolute cost advantage or an economies-of-scale advantage over a potential entrant, it may be able to adopt a limit pricing strategy in order to forestall entry (Bain, 1956). The limit price is the highest price the incumbent can charge without inviting entry; in other words, the price that leaves the potential entrant with a market share from which it is impossible to earn a normal profit. Early theoretical models of limit pricing depend crucially on the so-called 'Sylos postulate': the assumption that the potential entrant expects the incumbent to maintain its output at its pre-entry level, even after entry takes place (Sylos-Labini, 1962).

An incumbent operating with horizontal average costs and an absolute cost advantage over potential entrants that is constant at all levels of output can simply charge a price equal to the entrant's average cost. If the potential entrant assumes that the incumbent maintains the same output post-entry, then the entrant's output is a net addition to industry output, causing the market price to fall to a level below the entrant's average cost. Similarly, an incumbent operating in an industry in which a minimum efficient scale

(MES) has to be achieved in order to produce at minimum average cost could charge a price and produce at a level of output such that if the entrant produces at the MES, then total output will rise by an amount that causes price to fall below the minimum average cost, so preventing the entrant from earning a normal profit. If the entrant operates below the MES, total output increases by less and price falls by less, but the entrant still fails to make a profit because it does not reap the full benefits of economies of scale.

As already noted, the success of a limit pricing strategy as a means of deterring entry is dependent upon the entrant's adherence to the Sylos postulate: the entrant's assumption that, if it did enter, the incumbent would be prepared to maintain its output at its current level even in the face of a falling market price. In other words, it depends on the credibility of the incumbent's commitment to sustain reduced profits or losses in order to prevent the entrant from securing a viable market share. A commitment on the part of the incumbent to pursue a policy of predatory pricing represents an even stronger threat. In this case, the incumbent would commit to starting a price war in the event of entry, reducing price in the short run in an attempt to force the entrant to withdraw, and expecting to return to the higher price post-withdrawal. By creating spare capacity, an incumbent can enhance the credibility of such threats (see below). This sends a clear signal to the potential entrant about the incumbent's intentions: if entry does occur, then the incumbent is willing and able to engage in a price war (Spence, 1977; Dixit, 1982).

Incumbent firms can also raise barriers to entry by maintaining large advertising outlays (Comanor and Wilson, 1967). There may be increasing returns from expenditure on advertising (which arise from increasing consumer awareness of the incumbent's product) or discounts on bulk advertising. Alternative non-price forms of entry barriers include loyalty discounts to customers, or exclusive deals that guarantee customer commitment. The extent to which incumbents can segment a market may influence the ease with which entry can take place. Successful segmentation by customer attributes or geographical location may enable an incumbent to engage in price discrimination. If successful, this may yield extra returns that can be used to fight entry in some future period.

Pre-emptive patenting can also be used to deter entry, by restricting a potential entrant's access to technology or ability to sell a product with particular characteristics (Gilbert and Newbury, 1982). Naturally, pre-emptive patenting is attractive if the cost of patenting is less than the profits preserved by discouraging entry. Exclusive control over other strategic resources also raises rivals' costs and deters entry. An incumbent may deliberately seek to acquire key human resources, such as managers, designers or technicians, in order to gain an absolute cost advantage over potential entrants (Salop and Scheffman, 1983). Finally, by packing the product space, or brand proliferation, the incumbent might attempt to fill the market with numerous closely related products or brands, making it difficult for an entrant to find a niche in the market (Schmalensee, 1978).

Geroski (1991) and Kay (1993) have made important contributions to the literature on entry barriers. Drawing on influential contributions from Schumpeter (1950) and Chandler (1990), and empirical evidence on entry and exit, Geroski (1991) reformulates the relationship between entry conditions and market structure within a dynamic framework. When markets are first created, there is considerable confusion due to brand proliferation, perhaps with large numbers of competing firms. As time goes by, consumers assess the usefulness of competing brands, and eventually a 'core' product becomes established.

> At some stage, a wide enough consensus amongst users develops to make an investment in large-scale production viable, and learning and economies of scale that lead to price cuts persuade even more consumers that they may as well climb on board. The emergence of these mass producers leads to sharp increases in market concentration, and these are the 'first movers' or dominant firms who often dominate their markets for decades. In short, much of what is interesting about what a market develops into and when it does so seems to be bound up with this process of standardisation.
>
> Geroski (1991, p. 268)

Domination does not last indefinitely, however, because as the industry matures, consumer tastes change and the 'core' products become obsolete. Klepper (1996) notes that over the product lifecycle, as a market matures the rate of product innovation declines, and increased process innovation takes place to improve the production of existing products. New firms enter by introducing new products, and the market undergoes a new phase of expansion and moves toward another equilibrium. Therefore, past patterns of entry determine the structure of markets at any time. Geroski assumes that firms leave the market relatively easily when their products are no longer demanded. On the other hand, when 'exit barriers are high, excess capacity does not leave the industry, and companies that lose the competitive battle do not give up; rather they grimly hang on' (Porter, 1980, p. 110).

Kay (1993) argues that firms can draw on what he terms 'distinctive capabilities', including architecture and reputation, in order to achieve a competitive advantage over competitors and achieve growth. 'Architecture' refers to the firm's internal organisation, and contracts with suppliers and distributors. For example, knowledge of the industry may yield substantial advantages that allow the firm to grow over successive periods. If market structure or production technologies change, however, this advantage may be quickly eliminated. Reputation effects can also provide advantages over competitors. If a firm has a reputation for providing high quality and service, this will help add value and generate more sales. It may be that reputation can be established only over long periods, making it difficult for entrants to compete on equal terms with a reputable incumbent. In industries in which selective firms can draw on 'distinctive capabilities', these firms are likely to grow and achieve dominance for long periods.

Contestability

During the 1980s, particular attention was devoted to the notion of contestability, first discussed by Baumol et al. (1982). If entry conditions are relatively free, and new entrants can withdraw from the market and recover their costs (in other words, if there are no sunk costs), then it may be in the interests of a monopolist to forestall entry by setting prices as if it were operating in a competitive market. The lower the entry and exit barriers, the more contestable and therefore the more competitive the market will be. The implication is that it is not the actual number of firms in an industry that determines whether prices are set at perfectly competitive levels. Rather, a high degree of contestability or a high level of potential competition may be sufficient to exert competitive discipline even in the most extreme case of an industry that consists of a single firm.

The notion of contestability presents a major challenge to the traditional SCP empirical methodology, because it implies that the conduct of incumbents is constrained by potential as well as actual competition. It therefore breaks the empirical link between observed concentration and observed profitability, because observed concentration does not necessarily reflect the extent of potential competition, which of course is not directly observable. It is potential rather than actual competition that actively constrains the equilibrium behaviour of the established firm(s), and ultimately dictates the structure of the industry.

Baumol et al. (1982) describe the perfectly contestable market (PCM), in which potential entrants have access to the same technology as incumbents, there are no sunk costs, and there is free entry and exit. In a PCM, it is possible for a new firm to enter, sell goods at prices below those of existing firms, and leave again. It can do so provided it can identify customers and complete the sale of products, cover all necessary costs, and exit before the incumbent firm has time to react. Baumol et al. (1982, p. 4) define this process as 'hit-and-run entry':

> ... in a PCM any economic profit earned by an incumbent automatically constitutes an earnings opportunity for an entrant who will hit and if necessary run (counting his temporary supernormal profits on the way to the firm). Consequently, in contestable markets zero profits must characterise any equilibrium even under monopoly and oligopoly.

According to the theory of contestable markets, therefore, the nature of entry or exit barriers is the most important structural characteristic influencing the conduct and performance of firms operating in the industry concerned.

Baumol et al. (1982) originally cited the airline industry as an example of a contestable market. Early empirical investigation of the usefulness on the notion of contestability focused particularly on airlines (Graham et al., 1983; Call and Keeler, 1985; Moore, 1986; Morrison and Winston, 1987). Hurdle et al. (1989) tested for contestability in 867 airline routes in 1985. Contrary to the predictions of the contestability literature, concentration was the most important factor determining the level of fares. Similarly, Strassman (1990) found that traditional structural variables, such as concentration and entry barriers play an important role in determining the prices charged on individual air routes. Overall, the extent to which contestability is a useful defining characteristic of the competitive structure of markets is questionable; the empirical evidence at best provides weak support for the theory.

> As often happens, a bright idea has been exaggeratedly oversold by its enthusiastic authors. The ensuing debate trims the concept and claims to their proper niche, taking their place among all the other ideas. In this instance, contestability offers insights, but it does not affect the central role of market structure.
>
> Shepherd (1997, p. 220)

The persistence of profit

Empirical research that focuses on the time series behaviour of firm profit rates presents an alternative to the essentially static approach associated with the SCP paradigm. Proponents argue that competition is really a dynamic phenomenon that unfolds over a period of time. Investigation of SCP relationships based on cross-sectional regression can provide only a snapshot taken at one moment in time, and can say little or nothing about competition as a dynamic process (Geroski, 1990). Results derived from cross-sectional regression do not contain sufficient information on which to formulate reliable policy decisions; for example, a monopoly profit earned in one period could disappear in the next, rendering anti-trust intervention by regulatory organisations unnecessary. This echoes the earlier critique of Brozen (1971), who points out that whereas the relevant microeconomic theory refers to structure–performance relationships when markets are in long-run equilibrium, there is no certainty that a profit figure observed at one point in time does represent an equilibrium value. If it does not, then there is no reason why its behaviour should conform to predictions derived from theories based on equilibrium assumptions.

The implicit hypothesis tested in the persistence of profit literature is that entry and exit into any market are sufficiently free to bring any abnormal profits quickly into line with the competitive rate of return. In other words, competitive forces are sufficiently powerful to ensure that no firm can persistently earn profits above the norm. Because each period brings new random shocks, profits are never the same for all firms. If markets are responsive to the signals sent by abnormal profits and losses, however, over time each firm's profit will tend to gravitate back towards the competitive level. The alternative hypothesis is that some firms possess special knowledge or other advantages that enable them to prevent imitation or block entry. If so, abnormal profits may tend to exhibit a high degree of persistence from one period to the next.

Typically, these hypotheses are tested by examining the coefficients of a first-order autoregressive model for firm profit:

$$\Pi_{it} = \alpha_i + \lambda_i \Pi_{it-1} + v_{it} \qquad [3.11]$$

Π_{it} is a measure of firm i's profits in period t relative to 'normal profit', typically measured as the average profit rate of all firms included in the sample. λ_i, the short-run persistence coefficient, measures the speed at which firm i's abnormal profits above (or below) the norm tend to be eliminated: $\lambda_i = 0$ implies there is no association between profit in successive periods, or zero short-run persistence, while the closer λ_i is to one, the greater the degree of short-run persistence of profits. $\pi_{ip} = \alpha_i/(1 - \lambda_i)$ represents the long-run equilibrium rate of abnormal profit for firm i, or the rate towards which firm i's abnormal profit is mean-reverting in the long run. $\pi_{ip} = 0$ for all i implies that all abnormal profits, and therefore all differences between firms' profit rates, tend to disappear over time. $\pi_{ip} \neq 0$ for some i implies that these firms have a tendency to earn abnormal profits indefinitely, so differences between profit rates tend to persist in the long run.

Mueller (1990) uses a sample of 551 US firms covering the period 1950–72 to test for short-run and long-run persistence of profit. In common with a number of other researchers, Mueller splits his sample into six equal-sized groups based on profitability at the start of the sample period, and finds that the average profitability of the six groups remains quite stable over time. This is interpreted as evidence of long-run persistence of profitability differences. The overall average short-run estimated persistence coefficient, $\hat{\lambda}_i = 0.167$, indicates a relatively rapid rate of convergence compared with estimates reported in other studies. This may reflect a relatively strong anti-trust regulatory tradition in the USA. In contrast, Odagiri and Yamawaki (1990) obtain an average $\hat{\lambda}_i = 0.470$ from an analysis of a Japanese manufacturing data set covering the period 1964–82. There is little evidence of persistent differences between firms' long-run equilibrium rate of profit, however. Cubbin and Geroski (1990) obtain an even higher average short-run persistence coefficient of $\hat{\lambda}_i = 0.491$, from a UK data set covering the period 1951–77. There is also some evidence of long-run persistence in this case.

Goddard and Wilson (1996, 1999) argue that in the persistence of profit literature, the standard test procedures, based on a set of individual estimations of equation 3.11 for each firm, allow only limited inferences to be drawn regarding values of λ_i. The relevant hypothesis tests do not have enough power to enable reliable inferences to be drawn concerning the distribution across firms of the true values of λ_i. Statistical procedures that pool data across firms should be capable of yielding stronger inferences. Some evidence is presented that $0 < \lambda_i < 1$ for most members of a UK sample of 335 firms with data for the period 1972–91. The possibility of zero short-run persistence of profits ($\lambda_i = 0$) and complete persistence of profits ($\lambda_i = 1$) cannot be ruled out, however, for up to 15% and 24% of the sample, respectively. A general conclusion that emerges from both this and earlier studies is that competitive pressure is not sufficiently strong to eliminate differences between firms in profitability, even in the long run.

DETERMINANTS OF MARKET STRUCTURE

Concentration and entry barriers

As seen earlier, research based on the SCP paradigm is based on the assumption that there is a causal link between market or

industry structure, the conduct of the firms operating in the industry, and their performance measured by profitability or other relevant indicators. Strict adherence to the SCP paradigm therefore requires that market or industry structure is treated as exogenous. In practice, however, it is easy to visualise ways in which the conduct or performance of firms may influence industry structure, making the latter at least partly endogenous. This section discusses four such mechanisms. First, if the number and size distribution of an industry's constituent firms is an important structural characteristic, then internally generated growth on the part of incumbent firms will have implications for the evolution of structure over time. Second, innovation and technological change may have an important role to play in creating monopoly power and raising entry barriers. Third, merger and take-over activity involving established firms in the same or different industries will inevitably have implications for the structures of the industries concerned. Fourth, strategic decisions taken by incumbent firms may also have implications for industry structure, for example influencing a potential entrant's assessment of the likely reaction of an incumbent, and thereby the entrant's judgement as to whether entry would actually turn out to be profitable. We begin, however, at a rather more abstract level, with a brief discussion of the transactions costs approach to industrial organisation. By attempting to identify the lines of demarcation between those transactions that take place in an uncoordinated or spontaneous manner within the sphere of the market, and those that take place inside centrally planned organisations known as firms, transactions costs economics raises and addresses a number of fundamental questions about the underlying determinants of market structure.

Transactions cost economics

In previous sections, the main focus has been on the behaviour of firms within an industry setting. The transactions cost school approaches the analysis of the conduct of firms from a rather different direction, by asking why firms exist at all. In all economies, there are essentially two ways in which resources can be allocated: through the unplanned and spontaneous interactions of large numbers of participants in the market, or through the conscious and coordinated decisions of the individuals who are in control of centrally planned institutions – 'firms'.

Coase (1937) assumed that information is imperfect, and trade within the sphere of the market does not take place in a world of certainty. As a consequence, economic agents participating in markets cannot behave in a fully rational manner because they do not have full access to all relevant information. There are bounds on rational behaviour, known as bounded rationality. Consequently there are costs of using the market to conduct transactions and allocate resources. Transactions costs include the time spent collecting information about the prices and qualities of products and services under offer, drawing up detailed proposals and contracts for transactions, and ultimately enforcing the contract in a court of law if need be. When transactions costs are high, it may be more efficient to bring the transaction out of the sphere of the market, and to settle it through the command structure of the firm.

These ideas have been developed subsequently by Williamson (1971, 1975, 1979, 1985, 1990) in a series of articles and books. Given that information is often one-sided, opportunities are available for individuals to act in an opportunistic manner. They can do this by failing to disclose facts that would make the transaction more efficient. It is likely to be more efficient to allocate resources within a firm when the transaction involved is complex and carried out frequently, when there is the potential for opportunism on one or both sides of the transaction; or when the transaction involves the utilisation of a specific asset. Asset specificity confers monopsony or monopoly power upon the buyer or seller, respectively, which adds to the difficulties the parties will tend to experience in negotiating a mutually acceptable price at which to trade.

By identifying the kinds of transactions that carry high transactions costs as those that are most likely to take place within firms (and, conversely, ones with low transactions costs as those that are most likely to take place between firms, or between firms and individual customers), Coase and Williamson make a brilliant contribution to our understanding of the determinants of the boundaries separating firms from one another, and the boundaries separating the firm from the market. Such insights carry obvious implications for questions concerning determinants of the level of industry concentration, or the number and size distribution of the industry's constituent firms. Some specific examples of the relevance of the transactions costs approach in this context will be found in the section on mergers and acquisitions later in this chapter.

Growth

A natural consequence of the development of managerial and organisational theories of the firm in the 1950s and 1960s was an increase in the amount of attention devoted to growth rather than profit as a company performance indicator. If managers are motivated by rewards such as salary, power, fringe benefits and prestige, which are associated mainly with the size rather than the profitability of the firm, and if managers have some discretion to pursue their own rather than their shareholders' objectives, then it may be realistic to assume that firms act so as to maximise size (in a static setting) or growth (in a dynamic setting) rather than profit as assumed in the traditional neoclassical theory of the firm. To suggest that managers enjoy some discretion to pursue their own objectives, however, does not imply that shareholders have no influence whatsoever. The shareholders' ultimate right to replace an unsatisfactory management team, or (amounting effectively to the same thing) the threat that a firm earning inadequate profits relative to the value of its assets may become the victim of a stock market take-over, may impose significant constraints on the managers' discretion. In developing managerial theories of the firm, it is therefore natural to use a constrained rather than an unconstrained optimisation framework. Typically, managerial firms are assumed to maximise size or growth subject to a minimum profitability constraint needed to preserve the managers' job security, rather than to maximise size or growth per se regardless of the implications for profitability.

Perhaps the best known theory of the firm of this kind is Marris's (1964) model of the managerial enterprise. Marris identifies growth in the demand for the firm's products, and growth in its capital (its capacity to supply the same products) as the two essential components of a successful growth strategy. In the long run, firms must achieve a balanced growth path, along which demand and capital are growing at the same rate. Marris's discussion of the growth of demand draws on earlier contributions by Downie (1958) and Penrose (1959). In the long run, the demand for the firm's existing products tends to be constrained by limits to the potential size of the markets for these products. Ultimately, this constraint can be overcome only through a successful policy of diversification. The size, experience and abilities of the firm's existing management team imposes a further constraint, however, on the rate at which growth can be achieved through diversification. If the firm attempts to grow too quickly, its managers will become overstretched. Mistakes and failures will ensue, causing profitability to fall. Attempting to overcome the managerial constraint by expanding the management team through further recruitment is likely to prove counterproductive, because it takes time for new managers to become effective after they join an organisation. In the short term, the management team may become less rather than more effective if the attentions of the existing managers are diverted. The main conclusion that emerges from the discussion of the growth of demand, therefore, is that growth beyond a certain rate tends to have a detrimental effect on profit.

Growth in the firm's capital or productive capacity depends upon the rate at which funds can be raised in order to finance the purchase of new capital equipment. Finance may be raised in the form of loans, new equity issues or retained profits. In the long run, however, the firm's capacity to raise finance from any of these sources depends upon its continued profitability: the higher the rate of profit, the faster the firm can grow. It might appear that rapid growth could be maintained, even in the event of falling profitability, by reducing dividends and increasing the ratio of retained to total profits. To do so, however, would compromise the managers' job security objective: a reduction in dividends would tend to depress the firm's share price and leave it vulnerable to take-over. There is therefore no escape from the need for a continuous stream of profits to finance growth in the firm's capital in the long term.

Bringing together the analyses of growth of demand and growth of capital, the firm's balanced growth path is achieved by selecting a rate of growth of demand that produces profits lower than the maximum that would be attainable if growth were slower, but still sufficient to permit the firm's capital to grow at the same rate without jeopardising the managers' job security. Although the firm does not seek to maximise profit, in the Marris model growth and profit are so heavily interdependent that the practical consequences of the shift of emphasis from profit towards growth may be limited. The kinds of factor that influence the firm's profitability are therefore likely to exert a similar influence on its capacity to grow. In particular, the firm's current size may be correlated with the growth it is likely to achieve in the future if large firms earn high profits, enabling them to finance diversification into new markets, either through the exercise of market power (the 'collusion hypothesis') or as a result of being more efficient because of economies of scale or scope (the 'efficiency hypothesis').

An alternative school of thought points out that collusion or efficiency advantages for large firms are not an essential component of any explanation for the highly skewed appearance of actual firm size distributions in many industries. In a seminal work, Gibrat (1931) formulated what has since become known as the law of proportionate effect (LPE). Although there are numerous factors that influence growth, including product characteristics that determine the extent of the potential market, managerial talent, the firm's capacity to innovate, and the firm's ownership and management structures that determine the extent of managerial discretion, none of these factors is necessarily related to firm size. If so, a large firm has exactly the same probability of growing at a given rate in any year as a small firm. Over time, however, some firms will be lucky and enjoy above-average growth over several successive periods and so become very large, while others will remain the same size or decline. This will eventually create a skewed firm size distribution, with a tendency for the industry to be dominated by a small number of large firms. A number of researchers have found that this description accords with the actual firm size distribution of firms observed in many industries. Chapters 7 and 8 review the previous empirical evidence on the usefulness of the LPE as a descriptor of growth patterns in manufacturing and banking, and Chapter 9 presents some new empirical evidence on the extent to which the LPE provides a suitable description of patterns of growth in European banking during the early and mid-1990s.

Innovation and technological change

Famously, Schumpeter (1928, 1943) has likened the role of technological change to a 'gale of creative destruction' that blows continuously through all sectors of the economy, challenging and disrupting established industrial structures and practices. Firms that successfully adopt new technologies can establish themselves at the expense of competitors still reliant on older or obsolete methods. Any advantages that these firms gain will be temporary, however, because sooner or later further changes in technology will lead to more creative destruction. Over the long term, ongoing competition between existing and new firms to innovate successfully is the main driving force behind improvements in the range and quality of products, and in the efficiency of production in capitalist economies.

The process of technical change can be broken down into the invention, innovation and diffusion stages. Invention is the initial development of new technologies, which may or may not have the potential for commercial application. Innovation is the initial commercial production of successful inventions. There are two basic types of innovation: product innovation (the introduction of new or improved products), and process innovation (the introduction of new or improved methods of production). Diffusion takes place when a successful innovation is copied or adapted by other producers. Ultimately, the speed of diffusion determines the rate of technical change at industry level.

Factors that influence the speed of diffusion are discussed by Mansfield (1969), Romeo (1975), National Economic

Development Council (1983), Lintner et al. (1987), Patel and Pavitt (1987), Geroski et al. (1993) and Schankerman (1998). These include:

- age of the existing capital stock;
- degree of risk associated with the new technology;
- liquidity and the ease with which firms can raise the finance needed for investment in the new technology;
- extent to which trade unions have the ability or desire to resist the adoption of new technology;
- characteristics of management, such as dynamism or inertia;
- extent of cooperation and knowledge sharing between firms;
- extent to which it is possible to prevent the spread of a new technology through retention of specialised staff, or through patenting.

Chapter 6 explores the nature of technological developments that are currently under way in the banking industry, and reviews empirical evidence on their impact on the industry's cost structure. At a more general level, Kamien and Schwartz (1982) discuss the implications of market structure for the speed of diffusion. Broadly speaking, there are two competing hypotheses. On the one hand, a high level of competition may create pressure for firms to adopt new ideas quickly, in order to gain a competitive advantage over rivals. On the other hand, highly concentrated industries with significant entry barriers may be conducive to a rapid rate of technical change for the following reasons:

- large firms may benefit from economies of scale in research and development;
- large firms may have access to cheaper sources of finance;
- research and development may represent an important type of rivalrous activity in oligopolistic industries;
- investment in research and development is protected by the absence of actual or potential competition.

Some economists have argued in favour of an 'inverted U-shaped' relationship between concentration and innovation: research and development effort is likely to be low under the extremes of perfect competition and monopoly, and high under oligopoly. In perfect competition, firms do not have any uncommitted resources to devote to research and development, and any gains may be eroded rapidly through the spread of information and the effects of free entry. In monopoly, the firm is insulated from competitive pressure, and may therefore have little incentive to invest in research and development. In oligopoly, high competitive pressure creates incentives for research and development effort, while imperfect information and entry barriers afford a degree of protection to the successful innovator (Scherer, 1992).

The extent to which research and development and technological change affects the structure of industries is open to debate. According to Schumpeter, the desire to forge a position as a monopoly supplier is the main source of incentive for research and development. On the other hand, the process of creative destruction ensures that in the very long term, no monopoly position is ever secure. Monopoly may exist temporarily, but eventually there is always a tendency for reversion towards competition. In the early 1970s, Blair (1972) suggested that, over time, innovations in areas such as electronics would tend to reduce the MES across a wide range of industries. More recently, this view has gained empirical support: 'Our results suggest that innovative activity does affect the evolution of market structure in particular industries, and that innovation plays a deconcentrating role wholly consistent with Blair's hypothesis . . .' (Geroski, 1994, p. 40).

Nelson and Winter (1982) use simulation analysis to identify the impact of different types of innovative behaviour by firms on industry structures. In their model, firms can invest either in innovation or imitation. The more firms invest in research and development, the more likely they are to achieve success. By producing at high output levels to meet the demand for their product, successful firms will gain economies-of-scale advantages over rivals, enabling them to expand further, and leading ultimately to increased concentration. Scherer and Ross (1990) suggest that the speed at which a firm innovates will determine the success or otherwise of any investment. Early innovation allows the firm to exploit the market over a longer period of time, and improves the firm's position relative to its rivals. If the firm innovates too quickly, however, mistakes can cause costs to increase.

Mergers and acquisitions

Although mergers (when two firms combine to form a new entity) and acquisitions (when one firm takes over another) are distinct in theory, it can be difficult to distinguish between the two in practice. In this section, and elsewhere in this book, the term 'merger' will be used in both cases. The three types of merger are: horizontal, involving firms producing the same product; vertical, involving firms producing at successive stages of the same production process; and conglomerate, involving firms producing different products.

Economic theory suggests a variety of profit and non-profit motives for merger. Profit motives include the pursuit of economies of scale or scope, and the enhancement of market power. Horizontal integration may create a monopoly for the merged entity, enabling higher prices to be charged than those that prevailed when the two firms were separate entities. Vertical integration may enable a firm to acquire its inputs more cheaply, or may confer advantages at the distribution and retail stages. Another possibility is that a profit-maximising firm may regard a merger as an opportunity to acquire productive resources cheaply if, for example, its partner (or victim) is not maximising its own profits, perhaps because it is pursuing managerial objectives or simply because it is operating inefficiently.

Non-profit motives for merger include the pursuit of size or growth for its own sake: managerially controlled firms may seek to merge in order to become bigger if managerial objectives such as salary, power or status depend primarily upon firm size. For managers, conglomerate merger may represent a means of achieving greater job security through diversification. The same kind of consideration should not apply to shareholders, however, since if the latter wish to spread risk, they can do so by holding a diversified share portfolio. Finally, it may be that at certain times, merger simply becomes seen as a fashionable type of entrepreneurial activity. In this case, merger decisions may be driven mainly by peer pressure or hubris, and may not be explicable in terms of rational economic calculus.

The impact of merger on market concentration and structure has received some attention in the early empirical literature. Weiss (1965) examined the effects of merger on concentration for six US manufacturing industries over the period 1926–59, and found that internal growth and exit had a greater effect on concentration than did mergers. Hannah and Kay (1981, p. 312) found that mergers played an important role in raising concentration in the UK over the period 1957–69: 'Merger has been the dominant force in increasing concentration in the UK since 1919 . . . Its role has been growing and it now accounts for essentially all of currently observed net concentration increase.' Hart (1981) suggests, however, that Hannah and Kay exaggerate the role of mergers in raising concentration, and argues that internally generated growth is probably more important in this respect.

More recently, the strategic motives for vertical integration have received considerable attention in the industrial organisation literature. Firms may decide to integrate vertically in order to increase joint profits at successive stages of the production process. Should firms exploit their increased market power, such action may result in a loss of welfare and a reduction in efficiency. Alternatively, vertical integration may increase welfare and efficiency if coordinated activity leads to lower costs of production.

Firms may consider backward vertical integration in order to ensure a steady supply of inputs. Adelman (1955) and Langlois and Robertson (1989) suggest that the level of vertical integration may also be dependent on the stage reached in the industry's lifecycle. In the early stages, firms must vertically integrate backwards to develop their own specific components, and integrate forwards to ensure efficient distribution of the final product. As the industry matures, supply industries and independent distribution channels evolve, allowing firms to divest themselves of upstream and downstream activities. As the industry reaches maturity or decline, vertical integration may be motivated by defensive considerations, as firms seek to protect themselves by enhancing their market power.

Williamson's (1971) transactions costs approach seeks to locate several of these explanations within a unified logical structure. Transactions costs are those associated with market transactions between buyers and sellers. These include costs incurred in nego-tiating contracts, monitoring performance, enforcing contractual promises and pursuing litigation in the event of breach of prom-ises. Several of the traditional explanations for vertical integration can be developed and interpreted in terms of the reduction or elimination of transactions costs:

- The relationship between firms in successive stages of produc-tion, for example, is subject to uncertainty. One of the major sources of uncertainty is incomplete information. Vertical inte-gration may help to reduce uncertainty, and therefore reduce transactions costs (Helfat, 1987).
- Specificity arises when a firm invests in the production or dis-tribution of custom-made products for specific clients. This may leave the firm vulnerable to threats from clients in the event of disputes. Asset specificity occurs when two firms are 'tied' or dependent on one another, by investments in specific physical capital, human capital, sites or brands. The specialised nature of the asset causes a situation of bilateral monopoly to arise, with one firm buying and one firm supplying the input. As a conse-quence, firms may integrate in order to prevent any future disputes.
- Similarly, when successive stages of a production process are linked by potentially complex legal relations, it may be more efficient to integrate vertically. Otherwise, buyers of tech-nologically complex and strategically important inputs could find themselves at the mercy of their suppliers (Monteverde and Teece, 1982).
- A firm contracted by other firms at different stages of produc-tion may be subject to moral hazard if it is able to share or pass on the costs of its own inefficiency to the other firms. In this case, vertical integration may help eliminate the transactions costs arising from moral hazard, by providing incentives to maximise revenue or minimise costs at all stages of the production process.

A number of researchers have attempted to identify principal reasons for vertical integration, drawing mainly on evidence from industry- and firm-level case studies. Spiller (1985) attempted to determine which of two competing hypotheses best explained the rationale for vertical integration: first, that firms integrate vertically in order to gain economies of scope, reduce risk or avoid taxes or price controls; and second, that firms integrate vertically in order to reduce transaction costs arising through asset specificity. The capital assets pricing model was used to assess the gains arising from the first type of factor, while the extent of asset specificity was inferred from the location of vertically related plants and the extent of correlation between firm-specific shocks. On the whole, Spiller's US evidence, based on 29 cases, seems to favour the asset specificity rationale.

Krickx (1995) tests the argument that increased vertical integration is expected when asset specificity is higher. Using data on ten major computer mainframe manufacturers between 1950 and 1970, Krickx analyses three major components used in the computer industry: receiving tubes, transistors and integrated circuits. As the specificity of the components increased, so did the tendency towards vertical integration. By the late 1960s, the top six firms had all integrated upstream into the integrated circuit industry. Krickx concluded that patterns of vertical integration were consistent with both the transaction cost and production cost arguments. Factors such as technology appropriability (the ease with which a new technology can be copied) and industry maturity also played an important role in determining whether a firm would integrate vertically.

Strategic decisions by incumbent firms

The use of game theory to formulate theories to explain the behaviour of firms is central to a field of enquiry that has become known as the 'new industrial organisation'. The new industrial organisation models the strategic behaviour of firms with respect to decisions concerning both price and non-price variables. The game-theoretic approach can be defined as 'a way of modelling and analysing situations in which each player's optimal decision depends on his belief or expectations about the play of his opponents'

(Fudenberg and Tirole, 1989, p. 261). In game theory, opponents do not hold a priori beliefs about one another, but instead try to predict the other player's moves using previous knowledge of past encounters, assuming that their opponent's decisions are rational. Schelling (1960, p. 160) defines a strategic move as:

> . . . one that influences the other person's choice, in a manner favourable to one's self, by affecting the other person's expectations on how one's self will behave . . . The object is to set up for one's self and communicate persuasively to the other player a mode of behaviour (including responses to other's behaviour) that leaves the other a simple maximisation problem whose solution for him is the optimum for one's self, and to destroy the other's ability to do the same . . .

Game theory has been used extensively to examine competitive behaviour in situations where threats, commitments, credibility and reputation are important. Any strategy adopted by a firm must appear credible to its rivals. It therefore pays a firm to build up a reputation for 'toughness' over time, in order to gain credibility (Axelrod, 1984). Making an irreversible commitment is one means of establishing credibility. As described above, incurring unrecoverable sunk costs through expenditure on product-specific capital equipment, research and development or advertising represents one method by which an incumbent can signal commitment.

This section will not attempt to review the voluminous literature on the applications of game-theoretic models to all kinds of problems in industrial organisation. To provide a flavour of this literature, however, one typical application in an area already discussed in some detail will be outlined. Dixit (1982) applies game theory to the problem of entry deterrence. In this model, the incumbent can choose between a *passive* strategy, in which it does not prepare to fight a price war if entry takes place, and a *committed* strategy, in which it incurs nonrecoverable costs (for example, in building up spare capacity) in order to prepare to a fight a price war in the event of entry.

If the incumbent remains passive and does not prepare to fight, the pay-offs are as follows. If the entrant stays out, the incumbent earns monopoly profits, Pm, while the entrant earns zero. If the entrant comes in, the incumbent must decide whether to fight by starting a price war, in which case both firms earn negative profits,

Pw, or share the market, in which case both firms earn positive profits, Pd (Pm > Pd > 0 > Pw). If entry does take place, the incumbent clearly has no incentive to fight. The original threat to fight is therefore not credible. The outcome is that entry takes place, and the incumbent and the entrant share the market, each earning profits of Pd.

In order to demonstrate commitment, however, the incumbent can incur expenditure of C, which does not affect the incumbent's pay-off if a price war occurs, but which reduces the pay-off by C otherwise. It is shown easily that if (Pm – Pd) > C > (Pd – Pw), then it is better for the incumbent to commit than to remain passive, and if entry does subsequently take place, it is better for the incumbent to fight than to refrain from fighting. This time, the original threat to fight is credible. The outcome is that entry does not take place, and the incumbent earns profits of (Pm – C). In other words, by taking the strategic decision to commit, and assuming that the commitment is visible and irreversible, the incumbent creates an effective barrier that enables it to deter entry, even though there is no change in the industry's underlying cost structure.

Although some researchers argue that game theory strengthens the theoretical framework upon which industrial organisation is based (Tirole, 1988), it is worth noting that others are critical of the game-theoretic approach. According to Schmalensee (1990, pp. 140–146), when game theory is applied to competition analysis 'anything can happen!':

> Game theory has proven better at generating internally consistent scenarios than at providing plausible and testable restrictions on real behaviour . . . Until game-theoretic analysis begins to yield robust, unambiguous predictions or is replaced by a mode of theorizing that does so, any major substantive advances in industrial organization are likely to come from empirical research.

CONCLUSION

This chapter has reviewed, at a general level, the industrial organisation literature most relevant to the economic analysis of the banking industry that follows in subsequent chapters. Following a brief description of the early development of the neoclassical theory of the firm, important stages in the post-war development of the field of (mainly) empirical enquiry now known as industrial organisation have been identified. Following the SCP paradigm, particular attention has been devoted to studying the implications of structural characteristics of markets, such as concentration, and entry barriers for conduct and performance indicators, such as price and profitability. Since the Second World War, however, the (explicit or implicit) ordering of variables implied by SCP has come under increasing attack. The challenges to SCP from a wide variety of angles, including managerial and organisational theory, transactions cost economics and game theory have given rise to many new and important insights, and have contributed much to our current understanding of the economics of industries and firms. Our attention now turns to some specific applications of these ideas in the field of banking.

Chapter 4

Market structure and the growth and performance of banks

INTRODUCTION

This chapter provides a general review of the economic analysis of the banking sector, drawing on many of the ideas and theories described in the previous chapter. The review begins with a description of applications of the structure–conduct–performance (SCP) paradigm to banking. A topic that received particular attention from early banking researchers was the 'collusion versus efficiency' debate, concerning the most appropriate explanation for any positive relationship between concentration and profitability observed in banking markets. We consider the evidence on the sources of efficiency and inefficiency within the banking firm. The next section outlines the nature of barriers to entry and exit in banking, and examines the extent to which banking markets may be considered contestable. We then discuss the determinants of market structure and concentration in banking, including economies of scale and (more generally) the industry's cost structure; technological change and the industry lifecycle; merger and

collusion – Secret agreement especially en order
to do dishonest or to deceive people.

acquisition activity; the strategic behaviour of incumbent banks; and government regulation.

MARKET STRUCTURE, PERFORMANCE AND EFFICIENCY IN EUROPEAN BANKING

This section reviews empirical research that uses the SCP paradigm to investigate the relationship between market structure and various conduct and performance variables in banking.

> Analysis of the SCP relationship in banking is used to help evaluate the main policy issue of which type of banking structure best serves the public in terms both of cost and the availability of banking services. In general two main objectives have been sought; firstly, the attainment of an 'efficient' banking system which in some way, secondly, minimises the likelihood of bank failure.
>
> Molyneux et al. (1996, p. 93)

The collusion and efficiency hypotheses

As seen in the previous chapter, among the most important characteristics that define the four main theoretical market structures are the number of firms, the degree of product differentiation, and the height of barriers to entry. The number and size distribution of firms are usually the most easily quantified aspects of market structure. Defining what constitutes the 'market' is, of course, problematic in banking, in view of the multiproduct nature of the modern-day financial services firm. Nevertheless, the most commonly used measures are the three- or five-firm deposits or assets concentration ratio (Molyneux et al., 1996). The assumption underlying much of the earliest research based on application of the SCP paradigm to manufacturing industries – that there is a strong causal link between market concentration and the performance of the firms operating in the market concerned – also informs many of the early banking SCP studies. According to the collusion hypothesis, if a small number of banks dominates a banking sector, then it is easier and less collusion - disapproving.

costly for them to collude (implicitly or explicitly) than if the number of banks is large. Collusion may result in higher rates being charged on loans, less interest being paid on deposits, higher fees being charged, and so on than if there was genuine competition between a larger number of banks.

Most of the US and European banking research that has sought to test the SCP paradigm comes to the conclusion that there is some association between concentration and profitability (Gilbert, 1984; Molyneux et al. 1996). Short (1979) is characteristic of early SCP studies in banking. Short tests whether profits are a function of ownership type, concentration levels, growth in assets and capital scarcity for a sample of 60 banks from Canada, Western Europe and Japan. A positive relationship between profits and concentration is found, suggesting that banks are able to earn high profits through collusion or the exercise of market power. Scarcity of capital also appears to provide banks with the opportunity to grant loans at higher interest rates. The rate of company growth appears to exert a negative influence on profitability, however, and privately owned banks tend to be more profitable than state-owned banks. The results 'support the view that greater market power leads to higher bank profit rates' (Short, 1979, p. 214).

Nevertheless, the empirical evidence is by no means overwhelming. Of 45 published studies reviewed by Gilbert (1984), most of which referred to the US banking sector, only 27 found evidence that the traditional SCP paradigm holds. A rather smaller number of European studies, however, do tend to support the SCP paradigm. Even so, the results have to be treated with considerable caution. Even when a positive relationship between concentration and profitability is found, the explanatory power of the estimated models tends to be quite low: variation in concentration typically explains less than 20% of the variation in industry profitability.

Furthermore, as seen in the previous chapter, even if there is at least a weak relationship between concentration and profitability, this finding cannot be interpreted unambiguously as the result of collusion and the exercise of monopoly power. According to the efficiency hypothesis, it may simply reflect the fact that the larger firms are more efficient than their smaller counterparts. In other words, it is questionable whether the high profits enjoyed by large banks are a consequence of concentrated market structures and collusive price-setting behaviour, or of superior production and management techniques that allow larger banks to keep costs low and make high returns. If so, the more concentrated banking sectors containing a high proportion of large banks will tend to have higher profitability on average, because the large banks are more efficient than their smaller counterparts operating in more competitive sectors.

The existence of the competing collusion and efficiency interpretations of the concentration–profitability relationship has spawned a substantial body of research that seeks to resolve the issue using empirical criteria. Smirlock (1985), for example, investigates the relationship between profits, market share and concentration for a sample of 2700 US banks. The model includes a set of control variables that reflect differences in the size and growth of the banking sector, varying sources of finance, bank size and holding company affiliations. Smirlock finds a positive relationship between market share and profitability; an insignificant relationship between concentration and profits; and a negative relationship between the interaction of concentration and market share with profits. These results suggest rejection of the collusion hypothesis.

Larger banks are found to be slightly less profitable than smaller banks, perhaps as a result of advantages through diversification, which reduce risk and permit them to settle for a lower return on capital. Regarding the link between market growth and profitability, on the one hand given that entry of new banks is tightly regulated, a growing market that is uncontested will naturally represent a fertile source of new demand for an incumbent bank. On the other hand, one might expect an inverse relationship between growth and profit if incumbent banks find it difficult to expand in order to meet increased customer demand, leading ultimately to inefficiencies or the entry of other banks. Overall, Smirlock concludes that no relationship between concentration and profits is evident after controlling for market share, and that successful banks are profitable through efficiency advantages.

A similar analysis is carried out by Rhoades (1985) on a large sample of US banks using data covering the period 1969–78. Rhoades splits his sample into deciles based on concentration in order to examine the relationship between profits, concentration and market share. A positive relationship is found between profitability and market share, and between profitability and concentration. To test whether the same relationship holds within concentration deciles, Rhoades looks at the market share–profitability relationship for the top and bottom 10% of banks based on market share. Banks with higher market shares tend to make higher profit, regardless of the concentration decile membership. Rhoades also finds a positive relationship between risk and profit, and a positive relationship between market growth and profit, which seems to arise from entry barriers. Rhoades suggests that the positive association between market share and profit does not reflect differences in efficiency between banks, but rather product differentiation advantages, which allow some banks to charge higher prices than others.

Evanoff and Fortier (1988) compare the collusion and efficiency hypotheses using a sample of 6300 banks located in 30 US states, with 1984 data. Their model includes concentration and market share as determinants of profit, as well as a set of control variables that account for differences in risk, costs and demand factors. Evanoff and Fortier examine the effects of regulation on bank performance, by estimating separately for markets that are more strongly and less strongly protected from entry through regulatory barriers. Market share has a strong influence on profitability, especially when regulatory barriers to entry are high. Market growth has a negative effect on profitability for banks that are not protected by regulatory barriers. Overall, Evanoff and Fortier conclude that there is some evidence that the efficiency hypothesis holds in US banking.

Bourke (1989) examines the determinants of profitability using a sample of 90 of the largest banks operating in 12 countries with data for the period 1972–81. The explanatory variables are grouped into those that are specific to the bank itself (internal) including capital and liquidity ratios, and those that are general to all banks in the sector (external), including concentration, market growth, capital scarcity, inflation and regulatory indicators. Using three separate measures of bank profitability, concentration, capital ratios, liquidity ratios and interest charges are all associated positively with profit. Little evidence is found to support the collusion hypothesis.

Using a sample of 156 US banks, with data covering the period 1982–87, Amel and Froeb (1991) adopt an approach similar to that of Schmalensee (1985) described in Chapter 3. Amel and Froeb find that the within-market variation in profitability between banks is greater than the between-market variation. It is suggested that this finding also tends to support the efficiency rather than the collusion hypothesis.

Berger and Hannan (1989) suggest an alternative way of investigating the collusion hypothesis, by focusing on the relationship between concentration and price. If banks do exploit market power, prices should be higher in concentrated sectors than in competitive ones. Using quarterly data for a sample of 470 US banks covering the period 1983–85, a negative relationship between concentration and deposit interest rates was found. This suggests that banks in concentrated markets tend to exercise market power by paying lower rates of interest to depositors. In contrast, Jackson (1992) analyses a sample of 221 banks in 104 different local banking markets in the USA with monthly data from 1983–85, and finds that banks in highly concentrated markets pay higher deposit interest rates than banks in less concentrated sectors. This could be attributed to the superior efficiency of the banks concerned.

Molyneux and Thornton (1992) analyse a sample of banks from 18 European countries with data for the period 1986–89. They use various measures of profitability, including before and after tax returns on total assets and total equity. Explanatory variables in the profit equations include concentration, capital and liquidity ratios, inflation, growth in money supply and staff expenses. Concentration, interest rates and staff expenses are all related positively to profitability, while for liquidity there is a negative association. Molyneux (1993) also incorporates market share variables. The results for Belgium, France, Italy, the Netherlands and Spain tend to support the collusion hypothesis, while those for Norway favour the efficiency hypothesis. In a separate study, Molyneux and Forbes (1995) find market share to be insignificant as a determinant of profitability in every model estimated, while there is a significant and positive association between concentration and profitability. 'The results suggest that concentration in European banking markets lowers the cost of collusion between banks and results in higher than normal profits for all market participant' (Molyneux and Forbes, 1995, p. 158).

Overall, there is no definitive evidence to resolve the collusion versus efficiency debate in banking. Furthermore, at times, reservations have been expressed about the application of SCP methodology to banking data. Gilbert (1984) finds deficiencies in the theoretical basis of the models estimated, the measurement of structure and performance variables, and the specification of the regression models. Gilbert argues that much of the banking literature pays inadequate attention to the regulated nature of banking markets. Heggestad (1984) argues, however, that the kinds of regulatory dummy variables typically employed are adequate: because SCP studies are cross-sectional in nature, changes in regulation over time are of little concern. As seen in Chapter 3, the static nature of models based on cross-sectional regression analysis is itself open to criticism (Geroski, 1990; Berger, Bonime et al. 1999).

Most SCP studies also experience difficulties in measuring structure and performance variables adequately. Using the price of a single banking product as a measure of performance may be misleading because most large banks are multiproduct firms. Profit measures may be more informative in this respect, but may also be more difficult to interpret because of the complexity of the accounting procedures involved. Difficulty in identifying the objectives of bank owners and managers may also tend to make SCP relationships tenuous. For example, if banks are sacrificing potential profits in order to reduce risk by investing in more secure activities, then researchers should be more interested in variability in profit and not in profit per se (Neuberger, 1998). Alternatively, if managers are maximising utility through expense preference behaviour, then large banks in concentrated markets will not necessarily make abnormal profit (Berger and Hannan, 1998). Indeed, Berger (1995) argues that many of the regression models used to test SCP relationships may be misspecified due to omitted variables.

Determinants of efficiency: economies of scale and scope, and productive efficiency

The focus on bank efficiency has spawned a substantial literature examining scale (size), scope (product mix) and productive
efficiency (technical and economic efficiency). This literature is
reviewed in detail in Chapter 5. Generally speaking, research
using banking data for periods before the mid-1980s found that
scale economies tended to be apparent at relatively low asset
size levels, but became exhausted as size increased (Molyneux
et al., 1996). More recent US and European studies, however,
have found stronger evidence of economies of scale for large
banks (European Commission, 1997; Berger and Humphrey,
1997). Empirical estimates of scope economies in banking tend
to be mixed – and not necessarily very reliable. The main empirical regularity that does appear widely in the efficiency literature, however, is that productive inefficiencies are much larger
than scale economies. This means that banks can improve their
overall efficiency to a greater extent by emulating industry best
practice (by improving managerial efficiency and their use of
technology) than by increasing their size. In a review of 133
financial-sector efficiency studies, Berger and Humphrey
(1997) found some evidence to suggest that large banks are
more efficient than smaller banks, but there is less evidence to
suggest that large banks benefit significantly from scale
economies.

On balance, the empirical literature, based mainly on data for
the US banking sector, suggests that large banks are relatively
more efficient than their smaller counterparts. In the case of small
banks, there tends to be much greater variability in costs relative
to best practice. When interpreting the empirical literature, it is
also important to be aware of a number of limitations with the
econometric estimation of all types of efficiency in banking, discussed by Molyneux et al. (1996).

While European research on bank efficiency has not matched
the volume of the US literature, a number of recent studies have
sought to redress the imbalance. Vander Vennet (1998), for
instance, compared the efficiencies of European universal and

specialist banks measured in both cost and revenue terms. Using a sample of 2375 European Union (EU) banks from 17 countries for the years 1995 and 1996, Vander Vennet finds that in terms of revenues, financial conglomerates are more efficient than their specialised competitors, and universal banks are more efficient than non-universal banks. In estimates based on traditional inter-mediation outputs (loans and securities), the average bank incurred costs 30% higher than the most efficient bank. In estimates based on non-traditional outputs (interest and non-interest revenue), the corresponding average inefficiency score was 20%. For diversified banks, inefficiency is uncorrelated with size; however, small specialised banks appear to be relatively inefficient. Vander Vennet's results are broadly in accordance with Allen and Rai's (1996) cross-country comparison of universal versus specialist banking systems. Scale economics were found only for the small-est banks, with assets under ECU10 billion, with constant returns thereafter and diseconomies for the largest bank, with assets exceeding ECU100 billion. Vander Vennet suggests that the bank sizes for which no diseconomies are found are higher than in the 1980s, a result that was also reported for US banks by Berger and Mester (1997).

Altunbas, Gardener et al. (2001) estimate scale economies, efficiency and rates of technical change for a large sample of European banks between 1989 and 1997. The results reveal that scale economies are widespread across different countries, and that they increase with bank size. Cost elasticities with respect to output range between 90% and 95%, suggesting that cost penalties of between 5% and 10% are incurred through failing to realise economies of scale. Productive inefficiency measures, however, are much larger at around 25%. Productive inefficiencies also vary to a greater extent across different banking sectors, over different bank size groups, and over time. Altunbas et al. also show that technical progress has had a similar influence across all European banking markets between 1989 and 1996, reducing total costs by around 3% per annum. The impact of technical progress in reducing bank costs is also shown to increase systematically with bank size. Overall, these results indicate that Europe's largest banks benefit most from scale economies and technical progress. Altunbas et al. conclude that these are important factors promoting the current trend for consolidation within the banking industry.

While most of the literature described above draws conclusions that seem conducive for concentration within European banking sectors to tend to increase, there have been no studies, as far as we are aware, that attempt to examine the relationship between bank size, efficiency and market concentration and bank performance in Europe. Berger (1995), however, has investigated these relationships for the USA by evaluating the influence of market structure (measured by concentration), firm size and efficiency on bank performance. Berger estimates a range of equations along the following lines:

$$\text{ROE or ROA} = a + b\ \text{CONC} + c\ \text{MS} + d\ \text{X-EFF} + e\ \text{S-EFF} + u$$
$$[4.1]$$

where ROE is the return on equity, ROA is the return on assets, CONC is the Herfindahl index (a deposits market concentration measure), MS is the bank's deposits market share, X-EFF is the bank-specific productive efficiency measure, and S-EFF is the bank-specific scale economies measure.

Berger found that only the MS and X-EFF variables are significant in explaining US bank performance, both having a positive effect on profitability. Larger banks tend, on average, to earn higher profits, and those that are more efficient also earn higher profits. Berger interprets these results as providing evidence that larger banks can do better because they have relative market power, brought about partly through product differentiation. More efficient banks (irrespective of size) earn higher profits because they have superior management and technology. Concentration and economies of scale are found to be unimportant in influencing bank performance. In a later study, Berger and Hannan (1998, p. 464) examine the relationship between operational efficiency and concentration, to test the hypothesis that 'market power exercised by firms in concentrated markets allows them to avoid minimising costs without necessarily exiting the industry.' In the empirical model, bank efficiency is determined by concentration and a vector of dummy variables that control differences in ownership structure and geographic location. The evidence suggests that banks in highly concentrated markets are less efficient. It is suggested that these results could support reinforcement of anti-trust policy.

In interpreting these results, however, Berger (1995, pp. 428–429) sounds a note of caution, by pointing to the weak explanatory power of his models:

> Despite the limited support for the two hypotheses (MS and S-EFF positively influencing profits), it does not appear that any of the efficiency (S-EFF and S-ESS) or market power (MS and CONC) hypotheses are of great importance in explaining bank profits . . . The efficiency and market power variables explain relatively little of the variance in profitability (median R-squared below 10%), and the coefficients of the probability equations suggest that very large increases in efficiency and market share would be needed to raise expected profits significantly . . . The evidence does not rule out the possibility of large, relatively certain increases in profits from mergers or other action, but it does suggest that firms should look beyond the simple market structure and efficiency variables . . .

These findings for the US banking sector are clearly at odds with the collusion hypothesis, which suggests that high concentration enables banks to earn abnormal profits. In order to investigate the same relationships with European banking data, we present below an analysis similar to that of Berger (1995) based on banking data from 15 European countries covering the period 1989–96. Estimates of bank-specific efficiency and scale economies were obtained by estimating a Fourier-flexible stochastic cost frontier, using a three-output (loans, assets and off-balance-sheet business) and three-input (labour, physical capital and deposits) model. The data were obtained from BankScope. The results for the ROA performance measure were:

$$ROA = 0.359 + 4.198\ *CONC - 0.134\ *MS + 0.857\ *X\text{-}EFF$$
$$+ 1.234\ *S\text{-}EFF + u \qquad [4.2]$$

R^2 (adjusted) = 0.05
Number of observations = 16 820
* = Significant at the 5% level

These results suggest that there is a positive relationship between concentration and profitability in European banking. In addition, both scale economies and productive efficiency are related positively to profits. Market share, however, appears to be related inversely to profitability, suggesting that, on average, smaller banks are more profitable than their larger counterparts. In contrast to Berger's results for the US market, concentration and scale economies appear to matter more in European banking. The explanatory power of our model is weak, however, indicating that these variables, while significant, explain relatively little of the variation in bank profitability. On the basis of these results, therefore, we concur with Berger's concerns about the capability of such models to explain variations in bank profitability.

ENTRY AND EXIT BARRIERS AND CONTESTABILITY IN BANKING

Intuitively, it seems likely that barriers to entry are likely to be important in banking. As we saw in Chapter 3, the early industrial organisation literature concentrated on four main types of entry barrier identified by Bain (1956): economies of scale, absolute cost advantages, product differentiation and capital requirements. Economies of scale are an entry barrier if a new bank cannot attain the minimum efficient scale (MES). The European Commission (1997) estimates that banks entering below the MES are likely to have average costs around 5% higher than those of established counterparts operating at (or beyond) MES. An absolute cost advantage arises if an established bank has a management team with superior ability or experience or preferential access to other essential inputs, or if there are learning economies of scale that cause the costs of offering banking services to fall over time.

Capital requirements can act as a barrier in two respects. First, the EU Second Banking Directive, passed in 1988, requires that any new bank must have a minimum capital base of ECU5 million. Second, large investments are required to invest in the technology needed to meet the day-to-day demands of banking business. Obviously, fulfilling the requirements to obtain a banking licence acts as a major entry barrier in all jurisdictions. Product differentiation advantages can create a barrier to entry in three ways. First, a bank that is established and has built up a reputation over time is likely to enjoy the loyalty of customers (Neven, 1990).

> It is hardly surprising that image plays such a decisive role in financial services. After all, confidence has always been a key element for a banking system based on fractional reserve. What we are learning now are the important side effects that this confidence may have. Public trust has always been advocated to foster the necessary stability of the financial system. In a deregulated environment enhanced reputation may also turn out to be a powerful competitive weapon for a particular organisation, if used wisely.
>
> Ballarin (1986, p. 223)

Second, barriers may arise if substantial switching costs are involved in moving from one bank to another (Klemperer, 1987; Vives, 1991a; Vives, 1991b). Third, if incumbent banks proliferate branches across geographical space, or products over product space, it becomes difficult for new banks to enter (Schmalensee, 1978). The latter is becoming less of an issue with the evolution of new delivery channels, such as telephone and Internet banking (see Chapter 6).

To some extent, the implications of the presence or absence of entry barriers may depend upon whether size of the total market is growing. If there is free entry, then rapid market growth is likely to attract entrants, intensifying competition and reducing concentration (Rhoades, 1980). However, if entry is restricted (as in many banking markets), then rapid market growth gives incumbent banks the opportunity to expand, enabling large incumbent banks to dominate increasingly concentrated markets (Smirlock, 1985). If the total size of the market is relatively constant (or in decline), then the presence or absence of entry barriers may be less important, as entrants are less likely to be attracted in either case.

Only a handful of studies have evaluated the impact of entry on bank performance. Rhoades (1980) examines the effects of entry on competition in various US banking markets, using two measures of the extent of competition: mobility and turn-over. Mobility is the number of times the top five banks changed their rank over the sample period, and turn-over is the number of times banks not in the top five moved into this category over the sample period. Entry is measured by the number of new banks entering minus the number of banks exiting, and the number of entrants as a percentage of the total population of banks operating. Concentration, market growth, market size, numbers of mergers, and dummies for unit and branch banking markets are also included as controls. Rhoades finds that entry does not affect competition. Concentration and mergers have a negative effect on competition, while market growth has a positive effect.

In contrast, Rose's (1987) survey of the US banking entry and exit literature finds that when entry barriers are relaxed or a new entrant appears, typically competition tends to increase, as does the level of risk. When new banks move into established markets, for example, deposit and loan pricing becomes more competitive, and the new entrant picks up the poorer credit risks. New entrants also tend to find it easier to obtain loan market share than deposit market share. New bank formation has mainly been in regions experiencing relatively high economic growth, where household incomes are above the national average. The US evidence also suggests that newly formed banks may also tend to cluster in a handful of (mainly large urban) regions where existing concentration is relatively low.

High concentration appears to act as a strong deterrent to new bank formation. Of course, it should be borne in mind that the studies reviewed by Rose (1987) cover a period when a banking presence required bricks-and-mortar offices. Nowadays, the threat of new entry is mainly through remote delivery channels, such as telephone and Internet banking. Here, brand image is probably more important than a physical presence. There is evidence that new remote providers do tend to pick up the more price-sensitive (interest-elastic and therefore high-risk) customers. In many cases, the new remote providers also tend to target high-income earners. So some lessons, at least, can be learned from the early US literature on bank entry and exit.

As seen in Chapter 3, recent developments in anti-trust economics question the rationale for examining structure–performance relationships in banking markets. As noted in a recent review article in the *Economist* (1998), this approach is subject to two main shortcomings: first, it is often unclear as to the appropriate market definition; and second, even when the scope of the market under investigation is clear, the relationship between concentration and market power is not. This has led economists to de-emphasise market share as a determinant of profitability. It has also focused critical attention on questions such as whether a merger between banks will necessarily drive prices higher than they otherwise would be.

As seen in Chapter 3, in recent years much attention has been focused on the notion of contestability. The theory of contestable markets was developed in an attempt to address many of the criticisms of the SCP approach. If banking markets are contestable, then incumbent banks will be unable to collude or exercise market power to raise prices. In other words, if entry and exit barriers are low, then banks are forced to adopt competitive behaviour because their actions are constrained by the threat of entry. If banking markets are truly contestable, then entrants are not deterred from entering a particular banking market, because even if they are unsuccessful they can withdraw without having incurred sunk costs. A high degree of contestability or potential competition may be sufficient to exert competitive discipline, even on firms operating within actual market structures that are monopolistic or oligopolistic.

In contrast to the SCP approach, empirical studies that seek to establish the extent of contestability in banking markets are concerned with drawing inferences about market structure indirectly from observation of conduct. This is because contestability, which depends on the extent of potential competition, is not observable directly. Evidence as to whether banking markets are contestable can be inferred by observing how banks' revenues adjust in response to changes in cost conditions. A typical empirical model is:

$$LTRASS = a + b\ LPL + c\ LPK + d\ LPF + e\ LASS + f\ LLNASS + g\ LCAPASS + h\ LIBTDEP + u \qquad [4.3]$$

where LTRASS is total revenue/assets, LPL is personnel expenses/assets, LPK is capital expenses/fixed assets, LPF is annual interest expenses/total funds, LASS is assets, LLNASS is loans/assets, LCAPASS is risk capital/assets ratio, and LIBTDEP is interbank deposits/total deposits.

All variables are in natural logarithms. LLNASS and LCAPASS are included to control for differences in risk, LASS controls for scale economies, and LIBTDEP controls for the structure of deposits. The Rosse–Panzar H statistic is the sum of the elasticities of total revenue with respect to input prices, i.e. $H = \hat{b} + \hat{c} + \hat{d}$. The inferences that can be drawn from the numerical value of H are as follows:

- $H < 0$ indicates a collusive oligopoly or a monopoly, in which an increase in costs causes output to fall and price to increase. Because the profit-maximising firm must be operating on the price-elastic portion of its demand function, total revenue will fall.
- $H = 1$ indicates a perfectly competitive industry, in which an increase in costs causes some firms to exit, price to increase, and the revenue of the survivors to increase at the same rate as the increase in costs.
- $0 < H < 1$ indicates the intermediate case of monopolistic competition, in which an increase in costs causes revenues to increase at a rate slower than the rate of increase in costs.

For a sample of New York banks, Shaffer (1982) obtains $0 < H < 1$, suggesting conditions of monopolistic competition. This finding suggests a high level of contestability: although the New York banking sector is highly concentrated, entry and exit conditions are relatively free. Nathan and Neave (1989) test for contestability for groups of Canadian banks, trust companies and mortgage companies with data for the period 1982–84. In each case the results indicate $0 < H < 1$. 'The significantly positive values of the elasticity measure indicate that Canada's financial system does not exhibit monopoly power' (Nathan and Neave, 1989, p. 576). Using European banking data for the period 1986–89, Molyneux et al. (1994) found $0 < H < 1$ for France, Germany, Spain and the UK, and $H < 0$ for Italy. In a later study using data for the period 1992–96, De Bandt and Davis (1998) obtained $0 < H < 1$ for France, Germany, Italy and the USA. Competition appears to be most intense in the USA, while small banks are found to enjoy some monopoly power in the German and French markets.

These empirical studies are quite consistent in suggesting that banking markets exhibit characteristics of contestability. As usual, however, some care needs to be exercised when interpreting the results. These studies test for evidence of competitive conditions assuming the banking market concerned is in long-run equilibrium. As seen in Chapter 2, all banking markets have experienced fundamental transformation in recent years. The common tendency for the results to suggest conditions of mono-polistic competition does not necessarily imply that the banking market is contestable. Further evidence of relatively free entry and exit is needed for the finding of monopolistic competition to be consistent with contestability. The results of such studies also need to be compared with other (more traditional) indicators of competitive conditions, such as bank margins, profitability and firm turnover rates, if they are to have any relevance from a policy-making perspective. For example, it can be argued that various additional consistency conditions, along the lines sug-gested by Bauer et al. (1997) in the efficiency literature, should be incorporated into empirical models like that shown on p. 81 that test for competitive conditions in banking markets. These are discussed in Chapter 5.

DETERMINANTS OF CONCENTRATION IN BANKING MARKETS

Several researchers have investigated trends in concentration in international banking markets over time. Aliber (1975), for ex-ample, examined changes in concentration over the period 1965–74. As a measure of concentration, Aliber used the percentage of total deposits of the world's 100 largest banks accounted for by the ten and 20 largest banks. Over the period, concentration amongst the top banks remained relatively steady. Tschoegl (1982) used assets data (at two-yearly intervals) for the world's largest banks, covering the period 1969–79. In contrast to Aliber, Tschoegl found that concentration fell during the 1970s in all countries.

Rhoades (1983) examines trends in concentration of banking deposits amongst the world's largest banks, and the stability of the rankings of various countries' banks within this group, using data covering the period 1956–80. The share of the top 100 in the total assets of the top 500 increased from 63.3% in 1956 to 70.5% in 1979. Subsequently, Thornton (1991) found that this ratio declined slightly between 1979 and 1989. Rhoades' country rankings, calculated as the proportion of the deposits of the 100 largest banks controlled by banks from each country, identify Japan, the USA, Germany and France as the highest ranked countries. Japanese banks achieved the largest increase in their share of total deposits over the period. Baer and Mote (1985) examined trends in banking concentration in Canada, France, Germany, Japan, the UK and the USA over the period 1930–80. Using CR_5, they found that concentration fell in Canada, Germany and the UK; concentration remained roughly constant in Japan, but increased significantly in the USA and France. Overall, most evidence suggests that aggregate concentration in international banking has fallen slightly over the past 20 years, but certain large banks may be increasing their share of total world deposits.

We have already reviewed empirical evidence concerning the relationship between market structure (often measured by concentration) and the performance of banks (often measured by profit). This section discusses a number of factors that may explain the size distribution of firms in a given banking sector, i.e. the factors that explain market structure. The factors considered include economies of scale and scope, technological change and the stage of the industry lifecycle, market growth, government regulation and the strategic behaviour of banks.

Economies of scale

The analysis of bank costs can yield useful information for several reasons, discussed by Molyneux et al. (1996). First, it can aid banks in making output decisions that mininise average costs. Second, the structure of costs determines the most efficient scale of production for incumbent banks and the number of banks that can operate efficiently in a given sector. Third, cost information can aid banks in taking strategic decisions, such as whether to diversify into new product areas, or whether to acquire another bank. Fourth, information on costs is relevant for the industry regulator when formulating policies that attempt to ensure an efficient and equitable allocation of resources. The range of output levels over which the long-run average cost curve is declining, constant or increasing with respect to output is, of course, a defining characteristic of any industry's cost structure. Consequently, much empirical research on cost structures in banking concentrates on identifying economies of scale.

Economies of scale result from cost savings that occur as banks change in size. Economies may be internal to the bank or branch. Revell (1987) classifies economies according to whether they arise from more efficient labour usage, technology, marketing or managerial functions. In principle, each bank can be decomposed into many branches, processes and divisions. Some branches will benefit from economies of scale, some may have excess capacity, and some may suffer from diseconomies of scale. Bank-level economies are therefore the summation of lower branch-level economies. Economies may also be identified at the industry level, for example if improvements in technology (such as automation) lead to lower costs for all banks.

If a bank can widen the scope of its activities by engaging in related types of production, average costs may fall. Economies of scope are cost savings arising when a bank produces two or more outputs using the same set of resources, which result in the costs for the group of goods or services being less than the sum of the costs if they were produced separately. Economies of scope permit the bank to spread fixed costs across a wider product range. The increased use of computing and telecommunications is an important source of economies of scale and scope in banking (Canals, 1993). Economies of scale can be realised because large banks handle thousands of transactions, making the average cost of a single transaction low. Economies of scope can be realised because computers possess excess capacity, so the information collected on clients can be used to service other accounts and provide additional services.

Extensive research has been conducted to examine the extent to which banks minimise long-run average costs. This literature is reviewed in detail in Chapter 5. Overall, the early (mainly US) research tends to show that scale economies are exhausted at low levels of production. More recent studies on US and

European banking have found stronger evidence of scale economies for large banks (Berger and Humphrey, 1997; European Commission, 1997). In a review of 133 studies, Berger and Humphrey (1997) note that in the majority of cases, larger banks are more efficient than their smaller counterparts. The literature also indicates that x-inefficiencies are significantly larger than scale economies. This suggests that banks can realise greater cost savings by emulating best cost practice rather than by attempting to increase output (Berger, Hancock et al., 1993; Berger and Humphrey, 1997; Berger, Demsetz et al., 1999). Having said this, however, there does appear to be some potential for European banks to realise scale economies. If they do so, European banking markets are likely to become increasingly concentrated (European Commission, 1997). The scale economies hypothesis concerns the number of banks that can operate given existing cost and demand conditions. It says little, however, about inequalities within the existing size distribution of banks. This suggests that other factors also need to be identified in order to account for industry structure.

Technological change and the industry lifecycle

In very broad terms, it is clear that changes in both consumer tastes and production technology can influence trends in concentration over the full course of the industry lifecycle. Revell (1987) identifies certain trends in the evolution of the banking industry that are common to all major industrialised countries. At the start of the twentieth century, banking activity was typically on a single (unit) bank basis. Larger banks played the main role in financing the activities of domestic and international business, while smaller banks concentrated on the financing of small firms and industries. As industry became progressively more concentrated over the first two-thirds of the twentieth century, the leading firms in most industrial sectors became bigger, and so banks had to grow in order to keep pace with the capital requirements of these firms. 'Just as banks became large to provide the funds needed by their large customers, so they had to spread their presence geographically . . . This was perhaps the first critical point in the development of a modern banking system' (Revell, 1987, p. 20).

Initially, most bank growth was generated internally, but as growth opportunities were exhausted and failure became more common, growth began to take place by merger and acquisition (as some smaller banks were rescued from failure by their larger counterparts). Banks operating in large towns generally had more growth potential, due to access to larger markets. Eventually, this led to the emergence of a core group of banks that were so big that governments could not allow them to fail, for fear that the rest of the financial system might crash (see Chapter 2). Naturally, the core banks in each country were particularly influential in the evolution and development of the financial system (Kindleberger, 1984).

Other researchers have also seen links between the evolution of manufacturing and the development of the banking system. Rybczynski (1988), for example, identifies three phases in the evolution of banking: the bank-oriented, the market-oriented and the securitisation phases. In the bank-oriented phase, industrial and service sector firms typically raised external finance in the form of loans from banks, and the banks decided which firms could grow. In the market-oriented phase, industrial firms raised some external finance directly on the open market. If successful, these firms gained access to large amounts of capital, and investors gained ownership stakes in the firms. Finally, in the securitision phase, industrial firms raise most of their capital through capital markets, while banks are involved in off-balance-sheet activities and the underwriting of equity issues.

Technology is crucial in dictating the pace at which the banking sector evolves. For example, although new technologies, such as electronic banking, create opportunities for banks to expand and exploit economies of scale and scope, they may also give smaller banks an advantage. As technology becomes less expensive, small banks can start to offer services similar to those of large banks. As the smaller banks do not incur the costs of maintaining a large branch network, they may be able to operate at lower average costs than the large banks. These and other technological developments currently affecting European banking are the main subject of Chapter 6. A more detailed discussion of the recent impact of technological change on banking is deferred until then.

Mergers and acquisitions

According to banking commentators such as Smith and Walter (1998) and Groeneveld (1998), merger activity has been motivated by a number of factors including the desire of banks to:

- gain access to information and proprietary technologies;
- increase market power;
- reduce unit costs;
- realise greater scale and scope economies;
- diversify risks;
- extend geographical coverage;
- benefit from tax advantages;
- realise senior management objectives;
- meet the demands of shareholders. *to move or make the move ∧ in a particular direction.*

There may also be an element of <u>herd</u> behaviour among banks (and other financial institutions) during periods when merger activity is considered fashionable. In some cases, achieving increased size by acquiring another bank may also be a defensive strategy if it helps to reduce the threat that one will be the victim of a hostile take-over. The desire to gain improved performance by achieving cost synergies, however, has probably been the most widely cited motive for bank mergers in recent years (Dermine, 1999).

To put this in context, the corporate finance literature summarises the motives for merger activity in any industry (see also Chapter 3) under three headings: synergy, hubris and agency. In deals for which the main motive is synergy, shareholders hope to realise gains through improved performance. This may accrue due to cost reductions from greater scale economies, vertical integration, or the adoption of more efficient production or

Part of anything covers the another things

organisational technology. Gains are expected to arise from the elimination of overlapping costs by combining head-office functions, branch networks, treasury business and various back-office functions. The realisation of greater scope economies through cross-selling products and services, as in deals involving banks and insurance companies, for example, may also help increase revenue. Increased performance can accrue through various merger accounting advantages, such as the use of under-utilised tax shields and other types of tax advantage. In addition, mergers may give the new bank greater market power in certain product segments, again enhancing revenues. Finally, of course, a possible source of gain relates to the elimination of inefficient management at the acquired bank.

As noted by Dermine (1999), the synergy motive is the usual and obvious justification given by senior management to justify merger activity. A feature common to many bank mergers, however, has been an overemphasis on cost reductions, with less attention placed on strategies to deliver growth in revenue. Typically, deals between banks and insurance companies stand out as the type of mergers that tend to focus on revenue growth, mainly because rationalisation opportunities and overlaps are relatively small. The merger between Citicorp and Travelers stands out as the only deal between US banks that emphasised revenue growth as a top priority before the merger took place, with the combined Citigroup focusing on cross-selling commercial banking, investment banking and insurance services to its large and diverse client base.

The hubris hypothesis suggests that managers make mistakes in evaluating target firms and overestimate potential synergies. This implies that bidding firms overvalue the possible gains by the two companies and simply pay too much for the target. Finally, according to the agency hypothesis, managers at acquiring banks deliberately overpay for their targets because this will benefit them personally, even if stock prices and shareholder wealth are affected adversely. For instance, there may be greater prestige associated with working in a larger organisation, promotion opportunities may be better, a merger may enable senior managers to avoid dismissal if their bank has been experiencing poor performance, and so on. In short, managers may be willing to overpay for an acquisition and sacrifice the market value of the firm in order to benefit from these personal gains.

The rather limited literature that examines the motives for bank mergers during the late 1980s and 1990s generally finds that the synergy motive is the most important (Zhang, 1995; Grabowski et al., 1995; Rhoades, 1998). This is also the case in studies of most non-bank mergers, although here some evidence is found in support of the hubris and agency hypotheses (Berkovitch and Narayanan, 1998). Studies of bank mergers either examine pre- and post-merger cost efficiency, or stock price reactions to merger announcements.

Rhoades (1986) used a sample of 4000 US banks to compare the performance of banks that were acquired over the period 1968–84 with those that were not, but he found no difference between the performance of the two groups. Spindt and Tarhan (1992), on the other hand, found that the profitability of many merged banks improved in the years after merger. Using case studies, Rhoades (1998) employed 16 financial ratios to examine the effects of merger on efficiency and profitability for a small sample of US banks. In each of the nine mergers studied, significant cost savings were achieved. Four of the merged entities also showed substantial efficiency gains relative to the average achieved by banks in the same peer group, while seven showed improvements in profitability.

Early European studies (Revell, 1987; Berg, 1992) found little evidence of efficiency gains through merger. More recently, Vander Vennet (1995) examined the implications for bank conduct and performance of 492 mergers classified into domestic majority acquisitions, domestic integral acquisitions (a large bank takes over a small bank), domestic mergers among equal partners, and cross-border acquisitions. Domestic majority acquisitions result in acquiring banks maintaining above-average performance as a result of enhanced market power, while acquired banks often underperform relative to industry averages. Among integral mergers, the combined values of the merged banks do not differ significantly from their premerger levels, but liquidity decreases. Vander Vennet suggested that managerial objectives often tend to motivate this type of deal. Among domestic mergers between banks of similar size, the combined bank experiences significant cost savings through economies of scale, and improved profitability. Cross-border acquisitions normally involve large profitable banks acquiring less efficient banks. Post-merger, the acquiring bank tends to remain profitable, while the acquired bank's performance improves. The acquired bank is also likely to adopt more aggressive lending policies, as technologies and managerial practices are transferred from one bank to another. As far as we are aware, there have as yet been no studies dealing with the recent spate of bank mergers in Europe.

Most US evidence suggests that in-market (or intracountry overlapping) mergers generate the largest cost savings, not only in terms of reductions in the number of branches and employees, but also through savings on systems and operations costs (Morgan Stanley Dean Witter, 1998c). European evidence, however, is mixed. Several major UK deals have been successful in improving efficiency ratios. HSBC's acquisition of Midland, for example, resulted in a reduction in the cost : income ratio from over 70% in 1992 to under 60% by the end of 1997. Lloyds/TSB's cost : income ratio fell by 12% over the same period. Some continental European banks, in contrast, seem to have been less successful. ABN AMRO reduced domestic branch and staff numbers in the years after merger, with an improvement in ROE after a time lag. Its cost : income ratio, however, remained virtually static throughout the 1990s. Most of ABN AMRO's improvement in profitability was derived from its investment banking and international operations. In Spain, the mergers that established Banco Bilbao Vizcaya and Banco Central Hispano were convoluted deals, which took between three and four years to generate significant cost savings and performance enhancement.

One possible reason for the mixed experience following in-market deals is the fact that competition is so intense in European banking. Consequently, it may be that cost savings are being passed on to consumers in the form of lower interest margins and keener fee and service charges. Intense competition from mutual savings and cooperative banks in many sectors partly accounts for this pattern. In addition, restrictive labour laws also prohibit (or severely limit) rapid reduction in employee numbers.

Efficiency gains and performance improvements from other types of merger (nonoverlapping, revenue or product enhancement, and cross-border deals) are much more difficult to identify. Several of the largest cross-border deals have taken place recently (including mergers between Merita and Nordbanken, and ING and BBL). The short-term stock price reaction to the announcement of these deals has been negative. It remains to be seen whether these will generate significant gains in the short-to-medium term. Vander Vennet (1996) and Altunbas et al. (1997) report evidence of limited efficiency gains from cross-border European bank deals. While the merger between UBS and SBC, to create the United Bank of Switzerland, was forecast to reduce costs by 20% over three years, the poor performance of some recently merged US banks provides evidence that such a target may be unrealistic (*Euromoney*, 1999). Hardly any large US bank merger deal announced in 1998 has managed to hit premerger forecast earnings. This, together with temporary concerns about Y2K compliance, helped to keep US bank stock prices depressed towards the end of 1999 and through 2000.

An alternative, econometric approach to the question of the impact of mergers on average costs is taken by Shaffer (1992), who examines the potential cost savings arising from hypothetical, simulated mergers using cost functions estimated from actual data. The majority of simulated mergers between members of a US sample of banks with total assets greater than $1 billion lead to an increase in costs. Using a similar methodology, Molyneux et al. (1996) examine potential cost savings arising from hypothetical mergers between banks in Spain, France, Germany and Italy. Mergers between Spanish banks are generally expected to lead to falling costs as economies of scale are realised, while for France, Germany and Italy, most mergers are expected to cause costs to increase.

In general, it appears that the motives for European and US bank mergers have changed gradually during the 1990s. In the case of the earlier deals, where modest take-over premiums were paid and cost-cutting plans were less dramatic, the synergy motive dominated: predicted cost savings were achievable, feeding through into higher earnings and improved shareholder value. As the merger movement accelerated in the latter part of the 1990s, however, premiums tended to increase and less realistic cost-cutting targets were set, suggesting that within a general mood of merger euphoria, hubris and perhaps even agency motives became more prevalent. Future European bank mergers are likely to refocus increasingly on creating realisable synergies, both on the cost and revenue sides. In the future, greater emphasis will be placed on allocating capital to the most dynamic areas of the merged bank's business, while at the same time developing strategies to enhance competitive advantage over the long term.

Overall, the empirical evidence on mergers suggests that in many cases there is little improvement in the efficiency or performance of the merged entities. The inability of the extant literature (in both the banking and non-banking fields) to find widespread evidence of improvement in performance as a result of merger activity is puzzling. This general pattern perhaps suggests that agency and hubris motives for mergers are just as important as those based on operational synergies. It also suggests that mergers must be studied on a case-by-case basis. Nevertheless, since merger activity inevitably tends to increase concentration, it is likely that the desire to increase market power is an important motive in many cases. Increased market power may, of course, be reflected in senior managers directing a larger proportion of revenues towards executive salaries, fringe benefits, and so on. Large banks may choose to adopt risk-averse strategies, as expressed in the 'quiet-life' hypothesis (Hicks, 1935) investigated recently in the context of US banking by Berger and Hannan (1998). It may also lead to an increase in the intensity of non-price forms of competition, such as product differentiation. Such possibilities may explain why increased market power resulting from merger is not reflected in improved efficiency, higher profits and greater shareholder returns.

Strategic behaviour of incumbent banks

While the notion of contestability was championed strongly during the 1980s and exerted a major influence on US anti-trust policy, concerns that sunk costs were in fact substantial in many merger cases has led economists to focus on (usually game-theoretic) models of strategic competition among oligopolists in order to evaluate outcomes in terms of changes in the size and distribution of market power. Typically, this approach uses sophisticated modelling of data on price and performance to evaluate the likelihood of collusion resulting from mergers. So far, such techniques do not appear to have been applied rigorously to any bank mergers. This is probably because of the complexity of mergers between multiproduct service firms, where detailed and standardised product and price data are not readily available. Furthermore, models of contestability (see above) probably describe the competitive structure of many banking business areas just as well as, if not better than, models of strategic competition between oligopolists.

A relatively simple example of how rivalry between large banks can be modelled is presented by Molyneux (1995), who tests for collusive behaviour between leading European banks. Molyneux finds that the traditional concentration–profits relationship holds, but is determined primarily by the behaviour of the top two banks. In particular, a large leading bank does appear to promote cooperation (collusion) with other leading banks, but the appearance of a large second bank seems to induce rivalry rather than cooperation with leaders. The presence of more distant rivals does not seem to affect the profitability of banks in the sector. Overall, these results suggest that policy makers should be concerned if the largest bank in the sector is substantially larger than its nearest competitors. Policy makers may well be justified in encouraging mergers between large banks so they can act as stronger competitors to market leaders. As far as we are aware, no other studies have investigated this type of behaviour in banking markets. It is therefore difficult to generalise as to whether the same pattern of behaviour would be evident in different time periods, or in other banking sectors (including the USA). Table 4.1 provides a crude indication as to the relationship between the relative size of the top two banks in a number of European banking sectors, and their relative performance.

Table 4.1 shows, for example, that Germany's largest bank in 1996 was larger than the second largest by a factor of 1.52 (in terms of assets), while ROE for these two banks was virtually the same. Although it is difficult to detect any clear pattern signifying that the larger the difference in size of the top two

Table 4.1 Relative size of top two banks and performance difference, 1996

Country	Asset size of top bank/ asset size of second bank	ROE of top bank/asset size of second bank
Belgium	1.24	0.66
France	1.34	1.53
Germany	1.52	1.01
Italy	1.11	0.86
Netherlands	1.23	1.34
Spain	1.15	0.86
UK	1.27	1.27

banks the larger is the difference in their ROE, a correlation coefficient of 0.3 nevertheless suggests that large market leaders may tend to enjoy a profitability advantage over the second largest bank, which is related to the magnitude of their size advantage. The sample size is so small, however, that these results, while interesting, represent only circumstantial evidence that having two similar-sized large banks is more competitive than having a market leader with a substantial size advantage.

The strategic management literature offers some insights into the possible components of an effective management strategy in banking. Drawing on the insights of Porter (1980), Canals (1993) develops the concept of the value chain in relation to banking. The value chain disaggregates a bank into its strategically relevant activities: those that reduce costs and those that are potential sources of differentiation. Activities can be split into primary and support activities. Primary activities are those that are associated with the physical creation of the product or service. Support activities are those that support the primary activities and each other, for example by providing purchased inputs, technology and human resources. Once the bank's activities have been disaggregated, the process of appraisal can take place. Each of the support activities is linked to each of the primary activities to a greater or lesser extent. The analysis examines how these links can be improved in order to increase the margins on each product. Gardener (1992) also applies Porter's work to the EU banking industry. For applications of Porter's ideas to the US banking industry, see Ballarin (1986).

According to this approach, a bank must select and follow a generic strategy in order to add value and gain a competitive advantage over rivals. Generic strategies consist of cost leadership, differentiation and focus. Cost leadership implies a bank attempts to keep its costs lower than that of the competition (Salomon Brothers, 1993). To do this, the bank must identify cost savings at some point in its value chain and produce at lower cost, or alternatively change the structure of the value chain. For example, the bank may be able to strike an exclusive deal with suppliers for raw materials, such as in the purchase of automated teller machines (ATMs). Differentiation requires some unique characteristic to be associated with a bank's product, leading to higher margins and profits relative to competitors. Finally, focus can apply to both cost leadership and differentiation. In both cases, the strategy requires the bank to focus on a particular segment of the market. Only banks following generic strategies will add value and gain a competitive advantage over rivals.

Competitive advantage can arise in four main areas within the banking industry: human resources, financial resources, physical assets and intangible assets. With human resources, banks can gain advantages through the quality of their workforce or through training. Banks can also build up financial resources to become large and exercise market power or realise efficiency gains from building up the capital base or total deposits. By using physical assets (such as branch networks, information systems and telecommunications systems) or intangible assets (such as brand image, experience, managerial talent, and product and service quality), banks can gain and sustain a competitive advantage over rivals. This will lead ultimately to a market structure in which a few large banks dominate.

Regulation

Government regulation of the banking sector is designed to increase the efficiency of banks, to protect the interests of depositors, and to ensure the stability of the financial system as a whole. Requirements for banks to maintain adequate reserves can be used to protect solvency. Deposit insurance schemes, the provision of lender of last resort facilities, and the rescue of failing banks can help protect individual depositors and maintain stability, though possibly with an associated risk that moral hazard may encourage some bank management teams to behave imprudently.

The three main types of regulation are structural regulation, conduct regulation and prudential regulation. Structural regulation includes the functional separation of banks into different activities (such as commercial and investment banking); the creation of entry barriers, including minimum capital requirements; and restrictions on the type of business banks can undertake. The regulatory authorities can restrict the number of banks directly, by limiting the number of bank licences granted. This type of regulation is also likely to raise entry barriers (Gual and Neven, 1993). Conduct regulation includes controls on the levels of interest rates, the value of loans granted, and the rate of branch expansion. Prudential regulation includes compulsory participation in deposit insurance schemes and provisions for the central bank to act as lender of last resort (Baltensperger and Derminc, 1990).

Relative to other industrial and service sectors, banking is of course highly regulated. The nature of regulation is likely to have a significant effect on the structural composition of any banking sector. Naturally, the extent to which regulation tends to increase or decrease concentration depends upon whether the regulator seeks primarily to promote competition (for example, by granting additional licences enabling new banks to enter) or to increase stability (for example, by imposing high minimum capital requirements).

CONCLUSION

Chapter 4 has reviewed various topics relating to the economic analysis of the banking sector. A topic that received particular attention in early SCP-based research in banking was the question as to whether the superior profitability of large banks or banks operating in highly concentrated markets should be attributed primarily to collusion or efficiency effects. In general, however, there is little evidence to suggest that market structure and bank size strongly influence performance. We have also considered the evidence on the sources of efficiency and inefficiency within the banking firm. On balance, the empirical evidence, which refers mainly to US banking, suggests that large banks are relatively more x-efficient than their smaller counterparts. In the case of small banks, there tends to be much greater variability in costs relative to best practice.

Despite the presence of various regulatory barriers, including strict capital and solvency requirements, a general conclusion that appears to emerge when analysing barriers to entry and exit is that banking markets may be reasonably contestable. This conclusion is currently being strengthened as a result of rapid technological progress, which is having a fundamental effect on the cost structure of the banking industry, as well as that of other financial services. Among the determinants of market structure, the evidence on the extent of economies of scale within banking is rather mixed. In contrast to manufacturing, there is some evidence that rapid growth leads to increased concentration. There is also some evidence that technological advance and changes in customer attributes are leading to increased concentration, as banks expand in order to meet new customer demands.

Chapter 5

Efficiency in European banking

by Barbara Casu* and Phil Molyneux

INTRODUCTION

In the previous chapter, we noted that the desire to realise scale or scope economies, or to achieve other efficiency gains, could be an important motive for consolidation in banking markets. Chapter 5 provides a more extensive analysis of efficiency issues in the banking sector. The structure of the financial services industry is changing rapidly, so it is particularly relevant to examine the efficiency characteristics of financial institutions. There has been a proliferation of banking efficiency studies during the 1990s.

The desire to investigate the efficiency characteristics of financial services institutions has been motivated by various groups, including academics and policy makers, as well as bankers. These groups are interested in investigating such issues because if financial firms are becoming more efficient, then we

* Dr Barbara Casu is currently Research Fellow at Aston Business School, Birmingham, UK.

might expect improved profitability, lower prices, and improved service quality for consumers, as well as greater safety and soundness if efficiency savings are directed towards improving capital buffers that absorb risk. Of course, the opposite is the case if structural changes result in 'less efficient intermediaries, with the additional danger of taxpayer-financed bailouts if substantial losses are sustained' (Berger et al., 1993, p. 2).

The recent flurry of activity directed at evaluating the performance of financial institutions reflects a variety of considerations. Cooper (1997) notes that, traditionally, the study of financial firm performance was neglected in the economics, finance and management literature. New methodologies have also been developed, however, that are suited well to the study of firm efficiency. Furthermore, institutional changes, such as deregulation and liberalisation, as well as a handful of high-profile bank failures that have been attributed partly to the failings of managers, have also contributed to interest in the topic.

In terms of modelling bank efficiency, the recent academic literature has focused mainly on using statistical techniques that construct an efficient frontier. This allows the researcher to estimate empirically how close each financial institution is located to the best-practice frontier. Broadly speaking, two different empirical approaches are employed, involving the estimation of either parametric or non-parametric frontiers. These approaches differ in respect of the assumptions the modeller makes regarding the shape of the efficient frontier, the existence of random error and, if random error is allowed, the distributional assumptions imposed on the inefficiencies and error to enable one to be disentangled from the other.

Nowadays, there is broad consensus that differences in technical efficiency among financial institutions exceed differences attributable to incorrect scale or scope of output (Berger, Hancock et al., 1993; Berger and Humphrey, 1997). There is, however, still no consensus as to the best method for estimating the best-practice frontier against which relative efficiencies are measured. A recent study by Bauer et al. (1997) argues that it is not necessary to have a consensus as to the best frontier approach for measuring efficiency. Instead, they propose a set of consistency conditions that the efficiency measures derived from the various approaches should meet in order to be most useful for regulators or other decision makers. In general, the efficiency estimates derived from the different approaches should be consistent in their efficiency levels, rankings and identification of best and worst firms. They should be consistent over time, and should also be in line with standard non-frontier measures of performance used by banking firms and analysts.

The financial institution efficiency literature is both recent and extensive. This chapter provides a non-technical review of this literature. Finally, we consider briefly some of the more practical issues surrounding efficiency management in banking.

BANKS' PRODUCTION PROCESSES: MEASURING INPUTS AND OUTPUTS

A financial firm is an entity engaged in the production of intermediation services between borrowers and lenders. These services are related directly or indirectly to the financial assets and liabilities held by the firm, such as loans and deposits. The financial services industry can be viewed as the aggregation of all firms that supply financial services and products, and as such it includes sectors such as banking, securities and insurance. More specifically, 'a bank is an institution whose current operations consist in granting loans and receiving deposits from the public' (Freixas and Rochet, 1997, p.15). This is the kind of definition used by regulators when deciding whether a financial intermediary has to submit to the prevailing prudential regulations for banks.

As for any other institution, the existence of banks is justified by the role they play in the process of resource allocation, and more specifically in the allocation of capital. In order to provide a better understanding of how financial intermediation improves resource allocation, it is necessary to examine the functions that banks perform. Contemporary banking theory classifies these functions into four main categories (Freixas and Rochet, 1997, p.15):

- offering access to a payment system;
- transforming assets;

- managing risk;
- processing information and monitoring borrowers.

Allen and Santomero (1998) argue that many current theories of intermediation focus too heavily on functions of institutions that are no longer crucial in many developed financial systems. Bhattacharya and Thakor (1993) provide a review of the relevant literature. Such theories are often unable to account for those activities that have become the central focus of many institutions, such as risk management and reducing participation costs, which are the costs of learning about using markets effectively, as well as participating in them on a regular basis.

Financial firms provide services rather than readily identifiable physical products, and there is no general consensus as to the precise definition of what banks produce and how service output can be measured. Unlike the outputs of manufacturing firms, banking firms' outputs cannot be measured by physical quantities. In addition, banks provide a wide range of services. Indeed, one of the major problems in the theory of the financial and banking firm is the specification of appropriate measures of outputs and inputs. The problem is compounded when financial firms, especially commercial banks, are treated as multiproduct firms.

Colwell and Davis (1992) note that, at a practical level, the obvious starting point in measuring banking sector output is to look at the way it is treated in the national accounts. Most banking studies, however, do not use national accounts measures. Instead, they have relied upon a variety of alternative approaches, resulting in the fact that measurement techniques have often outpaced the theory of what is to be measured.

The earliest cost studies in banking used very simple models that resembled ratio-based analyses. Each study, however, applied a different indicator of banking output. Some early studies proxied bank services by a single index that combined all services into a unidimensional measure; others measured each bank service separately. In addition, some researchers chose to measure output in terms of bank assets and liabilities by focusing either on only one side of the balance sheet, or on both sides at the same time. Others used bank revenues to measure bank output. Greenbaum (1967), for example, used the dollar market value of services rendered to measure output in an attempt to estimate the real social value of banking services. Gilligan and Smirlock (1984) measured output in dollars, either as demand and time deposits, or securities and loans. According to Humphrey (1985), the output produced by a financial institution might be viewed primarily as the number of deposits and loans accounts produced. This is because most banks' operating costs are incurred by the processing of deposits and loans documents, as well as by the debiting and crediting of deposits and loans accounts.

An alternative view of bank output focuses on the dollars in each account rather than the number of accounts. This view argues that while banks do indeed produce deposits and loans accounts, the production process is associated more closely with the costs incurred per dollar in that account. Kolari and Zardkoohi (1987) used the dollar value of accounts to measure bank output. They justified their choice by arguing that banks compete to increase their market share regarding dollar amounts as opposed to the number of accounts. In addition, they noted that as long as banks produce many services, dollar measurement was the only 'sensible' common denominator.

This problem of output definition has persisted since the earliest studies, and has continued to present problems to researchers as the empirical banking literature has developed during the last three decades. Another important issue is that bank outputs are generally defined in terms of stock variables that do not correspond with the fundamental nature of the bank production process. Bank production is a continuous process in which inputs are continuously transformed into a flow of services using existing technology. There are two main approaches to the choice of how to measure this flow of services: the production approach and the intermediation approach.

Under the production approach, banks are treated as firms that employ capital and labour to produce different types of deposits and loan accounts. Outputs are best measured by the number and types of transactions or documents processed over a period of time. Unfortunately, such detailed transactions' flow data are typically proprietary and not generally available. Therefore, data on the number of deposits or loan accounts serviced, or the number of transactions performed on each type of product, tend to be used instead.

Under the intermediation approach, banks are thought of as intermediating funds between savers and investors. The values of loans and investments are taken as output measures; labour, capital and deposits are regarded as inputs to the bank's production process. In this approach, deposits are included as a third input, along with capital and labour. As a result, operating costs, as well as interest costs, are taken into account.

According to Berger and Humphrey (1997), both approaches are imperfect because neither captures fully the dual role of financial institutions, which includes both the provision of transaction- and document-processing services, and the transfer of funds from savers to borrowers. Nevertheless, each approach has some advantages. The production approach may be somewhat better for evaluating the efficiencies of branches of financial institutions, because branches primarily process customers documents for the institution as a whole, and branch managers typically have little influence over bank funding and investment decisions. On the other hand, the intermediation approach may be more appropriate for evaluating entire financial institutions because this approach is inclusive of interest expenses, which often account for between one-half and two-thirds of total costs. Moreover, the intermediation approach may be superior for evaluating the importance of frontier efficiency to the profitability of financial institutions, since the minimisation of total costs (and not just production costs) is needed to maximise profits.

Other possible methods of assigning financial values to input and output categories are the value-added approach and the user cost approach. As noted above, under the intermediation approach, banks are considered only as financial intermediaries between liability holders and those who receive bank funds, while outputs are considered to be just loans and other assets (Sealey and Lindley, 1977). Berger and Humphrey (1990) have strongly criticised this approach, favouring instead the value-added approach, under which those factors having substantial added values are employed as important outputs. Under the value-added approach, all items on both sides of the balance sheet may be identified as inputs or outputs, according to whether they generate or destroy value. Berger and Humphrey (1992) found that (demand, savings and time) deposits and loans tended to generate value-added for banks, and so suggested that these should be considered as the appropriate bank outputs.

The user cost approach determines whether a final product is an input or an output on the basis of its net contribution to bank revenue. If the financial returns on an asset exceed the opportunity cost of funds, or if the financial costs of a liability are less than the opportunity costs of funds, then the instrument is considered to be a financial output (Hancock, 1985).

Proponents of all of these methods agree that loans and other major assets of financial institutions should count as outputs. There is no agreement, however, on the role of deposits. Deposits have input characteristics because they are paid for in part by interest payments, and the funds raised provide the institution with the raw material of investible funds. On the other hand, deposits also have output characteristics, because they are associated with a substantial amount of liquidity, safe-keeping and payment services provided to depositors (Berger and Humphrey, 1997). Some studies resolve this issue by using both the input and output characteristics of deposits; the interest paid on deposits is counted as part of costs and the rate paid is included as an input price, while the quantities of deposits are counted as outputs (Berger and Humphrey, 1991). Others have treated deposits as an input and then as an output (Favero and Papi, 1995). Comparisons between the results of these and other studies suggest that the measurement of efficiency is sensitive to the treatment of deposits. Since it appears that inferences may be affected by how outputs are measured, this aspect of model specification assumes particular importance for the researcher.

DEFINING BANKS' PRODUCTIVE EFFICIENCY

A fundamental decision in measuring the efficiency of financial institutions is which concept of efficiency to use. The terminology used to define efficiency in economics is varied, and can give rise to confusion. This section begins by defining the terminology that will be used throughout Chapter 5, allowing precise use of the term 'efficiency' than in a number of different contexts.

Productive efficiency is defined as the sum of two components: the purely technical or physical component, and the economic component. The purely technical or physical component refers to the ability to avoid waste by producing as much output as input usage allows, or by using as little input as output production requires. The analysis of technical efficiency can have an output-augmenting orientation or an input-conserving orientation. Technical efficiency is similar or equivalent to the concept of x-efficiency developed by Leibenstein (1966, 1980), although the latter's analysis of business efficiency extends beyond a purely neoclassical theoretical framework, whereas technical efficiency refers to the production of as much output as possible from *any* chosen set of inputs. Economic efficiency refers to the ability to select the optimal set of inputs to obtain a given level of output in the light of prevailing input prices.

Productive efficiency (the sum of the technical and economic efficiency components) is the main focus of attention in the banking efficiency studies reviewed in this chapter. It is important to distinguish productive efficiency from an alternative efficiency concept used by economists: allocative efficiency. Allocative efficiency refers to the social welfare gains that accrue if all production takes place under competitive market conditions, in which price is equal to marginal cost in long-run equilibrium. Allocative inefficiency arises when firms exploit monopoly power in order to restrict output, and to set price above marginal cost, creating a welfare loss from a social perspective. Allocative efficiency does not come under extensive scrutiny in the banking productive efficiency literature reviewed in this chapter. Concern about allocative efficiency, however, is of course implicit in the concentration–profitability literature reviewed in the previous chapter.

Debreu (1951) and Farrell (1957) introduced a convenient measure of technical efficiency. Their measure is defined as one minus the maximum equiproportionate reduction in all inputs that still allows continued production of given output (see Figure 5.1). A score of unity indicates technical efficiency, because no equiproportionate input reduction is feasible, and a score of less than unity indicates the degree of technical inefficiency.

While the concept of productive efficiency is straightforward, various difficulties arise when attempting to measure it.

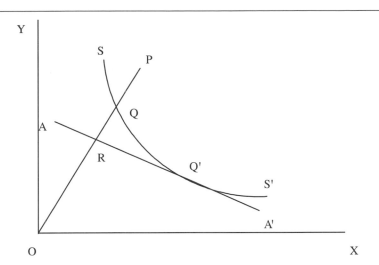

Consider, for the sake of simplicity, a firm employing two factors of production to produce a single product, under the conditions of constant returns to scale. Suppose that the efficient production frontier is known, i.e. the output that a perfectly efficient firm could obtain from any given combination of inputs. In the diagram above, the point P represents the inputs of the two factors per unit of output that the firm is observed to use. The isoquant SS' represents the various combinations of the two factors that a perfectly efficient firm might use to produce unit output. The point Q represents an efficient firm using the two factors in the same ratio as P. It can be seen that it produces the same output as P using only a fraction OQ/OP as much of each factor. It could also be thought of as producing OP/OQ times as much output from the same inputs. It thus seems natural to define OQ/OP as the technical efficiency of the firm P. This ratio takes the value of unity (or 100%) for a perfectly efficient firm, and will become indefinitely small if the amounts of input per unit output become indefinitely large.

However, one also needs a measure of the extent to which a firm uses the various factors of production in the best proportions, in view of their prices. If AA' has a slope equal to the ratio of the best prices of the two factors, Q' (and not Q) is the optimal method of production. This is because although both points represent 100% technical efficiency, the cost of production at Q' will be only a fraction OR/OQ of those at Q. It is natural to define this ratio as the price efficiency (economic efficiency in our terminology) of Q.

If the observed firm were perfectly efficient, both technically and in respect of their prices, its costs would be a fraction OR/OP of what they really are. It is convenient to call this ratio overall efficiency (productive efficiency in our terminology) of the firm, and one may note that it is equal to the product of the technical and price (economic) efficiencies.

Source: Farrell (1957, p. 245)

Figure 5.1 The Farrell measure of technical efficiency.

Essentially, it is necessary to derive the best-practice or production frontier, which depicts the maximum attainable performance. Existing firms are then compared with this standard. Ideally, actual firm performance would be compared with the true frontier. The latter is unobservable, however, and the best that can be achieved is an empirical or best-practice frontier generated from the researcher's data set. It is important to point out that in most practical economic analyses, relative productive efficiency (the distance from best-practice frontier) rather than absolute productive efficiency (the distance from the true frontier) is the more appropriate concept.

Another issue arises in determining the units of measurement for the best-practice frontier. Theoretically, output, cost and profit measures are all possible, although the output measure runs into difficulties if firms are multiproduct. Berger and Mester (1997) discuss what they consider to be the best economic foundations for analysing the efficiency of financial institutions.

The concept of efficiency as defined above is distinct from the concepts of scale and scope economies. Productive efficiency requires only that the firm operates on (rather than below) the highest attainable production function or the lowest attainable cost function, but not necessarily at the point of minimum average cost at which the full benefits of economies of scale are achieved.

Optimal firm size and product mix are important issues for an industry undergoing a restructuring process (see especially Chapters 2 and 6). Interest in the subject of scale and scope economies has been stimulated by the recent wave of bank mergers and acquisitions in Europe, the USA and elsewhere. One of the reasons commonly put forward to justify merger and acquisition activity relates to the potential gains that may result through larger size (economies of scale) and the ability to diversify (economies of scope). Technological change may also have important implications for the nature of scale and scope economies. For example, the application of new technologies often entails heavy expenditure, which becomes profitable only if a sufficient number of transactions takes place subsequently. There are also important policy issues relating to national consolidation and the impact on industry performance and competition.

ECONOMIES OF SCALE AND SCOPE

Economies of scale exist if, over a given range of output, costs per unit decline as output increases. Increases in costs per unit correspond to decreasing returns to scale. It is of interest to investigate whether there is potential for average cost savings if a firm were to produce at a higher or lower scale than at present. In order to produce at the lowest attainable average cost, a firm must produce at the point or points of constant returns to scale, where any change in output results in an equiproportionate change in costs.

These concepts are explained in Figure 5.2, which considers the case of a single-input and single-output production process. The assumption of constant returns to scale has been dropped, and the production process is now characterised by increasing returns up to point R, constant returns at point R, and decreasing returns for output levels above point R. The firm corresponding to point G fails to produce at the lowest attainable average cost for two reasons. First, there is technical inefficiency resulting from the

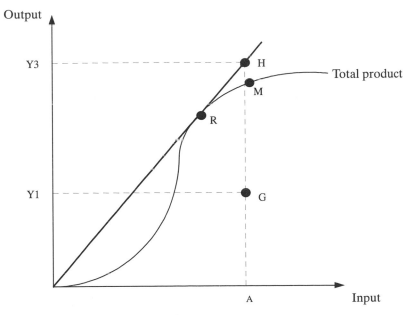

Figure 5.2   The concept of technical efficiency.
Source: Evanoff and Israilevich (1991, p.15).

underutilisation of inputs: the firm is operating beneath the total product curve. If inputs are fully utilised, the firm should produce the higher output level corresponding to point M. The output not produced because of technical inefficiency is GM. Second, there are decreasing returns to scale at point M, since this corresponds to an output level greater than that at point R. The output not produced because of the failure to benefit fully from economies of scale is MH.

For a single-product firm, the concept of scale economies (or returns to scale) refers to the rate at which output changes as all factor quantities are varied. Specifically, economies of scale are measured by the ratio of the proportionate change in output to a given proportionate change in all inputs. When a firm increases its output, there are economies of scale if the average cost per unit of output falls. Economies of scale can therefore be defined in terms of either the production function or the corresponding cost function.

The multiproduct nature of banks makes the analysis and interpretation of returns to scale more complex. When a firm is multiproduct, global scale economies are defined relative to a proportionate increase in the production of all outputs, the productive mix being held constant. Economies of scale can be measured by employing Baumol's (1982) concept of ray average cost (RAC). Alternative approaches to measuring scale economies are adopted by Humphrey (1985), Kolari and Zardkoohi (1987), Berger et al. (1987), Forestieri (1993) and Molyneux et al. (1996). According to Baumol's (1982) RAC approach, economies of scale are present when:

$$C(kQ)/k < C(tQ)/t \qquad \text{for } k > t \qquad [5.1]$$

where $Q = (Q_1, \ldots, Q_n)$ is a vector of outputs and $C()$ is the cost function.

Figure 5.3 illustrates the concept of RAC for a multiproduct firm in three dimensions. The point of minimum RAC, the output bundle q_0, corresponds to the most efficient scale (size) for the firm producing outputs in the proportion specified by the ray OR. Scale economies are measured as the elasticity of cost with respect to output, as the latter varies along the ray OR.

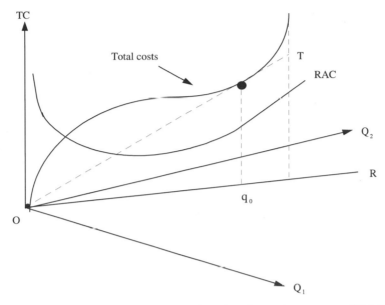

Figure 5.3 Economies of scale for multiproduct firms: the concept of RAC.
Source: Adapted from Baumol et al. (1988, p.50).

The concepts of RAC and multiproduct scale economies refer to proportionate changes in the quantities in the entire product set. However, a firm could change the production of a single output, holding the production of the other products constant. In order to define product-specific economies of scale, it is first necessary to introduce the concept of incremental cost. The incremental cost (IC_i) for product i at a vector of outputs Q* is the additional cost required to produce $Q_i = Q_i^*$ in place of $Q_i = 0$, i.e.

$$IC_i (Q^*) = C(Q_1^*, \ldots Q_i^*, \ldots Q_n^*)$$
$$- C(Q_1^*, \ldots Q_{i-1}^*, 0, Q_{i+1}^*, \ldots, Q_n^*) \qquad [5.2]$$

The degree of scale economies specific to a product is measured by the ratio of the average incremental cost of the product to its marginal cost (Forestieri, 1993).

Humphrey (1985) cautioned about the possible confusion between plant- (branch) and firm-scale economies. In the case of unit banks (one-branch banks), output can be expanded only by producing more of various banking services at a single office. Plant- and firm-scale economies are therefore identical. On the other hand, in a branch-banking organisation, scale economies for one office (plant-scale economies) may be quite different from those for the entire organisation or for all branches together (firm-scale economies). This is because branch banks can expand their output either by adding new services or by adding new branches. Plant-scale economies are calculated assuming that the expansion of output occurs with no increase in the number of branches, while firm-scale economies are calculated assuming that output expansion is accompanied by branch expansion. In the case of banks with a wide branch network, it is important to compute both plant- and firm-scale economies.

Additional cost advantages may result from producing more than one product. The impact of product diversification on banks' costs is captured in the notions of both cost complementarities and economies of scope. Cost complementarity means that the marginal cost of producing any product decreases with an increase in the output of any other product. If the cost of joint production is less than the sum of the costs resulting from independent production, then economies of scope are said to exist. Diseconomies of scope exist if joint production costs are higher than the sum of the independent production costs.

Consider two outputs, Q_1 and Q_2, and their separate cost functions, $TC(Q_1)$ and $TC(Q_2)$. If the joint cost of producing the two outputs is expressed by $TC(Q_1,Q_2)$, then economies of scope exist if:

$$TC(Q_1,Q_2) < TC(Q_1) + TC(Q_2) \qquad [5.3]$$

If the inequality is reversed, then diseconomies of scope are said to exist. A measure of economies of scope is:

$$\text{Scope} = \frac{[TC(Q_1) + TC(Q_2) - TC(Q_1,Q_2)]}{TC(Q_1,Q_2)} \qquad [5.4]$$

Figure 5.4 shows that the concept of scale economies involves a comparison of $TC(Q_1{}^*,0) + TC(0, Q_2{}^*)$, the sum of the heights of the cost surface over the points on the axes corresponding to $Q_1{}^*$ and $Q_2{}^*$, with $TC(Q_1{}^*,Q_2{}^*)$, the height of the cost surface at point $(Q_1{}^*,Q_2{}^*)$. If $TC(Q_1{}^*,Q_2{}^*)$ lies below the hyperplane OAB, which goes through the origin and points $TC(Q_1{}^*,0)$ and $TC(0, Q_2{}^*)$, then the condition for scope economies is achieved (Baumol et al., 1988).

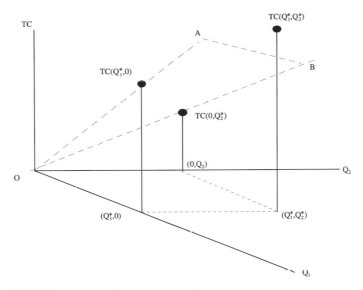

Figure 5.4   The concept of scope economies.
Source: Adapted from Baumol et al. (1988, p.72).

Berger et al. (1987) developed alternative scale and product mix measures: expansion path scale economies (EPSCE) and expansion path subadditivity (EPSUB), which compare the costs of firms that differ in both scale and product mix simultaneously. The expansion path measures costs relative to firms represented in the data, as opposed to the standard ray scale and scope measures, which compare the costs of firms that have the same product mix. Berger et al. (1987) identified the following potential sources of scope and product mix economies:

- spreading fixed costs;
- information economies;
- risk reduction;
- consumer cost economies.

According to Forestieri (1993), the hypothesis of the existence of scale and scope economies is usually grounded in one or more of the following:

- technology (Humphrey, 1985; Hunter and Timme, 1986; Evanoff et al., 1990; Landi, 1990);

- specialised labour (Bell and Murphy, 1968; Clark, 1988; Muldur, 1991);
- information economies (Arrow, 1971; Williamson, 1975; Berger et al., 1987; Shaffer, 1991; Humphrey, 1991);
- strategic and organisational flexibility (Berger et al., 1987; Gilbert and Steinherr, 1989; Litan, 1987; Muldur, 1990);
- demand side benefits (Herring and Santomero, 1990).

The methodology used to estimate scale and scope economies in banking has become increasingly complex. The choice of the functional form for the total cost or production functions reflects the problems in defining the characteristics of the bank production process. The Cobb–Douglas, constant elasticity of substitution (CES), translog, hybrid translog and Fourier-flexible functions have all enjoyed prominence. The methodological issues associated with estimating scale and scope economies are reviewed by, among others, Benston et al. (1982a), Kolari and Zardkoohi (1987), Berger et al. (1987), Forestieri (1993) and Molyneux et al. (1996).

Scale and scope economies: empirical evidence in US banking

This section reviews the results of some of the major studies investigating economies of scale and scope in US banking. Early investigations of the cost characteristics for banks of different sizes were relatively simple. Typically, these relied on accounting information to calculate financial ratios relating bank costs to output.

The first major systematic study of bank cost was undertaken by Alhadeff (1954), who compared the costs of Californian branch and unit banks of different size using data covering the period 1938–50. Output was measured as the ratio of loans and investments to total assets, to reflect the used capacity of the bank. Alhadeff found that branch banks produced greater output per dollar resources than unit banks. There was evidence of increasing returns to scale for both large and small banks, and constant returns to scale for medium-sized banks. Horovitz (1963) employed similar definitions of total costs and output, and reached similar findings using a data set covering the period 1940–60. Scale economies in banking appeared to be relatively small and did not outweigh diseconomies relating to branching.

A major criticism of these early studies related to the use of earning assets as a measure of output. Since this measure did not include all assets, this omission tended to exaggerate the average unit cost of large banks. In order to avoid this potential bias, Schweiger and McGee (1961) and Gramley (1962) used total assets as measure of bank output. Schweiger and McGee found that large banks had a cost advantage over small and medium-sized banks. Gramley found that average cost decreased as bank size increased, and therefore confirmed that larger banks had a cost advantage over small banks.

Benston (1965a, 1965b) marked the beginning of a new direction for the bank cost literature by employing a Cobb–Douglas cost function to investigate economies of scale in banking. Benston found that economies of scale were present, but were small for all banking services. Using a similar approach, Bell and Murphy (1968) found evidence of economies of scale for most banking services. Branching was found to be more costly than unit-banking operations. A number of studies that used alternative output definitions and input variables followed. Greenbaum (1967) reviewed the early literature on bank costs, and concluded that economies of scale were generally exhausted after banks exceeded $10 million in asset size. Banks with more than $10 million in assets were therefore inefficient, because of high overhead unit costs, high transaction costs, and the lack of sufficient specialisation and limited diversification.

In the 1970s, researchers sought to take into account technological change and other developments affecting the banking industry (Schweitzer, 1972; Murphy, 1972a; Murphy, 1972b; Daniel et al., 1973; Kalish and Gilbert, 1973; Longbrake and Haslem, 1975; Mullineaux, 1975; Mullineaux, 1978). From these studies, it emerged that if there were economies of scale in banking, then these were not sufficient to preclude small and medium-sized banks from viable competition. According to Benston et al. (1982a, p. 435), 'A consensus emerges from retrospective research into banking costs that there are constant economies of scale irrespective of the size of the bank.' At the start of the 1980s, however, this conclusion began to come under fire, on both theoretical and methodological grounds. Studies that used the Cobb–Douglas functional form were subject to various limitations. Many were based on modest samples, in which large banks were underrepresented. Furthermore, the Cobb–Douglas functional form allows neither for a U-shaped average cost curve, nor for the computation of economies of scope.

The first study to use a translog functional form to estimate scale economies was by Benston et al. (1982b). The translog offered at least two important advantages over the Cobb–Douglas functional form. First, it allowed for a U-shaped average cost curve or, more generally, for a cost curve that is not uniform for all sizes. Second, it dispensed with the ancillary hypothesis of an input elasticity equal to one, which is implicit in the Cobb–Douglas functional form. It also imposed fewer constraints on the structure of costs than the CES production function (Forestieri, 1993). It is therefore possible to test for any non-monotonic trend in the cost function, and for the relationship between multiproduct operations and costs. In general, the translog functional form appeared to be more suitable to represent the true nature of the activity of financial institutions.

Benston et al. (1982b) found evidence of the existence of U-shaped cost curves. US unit banks with more than $50 million in deposits recorded diseconomies of scale, while those operating in branching states experienced small economies of scale. Murray and White (1983) examined the production technology of credit unions in Canada, following Sealey and Lindley's (1977) intermediation approach. Evidence of economies of scale was obtained, and large multiproduct credit unions were found to be more efficient than small, single-product credit unions. From this point onwards, there was an increasing tendency for researchers to construct models of financial institutions as multiproduct firms. As such, the measurement of scope economies became a key issue in the analysis of the banking industry's cost structure.

The increasing use of the translog functional form led to a reappraisal of earlier results. The majority of studies from the

1980s, using either the production or the intermediation approach, reported the existence of scale economies up to a very low level of output (typically around $100 million). The estimated average cost function was often U-shaped, but the optimal bank size was typically small (Benston et al., 1982b; Benston et al., 1983; Gilligan et al., 1984; Berger et al., 1987; Humphrey, 1987; Mester, 1987). With the exception of Gilligan et al., these studies found little evidence of substantial scope economies.

One of the major shortcomings of the standard translog function is its indeterminacy when one or more products are produced. The Box–Cox transformation of a translog cost function (employed by Clark, 1984) or the hybrid translog function (Kolari and Zardkoohi, 1987) can solve this problem. A different, but commonly adopted, solution consists of assigning arbitrary low, positive values to the level of production of each service (Kim, 1986; Mester, 1987; Rossi, 1991). The translog function tends to give a poor approximation when applied to banks of all sizes, because it forces large and small banks to lie on a symmetric U-shaped ray average cost curve, and disallows other possibilities. McAllister and McManus (1993) also point out that the translog function may behave poorly away from the mean product mix, which can create problems in measuring scale economies because large banks tend to have very different product mixes from the average. The solution they proposed consisted of replacing the translog with one of several non-parametric estimation procedures.

In general, the translog studies suggested that average cost curves in US banking are U-shaped. Economies of scale exist only up to relatively low levels of output (between $25 and $200 million in deposit size). It is important to point out, however, that until the late 1980s, the majority of US banking cost studies tended to use only limited data on large institutions. Studies that used samples including large US banks generally found evidence of scale economies at higher output levels, well beyond $100–200 million in the deposit size range (Hunter and Timme, 1986; Shaffer and David, 1986; Kim, 1986; Hunter et al., 1990; Noulas et al., 1990). None of these studies, however, found much evidence of scope economies.

Berger, Hancock et al. (1993) point out a major difficulty in the scale economies literature, namely that most studies did not use a

frontier estimation method. In fact, they note that scale economies theoretically apply only to the efficient frontier, and the use
of data from banks off the frontier could compound inefficiencies
due to failure to achieve economies of scale with differences between firms in productive efficiency. Since the mid-1980s, considerable attention has been devoted to the estimation of
productive efficiency. This topic will be reviewed later in this
chapter.

The literature on scope economies seems to be even more
problematic. Berger et al. (1993) point out three major problems.
First, the translog functional form, on which many studies have
been based, is insufficiently flexible to describe an industry with
increasing returns to scale up to some point and constant returns
thereafter. It also has difficulties when firms tend to change product mix significantly as they change scale. The translog and the
Box–Cox approximation perform poorly in estimating scope
economies because they have trouble with estimations at or near
zero. Second, there are often little or no data on firms that spe-
cialise. Third, it is difficult to evaluate scope economies using data
that are not on the frontier. In order to address these limitations,
Berger et al. proposed the concept of optimal scope economies,
based on the profit function instead of the cost function. This
incorporates the revenue effects of output choices as well as the
cost effects of input choices, providing at least a partial solution to
the above limitations.

Scale and scope economies: empirical evidence in European banking

Early studies on the cost characteristics of European banking
began to appear in the mid-1970s (Maes, 1975; Lévy-Garboua
and Lévy-Garboua, 1975). These studies found evidence of substantial economies of scale in the French and Italian banking
sectors. More recent studies have also found evidence of economies of scale in both of these banking sectors. There is also
evidence that scope economies have become more prevalent.
Casu and Girardone (1998) found that slight scale economies

existed in the Italian banking market, and that banking groups realised greater scope economies compared with non-group banks. These findings are in line with other studies that found strong evidence of scope economies for large banks in many European banking sectors (European Commission, 1997).

Elsewhere in Europe, Fanjul and Maravall (1985) and Rodriguez et al. (1993) found evidence of both scale and scope economies for medium-sized saving banks, and diseconomies of scale and scope for larger institutions in Spain. Gathon and Grosjean (1991) found decreasing returns to scale for the four largest Belgian banks, with assets above 50 million BF, and increasing returns to scale in all other banks. Pallage (1991) found evidence of scale economies for small Belgian institutions, and diseconomies of scale as size increases, confirming the results of Pacolet (1986). Evidence of scope economies was found for the five largest Belgian banks.

UK studies have focused mainly on the building society sector. Gough (1979) and Barnes and Dodds (1983) both estimated linear average cost functions, and found no evidence of scale economies for UK building societies, using data covering the periods 1972–79 and 1970–78 respectively. Cooper (1980) found evidence of scale economies for building societies with assets of less than £100 million, and of diseconomies of scale for larger societies. Hardwick (1989, 1990) found evidence of scale economies for relatively smaller building societies and no evidence of scope economies.

McKillop and Glass (1994) employed a hybrid translog cost function to obtain measures of overall economies of scale, product-specific scale economies and economies of scope. The data were obtained from the 1991 annual returns for a sample of 89 national, regional and local building societies. There was evidence of significant augmented economies of scale for both national and local societies, but only constant returns to scale for those societies that are regionally based. There was no evidence of economies of scope or cost complementarities. Drake (1995) used a translog multiproduct cost function that allowed the first empirical test for expense-preference behaviour in UK building societies. There was no evidence of either scale or scope economies.

Several studies have investigated scale and scope economies across European banking markets. Molyneux et al. (1996) used the hybrid translog cost function to examine economies of scale and scope in France, Germany, Italy and Spain. There were noticeable differences in cost characteristics between countries. Scope and scale economies appeared to be evident in each country, however, over a wide range of bank output levels. The European Commission (1997) also investigated the cost characteristics of various European banking sectors, while assessing the potential gains brought about by the 1992 Single Market Programme (SMP). In all countries, there was evidence of both economies and diseconomies of scale. The preponderance of increasing returns to scale was found mainly for small banks, particularly in Germany and France. The existence of diseconomies of scale in several size bands suggested that, with the existing distribution of banks and current technology, the opportunities from exploiting economies of scale might be quite limited. There was clear potential for an SMP effect in that substantial economies of scale existed, especially for the small banks in more fragmented banking sectors. Strong evidence of large economies of scope was also found for Europe's largest banks.

RECENT APPROACHES TO MEASURING BANKS' PRODUCTIVE EFFICIENCY

As is apparent from the previous sections, scale and scope economies have been studied extensively, especially in the context of US financial institutions. However, more recently, greater attention has been paid to measuring what appears to be a much more important source of cost differences: productive inefficiency or deviations from the efficient production function or frontier. Productive inefficiencies derive from differences between the abilities of managers to control costs or maximise profits. There is a broad consensus that differences in average costs among financial institutions attributable to differences in productive efficiency exceed those attributable to failure to realise the full benefits of economies of scale or scope (Berger and Humphrey, 1997). There is, however, no consensus as to the preferred method for determining the best-practice frontier against which relative efficiencies are measured. At a broad level, the various methods can be classified into parametric and non-parametric approaches.

Parametric models

There are three main parametric approaches to the estimation of the best-practice frontier:

- stochastic frontier approach (SFA)
- distribution free approach (DFA)
- thick frontier approach (TFA).

The SFA specifies a functional form for the cost, profit or production function, and allows for random error. It generally assumes that inefficiencies, denoted μ, follow an asymmetric half-normal distribution, and that random errors, denoted ν, follow a symmetric standard normal distribution (Aigner et al., 1977). The total error term is given by $\varepsilon - \mu + \nu$. Both the inefficiencies and the random error are assumed to be orthogonal to the inputs, outputs or other exogenous variables specified in the estimating equation (Ferrier and Lovell, 1990; Timme and Yang, 1991; Bauer et al., 1993). The estimated inefficiency of any firm is taken as the conditional mean or mode of the distribution of the inefficiency term, μ, given the observation of the composed error term, ε.

It can be argued that the half-normal assumption for the distribution of inefficiency is rather inflexible, and that it presumes that most firms are clustered near full efficiency. Other distributions, such as the truncated normal or the gamma distributions, may be more appropriate (Greene, 1990; Yuengert, 1993; Mester, 1996; Berger and DeYoung, 1997). Allowing for more flexibility in the assumed distribution of the inefficiencies, however, may make it difficult to separate inefficiency from random error (Berger and Humphrey, 1997). Bauer et al. (1997) argue that any arbitrarily chosen distributional assumptions can lead to significant error in estimating individual firm efficiencies.

The SFA can be estimated using cross-sectional data. In contrast, the DFA requires a panel data set. Under this approach, the efficiency differences are assumed to be stable over time, but no specific distributional assumptions are required (Berger, 1991; Berger, 1993; Bauer et al., 1993; Berger and Humphrey, 1991; Berger et al., 1993). The estimate of inefficiency for each firm is the difference between its average residual and the average residual of the firm on the frontier, with some truncation performed to account for the failure of the random component to average out to zero. Another way to apply DFA is to use fixed effects estimation, with a separate dummy variable specified for each firm. Each firm's dummy variable coefficient represents its inefficiency score (Lang and Welzel, 1996). If efficiency is changing over time, DFA describes the average deviation of each firm from the average best-practice frontier, rather than efficiency at one point in time (Berger and Humphrey, 1997).

The TFA assumes that deviations from predicted costs within the lowest average-cost quartile of banks in a size class represent random error. Deviations in predicted costs between the highest and the lowest quartile represent productive inefficiencies (Berger and Humphrey, 1991; Bauer et al., 1993; Berger, Hancock et al., 1993). This approach imposes no distributional assumptions on either the inefficiencies or the random error, except to assume that inefficiencies differ between the highest and lowest quartiles, and that random error exists within these quartiles. The TFA itself does not provide exact point estimates of efficiency for individual firms, but does provide an estimate of the overall level of efficiency.

Non-parametric models

The main non-parametric approaches are data envelopment analysis (DEA) and free disposal hull (FDH). DEA employs mathematical programming methods to construct production frontiers and to measure efficiency relative to the constructed frontiers. The main difference between DEA and the parametric approaches described above is that the DEA production frontier is not determined by a specific functional form; instead it is generated directly from the actual data for the evaluated firms. The DEA frontier is formed as the piecewise linear combination that connects the set of best-practice observations, yielding a convex production possibility set (PPS). As a consequence, the DEA efficiency score for a specific firm (or decision-making unit, DMU) is not defined by an absolute standard, but is defined relative to other firms. Extensive reviews of the relevant literature on applications of DEA to banking can be found in Sciford and Thrall (1990), Lovell (1993) and Berger and Humphrey (1997).

The FDH approach, developed by Deprins et al. (1984), is a special case of DEA. Here, the hypothesis of convexity of the PPS is abandoned, and the PPS is composed only of the DEA vertices and the FDH points interior to these vertices. Because the FDH frontier is either congruent or interior to the DEA frontier, FDH will typically generate larger efficiency estimates than DEA (Tulkens, 1993). The FDH approach allows for a better approximation or envelopment of the observed data. DEA is a more efficient estimator than FDH, but only if the assumption of convexity is correct.

Both DEA and FDH permit efficiency to vary over time, and neither method requires prior assumptions regarding the form of the distribution of inefficiencies across observations, except that undominated observations are 100% efficient (Berger and Humphrey, 1997). A drawback of non-parametric approaches, however, is that they generally assume there is no random component affecting a firm's performance. There have been a number of attempts to generalise and extend the standard DEA non-parametric approach. These include the polyhedral cone-ratio DEA model (Charnes et al., 1990; Brockett et al., 1997; Resti, 1996); the assurance region DEA model (Thompson et al., 1997; Taylor et al., 1997); the non-parametric Malmquist Index method of productivity measurement (Griffell-Tatjé and Lovell, 1994); and tests of the sensitivity of DEA and FDH efficiency models to different radial and non-radial measurement techniques (Ferrier et al., 1994; Pastor, 1995; DeBorger et al., 1995).

Bergendahl (1995) has suggested the concept of a composite frontier: the DEA frontier should be composed of the most efficient parts of banks within the sample, forming a composite or representative firm, instead of being composed of separate and individual firms. The composite frontier would indicate the efficiency that had been achieved within the sample, though not necessarily within a single institution. In this way, the frontier would represent best practice, without confounding efficient results achieved in one specific area with inefficiencies elsewhere.

Is there a 'best' frontier method?

Frontier analysis is essentially a way to benchmark the relative performance of production units. Most institutions – and not only financial institutions – benchmark themselves against a certain standard in order to evaluate their performance. There is widespread consensus that frontier analysis outperforms the standard financial ratios from accounting statements for most regulatory and other purposes (Bauer et al., 1997). This is because frontier efficiency measures use statistics or programming to remove the effects of differences in input prices and other exogenous market factors affecting the standard performance ratios, in order to obtain better estimates of firm-level efficiency. These approaches allow the researcher to focus on the quantitative effects on costs, input use, and so on that regulatory changes (or other factors) are likely to cause (Bauer et al., 1997).

Despite intense research effort, however, there is still no consensus as to the best method or set of methods for measuring frontier efficiency. Parametric approaches impose a particular functional form that presupposes the shape of the frontier. Consequently, if the functional form is misspecified, measured efficiency may be confounded with specification error. On the other hand, non-parametric approaches impose less structure on the frontier, but do not allow for random error. If random error exists, measured efficiency may be confounded with these random deviations from the true efficient frontier. Berger and Humphrey (1997) argue that it is not possible to determine which of the two major approaches dominates the other, since the true level of efficiency is unknown. A possible solution would be to add more flexibility to the parametric approaches, and to introduce a degree of random error in non-parametric models. By addressing the main limitations of each approach, it should be possible to obtain efficiency estimates that are more consistent across various approaches.

Some researchers have experimented with more flexible functional forms using parametric models. Among others, Mester (1992) has estimated hybrid translog functions. Berger, Hunter et al. (1993) used a Fuss normalised quadratic variable profit function. More recent studies have used the Fourier-flexible functional form, which adds Fourier trigonometric terms to a standard translog function (Spong et al., 1995; Mitchell and Onvural, 1996; Berger et al., 1997; Berger and Mester, 1997; Altunbas et al., 1999). The Fourier-flexible functional form is attractive as it increases the flexibility of the frontier by allowing many inflection points and including orthogonal trigonometric terms that help fit the frontier to the data wherever it is needed most. In one study, Berger and DeYoung (1997) found that using the Fourier-flexible form instead of the translog reduced the amount of measured inefficiency by as much as 50%, since the Fourier was able to produce a much closer approximation to the data.

In the field of non-parametric approaches, researchers are following two main directions. The first tries to provide a statistical basis for DEA. The second seeks to implement a version of DEA that allows the estimates to contain a stochastic or random component. In the first case, analytical research is seeking to provide a theoretical foundation for hypothesis testing based on DEA. The main issue concerns the specification of the distribution of efficiency across firms (Simar, 1996). Hypothesis testing can be conducted only after the data-generating process has been specified, and in a multidimensional non-parametric setting in which the inefficiencies are one-sided, this is a complex matter. The sampling distributions of DEA efficiency estimators remain unknown, although resampling techniques such as bootstrapping may be used to obtain an empirical approximation. Once the underlying distribution is approximated, statistical inference can be conducted. Careful attention, however, needs to be paid to the specification of the data-generating process (Simar and Wilson, 1995).

In the empirical area, researchers are seeking to develop a stochastic version of DEA. Here, inequality constraints describing the structure of the non-parametric DEA technology are converted into chance constraints, which, due to noise in the data, are allowed to be violated by a certain proportion of the observations. If probability distributions are specified for these violations, the constraints can be converted into certainty equivalents, and chance-constrained DEA models emerge as non-linear programming problems. Although the chance-constrained DEA model remains deterministic, it incorporates noise in the data (Grosskopf, 1996).

While research is evolving along a variety of directions, Bauer et al. (1997) have argued that it is not necessary to have consensus on which is the single best-frontier approach for measuring productive efficiency. Instead, they proposed a set of consistency conditions that efficiency measures derived from various approaches should meet so as to be useful for regulators or other decision makers:

- Efficiency scores generated by the different approaches should have comparable means, standard deviations and other distributional properties.
- Different approaches should rank the institutions in approximately the same order.
- Different approaches should identify mostly the same institutions as best practice and worst practice.
- All approaches should demonstrate reasonable stability over time.
- Efficiency scores generated by different approaches should be reasonably consistent with competitive conditions in the market.
- The measured efficiency from all of the useful approaches should be reasonably consistent with the standard non-frontier performance measures, such as return on assets or equity, or cost to income or assets ratios.

The first three consistency conditions may be thought of as measuring the degree to which the different approaches are mutually consistent, while the others may be thought of as measuring the degree to which the efficiency measures generated by different approaches are consistent with reality or are believable.

PRODUCTIVE EFFICIENCY IN BANKING: EMPIRICAL EVIDENCE

In recent years, there has been a proliferation of academic studies of the efficiency of financial institutions. Berger and Humphrey (1997) surveyed 130 such studies, which employed at least five major techniques, using data on at least 21 countries and four types of financial institutions: commercial banks, savings banks, credit unions and insurance companies. Within this survey, applications of parametric techniques (60 applications) and non-parametric techniques (69 applications) were split fairly evenly. Most studies relate to US banking (which accounted for 66 out of 116 single-country studies), but European research is developing rapidly (Molyneux et al., 1996).

Applications of efficiency analysis seek not only to provide information for policy makers (identifying the efficiency implications of deregulation, financial institution failure, mergers, and so on) but also to investigate a host of other issues, such as those relating to corporate control and the impact of risk on efficiency (Altunbas et al., 2000; Altunbas, Evans et al., 2001). Some studies have investigated the stability of bank efficiency over time, while others have suggested ways to help managers improve performance. Any classification of the studies according to the specific issues they raise is to some extent arbitrary, since the conclusions drawn are often of interest to more than a single party. Moreover, the distinction between studies that employ parametric and non-parametric approaches has recently started to become blurred, as increasing attention has been devoted to comparisons between different methods (Ferrier and Lovell, 1990; Giokas, 1991; Ferrier et al., 1994; DeBorger et al., 1995; Resti, 1997; Eisenbeis et al., 1996; Casu and Girardone, 1998).

Overall, the empirical evidence from the recent literature suggests that the efficiency estimates from parametric and non-parametric approaches are quite similar, but the non-parametric methods generally yield slightly lower mean efficiency estimates and seem to have greater dispersion. More specifically, Berger and Humphrey (1997) found that for the US studies that used DEA and other non-parametric methods, the average efficiency score was 0.72 overall. The standard deviation of efficiencies in these studies was 0.17, and the efficiencies ranged between 0.31 and 0.97. The average efficiency scores for the non-US studies that used non-parametric methods was 0.71. Studies that employed parametric methods reported an overall mean efficiency of 0.84 for the US banking, with a standard deviation of 0.06, and efficiency estimates ranging between 0.61 and 0.95. As Berger and Humphrey (1997) pointed out, however, the similarity in average efficiency values across different methods does not carry over strongly into similarities in the efficiency rankings of individual firms. This suggests that the confidence intervals surrounding individual firm or branch efficiency estimates are substantial. Table 5.1 shows the main empirical findings from recent US studies.

Berg, Forsund et al.'s (1993) DEA study of bank efficiency in Finland, Norway and Sweden in 1990 was possibly the first cross-country European study. Within countries, efficiency differences between banks were most important in Finland and Norway, and least important in Sweden. The largest Swedish banks were among the most efficient units in the pooled sample, whereas only one large Finnish bank and no large Norwegian bank had efficiency scores above 0.9. More recently, Berg et al. (1995) used DEA to investigate efficiency in the banking sectors of Denmark, Finland, Norway and Sweden. The study found that the largest Danish and Swedish banks were among the most efficient units in the pooled sample. Danish and Swedish banks appeared to be in the best position to expand in a common Nordic banking market.

Pastor et al. (1995) analysed productivity, efficiency and differences in technology, using non-parametric methods for eight European countries in 1992. France, Spain and Belgium appeared to have the most efficient banking sectors (with average efficiency scores of 0.950, 0.822 and 0.806, respectively), while the UK (0.537), Austria (0.608) and Germany (0.650) were the least efficient. Allen and Rai (1996) used both the SFA and DFA on a sample of 194 banks from 14 Organization for Economic Cooperation and Development (OECD) countries (including nine in the

Table 5.1 Review of US studies on bank productive efficiency

Study	Data	Model	Findings
Sherman and Gold (1985)	Data on a savings bank branch with 14 branch offices for 1982.	DEA	DEA identified 6 of the 14 banks to be relatively inefficient, with an average efficiency of the sample equal to 0.96.
Parkan (1987)	Data on 35 branches of a major Canadian bank.	DEA	DEA identified 11 of the 35 branches to be relatively inefficient.
Rangan et al. (1988)	Data on 215 independent banks.	DEA	The average value of efficiency for the sample was 0.70.
Elysiani and Mehdian (1990a)	Data on a random sample of 144 US banks for the period 1980–85.	DEA	The average value of efficiency for the sample was 0.90.
Elysiani and Mehdian (1990b)	Data on a sample of 191 large US banks for the period 1980–85.	DEA	The average value of efficiency for the sample was 0.88, revealing an inward shift of the frontier due to technological advancement.
Aly et al. (1990)	Data on a sample of 322 independent banks from the call reports for 1996.	DEA	The results indicated a low level of overall inefficiency, which was more technical (0.75) rather than allocative (0.81).
Ferrier and Lovell (1990)	Data on 575 banks for 1984.	DEA and SFA	Overall inefficiency was 21% according to DEA, and 26% according to SFA.
Berger and Humphrey (1991)	Data on US banks for 1984.	TFA	The authors suggested that their efficiency results (0.81) showed operational inefficiencies.
Yue (1992)	Data on 60 Missouri banks for the period 1984–90.	DEA	Overall efficiency of 0.8. It appeared that scale inefficiency was not a major source of inefficiency.
Bauer et al. (1993)	Panel data on 683 large US branching state banks for the period 1977–88.	SFA and TFA	The average efficiency for the sample was 0.87. The levels of efficiency were found to be reasonably consistent between the two approaches and over time.

(*continued over*)

Study	Data	Model	Findings
Berger, Hunter et al. (1993)	Data on US commercial banks from the call reports for the period 1984–89.	DFA	Inefficiencies in US banks appear to be quite large (0.52 small banks; 0.65, medium-sized banks; 0.66, large banks). Larger banks appear to be substantially more efficient than smaller banks.
Kaparakis et al. (1994)	Data on 5548 banks with assets over $50 million for 1986.	SFA	Overall estimated inefficiency amounted to 10%.
Berger et al. (1994)	Data on 760 branches of an anonymous US bank over the period 1989–91.	DFA	Total efficiency averages 0.90 and 0.66 for the intermediation and the production approaches, respectively.
Wheelock and Wilson (1994)	Data on 269 banks participating in the FCA programme for 1993.	DEA	Results show considerable inefficiencies among banks in the sample (around 50%).
Hunter and Timme (1995)	Data on 317 banks with assets over $1 billion over the period 1985–90.	DFA	Overall inefficiencies in the range of 23–36%.
Kwan and Eisenbeis (1995)	Data on 254 bank holding companies, based on semi-annual data from 1986 to 1991.	SFA	The average small-sized bank is found to be relatively less efficient (0.81) than their larger counterpart (0.92). The average x-inefficiency appears to be declining over time.
Spong et al. (1995)	Data on 143 state banks for 1994.	SFA	The average bank in the least efficient group has an efficiency index of 0.71, while the average efficiency index for a bank in the most efficient group is 0.94.
Berger and DeYoung (1997)	Data on US commercial banks over the period 1985–94.	SFA	Overall average efficiency of 0.92 over the entire sample period.
Berger and Mester (1997)	Data on 6000 US commercial banks over the period 1990–95.	DFA	Failure to account for the equity position of a bank makes large banks appear to be more efficient than small banks.

(*continued over*)

Study	Data	Model	Findings
Thompson et al. (1997)	Data on a panel of the USA's 100 largest banks in asset size over the period 1986–91.	DEA	High levels of inefficiency were found: 0.81, 0.71, 0.61, 0.62, 0.57 and 0.65 for the years of analysis.
Bhattacharya et al. (1997)	Data on 70 Indian commercial banks over the period 1986–91.	DEA	Overall efficiency of 0.80; publicly owned banks seem to be more efficient (0.87) than their privately owned (0.75) and foreign-owned (0.75) counterparts.
Taylor et al. (1997)	Data on 13 Mexican commercial banks over the period 1989–91.	DEA	The average efficiency is 0.75, 0.72 and 0.69 for the 3 years of analysis, respectively.
Humphrey and Pulley (1997)	Data on a panel of 683 US banks, all having assets over $100 million in 1988. Three time periods: 1977–80, 1981–84 and 1985–88.	TFA	Overall average efficiency of 0.81, 0.82 and 0.85, respectively, in the 3 time periods. Apparently, deregulation brought about an improved business environment.
Brockett et al. (1997)	Data on the 16 largest banks in Texas over the period 1984–85.	DEA	Overall average efficiency scores of 0.97 both in 1984 and 1985 for the CCR DEA, 0.91 for 1984, and 0.89 for 1985 for the cone ratio DEA model.
Schaffinit et al. (1997)	Data on 291 Ontario-based branches of a large Canadian bank, subdivided into 4 groups according to size for 1993.	DEA	Overall average efficiency for the basic DEA model of 0.72, and 0.54 for refined DEA model.

European Union, EU) for the period 1988–92. Large banks operating in countries that prohibited the functional integration of commercial and investment banking had the largest inefficiency measures, amounting to 27.5% of total costs.

Using banks' balance sheet and income statement data for the period 1987–94, the European Commission (1997) estimated a pooled time-series cost frontier for all the main EU banking sectors. Overall, the study found average productive inefficiencies of around 20%. Results for individual countries, calculated from the pooled EU estimates, showed that Luxembourg banks appeared to be relatively more efficient (0.88) than their counterparts in other banking systems. Individual country estimates suggested that there had been no systematic change in productive efficiency following the implementation of the SMP in 1992. Pooled estimates, however, suggested a general movement towards the EU cost efficiency frontier between 1990 and 1994.

Pastor et al. (1997) carried out international comparisons by defining a common frontier that incorporated various country-specific environmental conditions. The common frontier is built under the assumption that the environment is likely to differ across countries more than banking technology. To test this hypothesis, DEA efficiency scores for each European country were obtained from a common frontier with and without environmental variables. With environmental variables omitted, the average efficiency scores were lower than when these variables were included. Overall, the results indicated that there were three groups: Denmark, Spain, Germany, Luxembourg and France had the highest average efficiency scores between 1.00 and 0.88; the Netherlands, Belgium, the UK and Portugal had average efficiency scores between 0.69 and 0.56; and Italy had the lowest average efficiency score (0.35).

Dietsch and Weill (1998) used unconsolidated accounting data of 661 commercial, mutual and savings banks from 11 EU countries covering the period 1992–96 to estimate changes in efficiency and productivity. Overall, the results suggested an increase in efficiency when measured using both a cost and a profit frontier. This trend, however, was not observed in all countries: France, Italy, Luxembourg and the UK experienced decreasing efficiency measured in terms of costs. Productivity results showed an increase in total productivity, mainly due to technological change. Overall, European integration appeared to have had a small but positive effect on efficiency in banking prior to 1996.

Altunbas, Gardener et al. (2001) used a Fourier-flexible functional form to estimate a stochastic cost frontier from which estimates of scale economies, productive inefficiencies and technical change were obtained for a sample of European banks with data covering the period 1988–95. The country estimates revealed that the relative inefficiency of various banking sectors (Austria, Denmark, Finland, Italy and the UK) increased over time. On average, inefficiencies appeared to be around 25%. Inefficiency was more variable across countries and bank size bands and over time than the scale economy estimates.

Maudos et al. (1999) examined efficiency for a sample of banks from 11 EU countries with data covering the period 1993–96 using both cost and profit frontiers and taking into account firms' specialisations in the measurement of efficiency. Using cluster analysis to group banks according to specialisation, efficiency estimates increased when separate frontiers were estimated for each cluster, instead of estimating a common frontier for all banks. Using the cost frontier, the average efficiency score for the whole sample was 0.44, compared with 0.74 when estimation of separate frontiers was carried out. Differences in product mix therefore seem to be important in explaining efficiency.

Berger and Humphrey (1997) suggest that there is a clear need for more work in the area of international comparisons. In Europe, it is a topic of growing interest in view of the trend towards closer integration of national markets in financial services as a result of the SMP and European Monetary Union (EMU). Table 5.2 summarises selected European bank efficiency studies.

BANK EFFICIENCY: MANAGERIAL ISSUES

The preceding sections of this chapter have focused on the academic literature that seeks to evaluate the presence of economies of scale and scope, and productive efficiency, in various banking sectors. While this research is of interest to academics and policy makers, it may seem somewhat detached from the practical issues facing bankers who wish to improve the efficiency of their own institutions. Of course, the various optimising techniques outlined above can be used to benchmark individual banks' efficiencies against major competitors. These techniques can also be applied to study the relative efficiency of banks' own branch networks.

Having said this, however, from a practical perspective the efficiency literature does not provide any panacea in guaranteeing improved overall efficiency. As we showed in Chapter 2, while cost : income ratios have been on a downward trend in various

Table 5.2 Review of European studies on bank productive efficiency

Study	Data	Model	Findings
Vassiloglou and Giolias (1990) (Greece)	Data on 20 Greek bank branches located in the vicinity of Athens.	DEA	Average annual efficiency estimate of 0.91.
Drake and Howcroft (1993) (UK)	Data on a sample of 190 branches drawn from one of the six largest UK clearing banks.	DEA	Overall average efficiency of 0.92, although there is considerable diversity across branches (standard deviation of 0.505).
Berg, Claussen et al. (1993) (Norway)	Data on 502 Finnish, 141 Norwegian and 120 Swedish banks for 1990.	DEA and Malmquist Index	Overall average efficiency of 0.58 for Finland, 0.78 for Norway, and 0.89 for Sweden.
Berg, Forsund et al. (1993) (Norway)	Data on 503 Finnish, 126 Swedish, and 150 Norwegian banks for 1990.	DEA	Overall average efficiency of 0.53 for Finland, 0.57 for Norway, and 0.78 for Sweden.
Tulkens (1993) (Belgium)	Data on 773 branches of a large, publicly owned Belgian bank for January 1987.	FDH	Out of the total of 773 branches, 136 are found to be inefficient. Inefficiency seems be more frequent in small branches than in large ones. Average efficiency appears to be quite high (0.97) due to the large percentage of observations that are 100% efficient.
Altunbas et al. (1994) (Italy)	Data on 516, 452 and 483 Italian credit co-operative banks for the years 1990, 1991 and 1992, respectively.	SFA	The mean inefficiency score was 13.1% in 1990, 15.9% in 1991, and 17% in 1992.
Grifell-Tatjé and Lovell (1995a) (Spain)	Data on nearly all Spanish savings banks over the period 1986–91.	DEA and Malmquist Index	Overall average efficiency of 0.78, 0.78, 0.79, 0.83, 0.83 and 0.83 for the 5 years of investigation, respectively. Average Malmquist Index 0.97.
Grifell-Tatjé and Lovell (1995b) (Spain)	Data on nearly all Spanish savings banks over the period 1986–91.	DEA and Malmquist Index	Overall average efficiency of 0.75, 0.74, 0.75, 0.80, 0.77 and 0.80 for the 5 years of investigation, respectively. Average Malmquist Index 0.945.
Berg et al. (1995) (Norway)	Data on 714 banks of 4 Nordic countries for 1993.	DEA	Largest Danish and Swedish banks are the most efficient.

(*continued over*)

Study	Data	Model	Findings
Maudos et al (1995) (Spain)	Data on a panel of Spanish savings banks over the period 1985–94.	SFA	The estimated average impact of technical change of average costs corresponds to an annual rate of 68%.
Pastor et al. (1995) (Spain)	Data on 168 US, 45 Austrian, 59 Spanish, 22 German, 18 UK, 31 Italian, 17 Belgian and 67 French banks for 1992.	DEA and Malmquist Index	Overall weighted average efficiency estimates of 0.81 for the USA, 0.89 for Spain, 0.93 for Germany, 0.92 for Italy, 0.92 for Austria, 0.54 for the UK, 0.95 for France, and 0.92 for Belgium.
Favero and Papi (1995) (Italy)	Data on a sample of 174 Italian banks for 1991.	DEA	Overall average efficiency equal to 0.96 for the production approach, and 0.95 for the intermediation approach.
Allen and Rai (1996) (Italy)	Data on 194 banks from 11 OECD countries (9 EU countries) for the period 1988–92.	DFA and SFA	Prevalence of cost inefficiencies on diseconomies of scale and scope. Input inefficiency amounting to 27.5% of total costs.
Resti (1997) (Italy)	Data on a panel of 270 Italian banks over the period 1988–92.	SFA and DEA	Overall average efficiency of 0.69 for the SFA and 0.74 for the DEA model.
European Commission (1997) (Europe)	Balance sheet and income statement data from 1987 (295 banks) to 1994 (1451 banks) obtained from the IBCA BankScope database for 10 EU countries.	SFA and DEA	Average efficiency levels in the EU of 0.72, 0.71, 0.73, 0.75 and 0.77, respectively for the 5 years under investigation, according to the SFA. According to the DEA, average efficiency levels are decreasing from 0.96 in 1990 to 0.93 in 1994.
Pastor et al. (1997) (Spain)	Data for 1993 for 24 Belgian, 29 Danish, 150 French, 203 German, 26 Italian, 68 Luxembourgian, 22 Dutch, 17 Portuguese, 28 Spanish and 45 British banks.	DEA	Average efficiency scores of 0.78 for Belgium, 0.71 for Denmark, 0.37 for France, 0.51 for Germany, 0.85 for Italy, 0.59 for Luxembourg, 0.71 for the Netherlands, 0.85 for Portugal, 0.82 for Spain, and 0.56 for the UK.

(*continued over*)

Study	Data	Model	Findings
Lovell and Pastor (1997) (Spain)	Data on 545 branch offices of a large anonymous Spanish bank for the first semester of 1995.	DEA	Overall average efficiency of 0.92. 60 bank branches out of 545 were found to be efficient.
Athanassopoulos (1997) (Greece)	Data on a sample of 68 commercial branches of a large bank in Greece.	DEA	The efficiency of the bank branches was estimated to be 0.90.
Casu and Girardone (1998) (Italy)	Data on 32 banking groups and 78 bank parent companies and subsidiaries for the year 1995.	DEA and SFA	SFA efficiency estimates equal to 0.927 for banking groups and 0.947 for bank parent companies and subsidiaries. DEA efficiency estimates of 0.887 for banking groups and 0.903 for bank parent companies and subsidiaries.
Maudos et al. (1998) (Spain)	Data on 879 European banking firms over the period 1993–96.	DFA	The results at 5% level truncation show a level of cost efficiency of 0.91 for the average of the 11 EU countries considered.
Dietsch and Weill (1998) (France)	Data on 661 commercial, mutual and savings banks form 11 EU countries for the period 1992–96.	DEA + Malmquist + Profit Efficiency	The results showed an increase in both cost and profit efficiency over the period. Increase in total productivity mainly due to positive technical progress.
Maudos et al. (1999) (Spain)	Data for a sample of banks (879 banks) form 11 EU countries for the period 1993–96.	Cost and profit translog functions	Average cost efficiency value obtained for the whole sample of 0.44; this value increases to 0.74 when bank specialisation is taken into account.
Altunbas, Gardener et al. (2001) (UK)	Data for a sample of European banks for the period 1988–95.	Fourier-Flexible	The country estimates show that the relative inefficiency of various banking markets has increased over time, averaging around 25% of total costs.

European banking sectors, not all banks have been successful in improving their efficiency during the 1990s. Also, a major limitation of the bulk of the academic literature is that it focuses mainly on the cost side of banks' operations, ignoring the revenue side. This is why some recent studies have tended to focus on modelling profit efficiency, so that both costs and revenues are taken into account.

This development is likely to be met with surprise (maybe derision) by bankers who have, for a considerable time, put their energies into trying to boost returns to shareholders by focusing on both costs and revenues. A critical element in improving revenues has been to focus on expanding high-margin/fee areas of business at the expense of low-margin/fee activities. Central to this has been the increased use of risk-adjusted performance measurement systems that help allocate capital more effectively, leading to better use of assets and higher risk-adjusted returns. In particular, European banks are aiming increasingly to boost their ability to generate revenues from a pool of assets, given the banks' capital backing and risk profile. This is seen as a critical element in boosting performance.

High-performing European banks have focused their strategy in three key areas:

- Banks have sought to improve operating efficiency by reducing staff and other costs. The more banks can adopt best-cost practice, subject to maintaining service quality and customer relationships, the stronger their competitive position and net income-generating capacity.
- The use of capital has been enhanced, with increasingly sophisticated internal risk-management tools used to direct capital resources to business areas that generate as much revenue as possible from a given level of capital, for a given level of risk. The more effectively scarce capital resources can be deployed, the greater the revenue that can be derived from a set pool of assets.
- Banks have sought to increase revenue by ensuring that the capital required to back assets is allocated efficiently, so that sufficient income is generated to meet both internal management and shareholder value requirements.

When macroeconomic growth and demand for banking products is sluggish, attention typically focuses on cost reduction, given the limited revenue-generating opportunities. This type of strategy was prevalent in the USA and the UK in the late 1980s and early 1990s. More recently, as these economies have emerged from recession and experienced a period of sustained growth, banks' ability to boost revenues by directing capital resources to higher-margin business has been a key element in improving performance. Many European banks appear to be following similar strategies as economic conditions improve and revenue opportunities grow. The positive relationship between asset productivity and returns for a variety of European banks is shown in Table 5.3.

Table 5.3 European banks: asset productivity and return on average equity, 1998

Bank	Asset productivity (%)	Return on average equity (%)	Bank	Asset productivity (%)	Return on average equity (%)
Lloyds TSB Group	9.8	31.0	ING Group	9.4	10.7
Abbey National	6.4	20.6	BNP	8.3	10.3
Bayerische Landesbank Girozentrale	6.0	20.3	UBS	4.3	10.2
Nat West	7.4	19.5	Deutsche Bank	6.3	10.1
NationsBank	7.7	17.6	Credit Agricole	7.8	9.7
Generale Bank	5.2	17.5	Landesbank Baden-Wuerttemberg	6.9	9.6
Barclays Bank	6.2	17.1	Deutsche Genossenshaftsbank	5.6	9.4
Halifax	7.9	16.3	Societe Generale	7.2	9.1
HSBC	9.0	15.6	Dresdner Bank	5.5	9.0
Banca Intesa	7.8	13.8	Credit Suisse Group	6.6	9.0
Banco Santander Central Hispano	9.9	13.1	Rabobank	6.6	8.2
Fortis (Banking)	7.8	12.9	Paribas	6.2	8.1
ABN AMRO	6.9	12.5	Westdeutsche Landesbank	6.0	7.5
San Paolo IMI	8.3	11.8	Bangesellschaft Berlin	6.6	7.0
Group Dexia	6.4	11.7	Groupe Caisse d'Epargne	6.2	6.1
			Credit Lyonnais	9.8	4.8

Source: Calculated from BankScope (1999).
Asset productivity = net revenue/total assets.

Overall, while European banks need to continue to focus on cost control, at the same time they also have to prioritise ways to increase revenue in order to boost returns. This needs to be borne in mind, especially given the overemphasis on cost efficiency in the academic literature.

CONCLUSION

Chapter 5 provides a non-technical review of the voluminous academic research into bank efficiency, from the earliest and (by later standards) relatively simplistic attempts, to the studies based on increasingly sophisticated econometric techniques that have appeared in recent years. While earlier studies concentrated mainly on analysing scale and scope economies, more recent literature has focused on estimation of productive efficiency, which measures how close financial institutions are to a best-practice frontier.

To date, there is broad consensus in the literature that differences in frontier efficiency among banks exceed differences attributable to failure to realise scale or scope economies. There is no consensus, however, as to the best method for estimating the best-practice frontier. The variety of parametric and non-parametric approaches that have been developed recently do not produce consistent results. This suggests that despite the large number of studies recently published on efficiency in banking, there is still a need for further research. Two main directions are currently being followed. For users of parametric models, the new developments include the specification of more globally flexible functional forms, the use of less restrictive assumptions on the distribution of inefficiencies, and the measurement of confidence intervals. For users of non-parametric models, the new developments include finding a statistical basis for the non-stochastic approaches, and allowing for a random component in performance when estimating the best-practice frontier.

While the majority of academic studies have focused on modelling efficiency using a best practice cost function, issues relating to revenue, profit and (even) the efficient use of capital remain substantially underinvestigated. As European and other banks focus increasingly on improving their revenue and use of capital, as well as their control of costs, it is likely that much greater attention will be paid to these areas in the future.

Chapter 6

Technological change in European banking

INTRODUCTION

Technological advances are currently having a dramatic impact on the structure, operations and economics of European banking markets. As noted in Chapter 4, technical progress is often cited as the main, if not the most important, driver of change in the banking industry. Naturally, developments in information collection, storage, processing, transmission and distribution technologies have a major impact on many aspects of banking activity.

Information technology (IT) developments affect banking in two main ways. First, they contribute to reducing costs associated with the management of information (collection, storage, processing and transmission), mainly by substituting paper-based and labour-intensive procedures with automated processes. Second, they alter the ways in which customers have access to banks' services and products, mainly through automated distribution channels such as Internet, telephone-based and other remote banking channels (European Central Bank, 1999). Overall, banks are involved with introducing new technology in four main areas:

- *Customer-facing technologies:* automated teller machines (ATMs), electronic funds transfer at the point of sale (EFTPOS), telephone banking, call centres, Internet banking, e-commerce and e-card business, and customer relationship management systems (CRMs).
- *Business management technologies:* data warehousing, data mining, middleware, and credit and risk systems.
- *Core processing technologies:* cheque processing, statement issuance, and interest and charging systems.
- *Support and integration technologies:* general ledgers, human resources systems, finance systems and technology support systems.

Banks spend an enormous amount on these technologies. For example, in 1999 European retail banks spent an estimated total of $21.7 billion, and US banks $23.49 billion (Datamonitor, 1999a, 1999b). Chapter 6 reviews recent developments in these areas and describes their impact on European banking. Customer-facing technologies are described first, then business-management technologies, core processing technologies and support and integration technologies are covered. Finally, a small number of academic studies of the long-term impact of technological change on banking cost structures are reviewed.

CUSTOMER-FACING TECHNOLOGIES

The application of new technology in the banking sector, especially in the customer-facing technologies, has advanced considerably over the last decade. The growing use of ATMs, cash dispensers and bank cards, and the effecting of automatic transfer payment and retrieval of basic account information by customers have also become common practice. In addition, EFTPOS and home banking developments have grown in importance. The broad embrace of new customer-facing technologies is forcing banks to provide multichannel delivery systems where banking services are offered via the branch, telephone, mail, Internet and interactive TV. This has led some commentators to talk about the evolution of the network bank, where multichannel delivery systems are integrated fully with back-office and middle-office activities and systems, with the ultimate objective of providing lower-cost and higher-quality customer service (Gandy, 1999a, 1999b).

Cash dispensers and automated teller machines

The rapid growth of cash dispensers and ATMs during the 1990s is one indication of the extent to which banks have developed this aspect of their customer-facing technology. Figure 6.1 shows the number of cash dispensers and ATMs per one million inhabitants for various European and other countries. The large number of machines in Canada was attributable to the dispersion of population and geographical size of the country. Figure 6.1 also reveals that since 1993, UK banks have been slower to add extra cash dispensers and ATMs compared with their counterparts in most other countries. For example, between 1993 and 1997, the number of machines per one million inhabitants increased by 64% in Germany and 42% in France, but only by 20% in the UK. Despite the relatively slow growth in the number of machines in the UK, however, the number of transactions per capita, shown in Table 6.1, is quite similar across countries. The

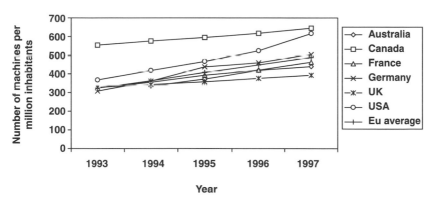

Figure 6.1 Cash dispensers and ATMs: number of machines per one million inhabitants (end of year).

Source: European Central Bank (1999), Bank for International Settlements (1998) and Bank for International Settlements (1999).

slower growth in machines in the UK has resulted neither in a significantly higher level of transactions activity per machine, nor in a large increase in the average value per transaction (Table 6.2).

Table 6.1   Cash dispensers and ATMs: number of transactions per capita

| | Number of transactions per capita | | | | | Change 1993–97* (%) |
	1993	1994	1995	1996	1997	
Australia	–	27	26	27	25	–7
Canada	37	41	46	49	53	+43
France	13	14	16	18	20	+51
Germany	–	11	13	15	–	–
UK	21	23	25	27	30	+41
USA	30	32	37	40	41	+37
EU	14	14	16	17	20	+46

* 1994–97 in the case of Australia.
Source: European Central Bank (1999, Table A1), Bank for International Settlements (1998) and Bank for International Settlements (1999).

Table 6.2   Cash dispensers and ATMs: average value per transaction

| | Average value per transaction (ECU) | | | | | Change 1993–97* (%) |
	1993	1994	1995	1996	1997	
Australia	–	67	73	85	95	+41
Canada†	46	43	40	42	47	+2
France	66	64	63	62	63	–6
Germany	–	133	150	146	–	–
UK	62	63	59	61	74	+20
USA	58	56	52	54	63	+9
EU	94	102	104	105	97	+3

* 1994–97 in the case of Australia.
† Average value of a cash withdrawal only.
Source: European Central Bank (1999), Bank for International Settlements (1998) and Bank for International Settlements (1999).

EFTPOS

The extent to which banks are developing their distribution channels is also reflected in the growth of ETPOS terminals. These are terminals typically found in supermarkets, petrol stations and other retailers that allow customers to debit their account (either a bank or credit card account) at the point of sale. Figure 6.2 shows the trends in the number of EFTPOS terminals, and illustrates that after France, the UK had the largest number of terminals per one million inhabitants in 1993, with the German and US markets looking especially underdeveloped. All the major banking markets experienced an increase in the number of terminals between 1993 and 1997, with the USA having the largest growth: the number of terminals increased by 708%. The French EFTPOS market seems to have reached capacity, in the sense that the number of terminals per one million inhabitants increased by only 4%. The same may also be true for the UK, where the number of machines peaked in 1996, before falling slightly in 1997. Despite the substantial growth in the number of terminals in most countries, both the German and US markets appear relatively underdeveloped. Table 6.3 shows that the number of EFTPOS transactions is increasing rapidly in all countries for which data are available (see also Table 6.4).

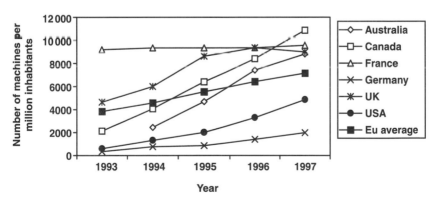

Figure 6.2 EFTPOS terminals per one million inhabitants (end of year).
Source: European Central Bank (1999), Bank for International Settlements (1998) and Bank for International Settlements (1999).

Comparisons between the number of transactions per capita data from Tables 6.1 and 6.3 show that those undertaken through EFTPOS machines are growing at a faster rate than those through cash dispensers and ATMs. This, of course, is hardly surprising, as the former are retail payments while the latter are cash withdrawals.

Table 6.3 EFTPOS terminals: number of transactions per capita

	Number of transactions per capita					Change 1993–97* (%)
	1993	1994	1995	1996	1997	
Australia	–	13	17	22	26	+100
Canada	3	6	13	23	34	+1033
France	27	29	32	36	39	+44
Germany	1	1	2	3	3	+252
UK	–	–	–	–	–	–
USA	2	2	3	4	5	+150
EU	9	10	11	14	16	+83

* 1994–97 in the case of Australia.

Source: European Central Bank (1998), Bank for International Settlements (1998) and Bank for International Settlements (1999).

Table 6.4 EFTPOS terminals: average value per transaction.

	Average value per transaction (ECU)					Change 1993–97* (%)
	1993	1994	1995	1996	1997	
Australia	–	33	30	34	36	+9
Canada	33	31	27	27	28	–15
France	49	49	48	48	46	–7
Germany	46	54	73	80	65	+40
UK	–	–	–	–	–	–
USA	20	21	22	25	31	+55
EU	57	59	61	66	62	+8

* 1994–97 in the case of Australia.

Source: European Central Bank (1999), Bank for International Settlements (1998) and Bank for International Settlements (1999).

e-Money

Another sign of the extent of technological development in retail payment is the growing use of electronic money or e-money. A distinction is usually made 'between card-based e-money (card-based products or electronic purses) and network e-money. Card-based e-money is stored value on cards or prepaid card products that allow customers to make (small-value) transactions . . . Network e-money refers to transactions conducted via telecommunications networks, primarily the Internet' (European Central Bank, 1999, pp.18–20). Table 6.5 illustrates the development of e-money cards and terminals in a selection of European countries. The large number of e-money cards in Germany reflects the fact that the electronic purse function is already included as a feature of many debit, eurocheque and ATM cards. While the number of e-money cards in Europe is still only a small proportion of the number of debit or credit cards outstanding, 'the fastest growth rates in the number of e-money/smart cards are recorded in Belgium, Germany, Spain, Austria and the UK' (European Central Bank, 1999, p.19).

Table 6.5 e-Money loading machines, purchase terminals and cards (end of year)

	Electronic money cards (thousands)			Number of loading machines			Number of purchase terminals		
	1995	1996	1997	1995	1996	1997	1995	1996	1997
France	–	–	–	–	–	–	–	–	–
Germany	–	22 000	35 000	–	75	20 000	–	1000	50 000
Spain	–	1344	3502	–	4123	10 942	–	48 524	77 092
Portugal	161	299	384	5484	7622	5129	30 760	55 646	55 646
UK	–	25	113	–	1340	1295		1922	3537
EU	1349	29 095	46 080	5897	15 753	50 347	34 042	123 342	239 331

Source: Adapted from European Central Bank (1999, Table A6).

Telephone banking

Another area where technological advances have impacted on customer-facing technologies is in the area of telephone banking. UK and French banks appear to be relatively advanced compared with many of their European neighbours. Table 6.6 shows telephone banking penetration in various EU countries. European Central Bank (1999) reports that the UK has experienced 'very high growth' in telephone banking in recent years. In many cases, banks offer call centres as well as tone- or voice-activated telephone banking systems, although there appears to be a stronger consumer preference for call centres using human operators.

Table 6.6 Indications of telephone banking penetration: selected EU countries, 1997–98

	Telephone banking penetration (%)
Belgium[1,2]	5
Germany[3]	6
Spain[1]	6
France[1,4]	10
Ireland[1]	5
Italy[3]	3
Netherlands[5]	5
Finland[1]	2
Sweden[5]	4
UK[1]	10

Source: European Central Bank (1999, p.10).
[1]Percentage of the retail customer base; [2]1996 figures; [3]percentage of retail bank accounts; [4]Minitel users; [5]percentage of payment transactions.

INTERNET BANKING

European banks have two main areas of interest in the Internet. The first is in using the Internet as a delivery channel for banking services. The second is to facilitate the rapidly developing market for e-commerce. An important strategic objective is to use the new technologies in both their production and distribution processes. The Internet provides European banks with major opportunities.

Transaction costs can be reduced significantly, estimates of the costs of Internet banking varying between 1% and 25% of the cost of the transaction being manually processed. The European Central Bank (1999) expects the biggest cost reductions in retail payments, deposit taking and lending areas, as well as in retail securities transactions. In addition to cost reduction, the Internet also offers banks new worldwide marketing and transactions instruments that provide opportunities to increase market share. Internet banking provides a more efficient way to process information related to the specific demands of customers. Since entry costs are low, it also provides opportunities for diversifying into new business areas, including e-commerce and non-financial services. The ultimate aim is to integrate these new technologies into European banks' internal processes, products and distribution channels, so as to help them gain competitive advantage, improve market share, improve efficiency and enhance their risk-management capabilities. Ultimately, this should feed through into improved performance and growth.

With Internet banking, as well as other new-technology delivery systems, the avoidance of direct human involvement in the sale, distribution and processing of transactions affects operating costs significantly. Staff costs are banks' single largest expense category, typically accounting for over half of operating costs. Some sense of the relative costs of different delivery channels can indicate the cost effectiveness of delivery through the Internet. Estimates suggest that Internet banking transactions are around 90% less costly than through a traditional branch network. The European Central Bank (1999) estimates that the unit transaction cost for a non-cash payment is $1.08 for a branch, $0.54 for a telephone bank, $0.26 for a PC bank, and just $0.13 for an Internet bank. These figures exclude set-up, installation and capital expenditure costs. The operating costs of an Internet bank are believed to be around 40% less than those of a traditional retail bank.

The expected cost reductions brought about through Internet banking are attributable to a range of factors:

- the lower costs of processing electronic transactions, compared with traditional labour-intensive methods;
- realisation of scale economies and the associated cost savings due to the centralisation of information collection and transaction processing;
- rationalisation of production and distribution structures, and the standardisation of banking processes;
- realisation of scope economies through the cross-selling of non-banking products, such as travel and insurance services.

In addition to lower costs, the Internet provides global banks with an alternative distribution channel: an additional front office. As such, it represents a relatively efficient addition to an existing operating structure. It need not even be separate from that infrastructure, and can be run off existing banking operations.

The decisions of European banks to develop their Internet banking capability rapidly, however, are not driven by cost considerations alone. Offering new services and service access possibilities is a way for banks to attract new customers and generate new revenue. New technologies allow banks to centralise information, including details of product preferences, on each customer. This allows banks to create specific products and services to meet customers' demands and, in theory, to create customer loyalty, as customers benefit from concentrating their banking and financial affairs in a single institution. Information about consumption patterns and lifestyles will be of increasing value for banks' target marketing.

Traditionally, the business model of retail banking seeks to emphasise the personal relationship with the customer by making available the full range of financial products through a variety of delivery channels. This approach attempts to highlight the importance of service and advice, rather than to sell a product purely on considerations of price. Furthermore, the wide range of financial products ensures that the provision of advice is a crucial element in the process of selling a product. Provision of advice normally requires face-to-face contact, however, and is therefore not susceptible to delivery via the Internet. As a result, transactions that are more process driven and price sensitive are more likely to be delivered through the Internet. Among conventional retail financial services, the products and services best suited to delivery via the Internet would include payments, transfers between accounts, basic insurance products, and savings products. The success of Charles Schwab in Internet retail securities broking, as well as the rapid growth of Internet mortgage brokers in the USA, also suggests that these are the kinds of products most amenable to Internet delivery.

The Internet provides greater transparency in the market for financial services making it easier for customers to shop around for the best deals. Some non-financial firms already perform the role of information brokers to assist consumers in their search for the best deals. The information-broking industry is expected to grow rapidly over the next few years. The growth of information broking and greater price transparency will result in heightened competition between European bank and non-bank firms.

Lower operating costs, greater price transparency, and the wider access to suppliers of financial services afforded by the Internet should lead to reduced margins on product pricing. This is most likely to impact on the more standardised, process-driven products, as mentioned above. In general, increased competition might be expected to create pressure for change in favour of more cost-based pricing and the reduction of cross-subsidisation. If new entrants gain market share at the expense of traditional providers, established banks may need to apply differential pricing according to different delivery systems in order to remain competitive.

While the market for financial services is expected to become much more competitive as Internet banking develops, it is expected that the lower costs and greater revenue opportunities afforded by the new technology will feed through into higher profits. For instance, the European Central Bank (1999) found that many EU banks saw the major influence of new technology on the revenue side rather than on the cost side. Retail banking is likely to be affected more than wholesale business, and the largest profitability increases are expected in retail payments, retail securities business, and retail lending. In contrast, deposit-taking business is expected to become less profitable as customers find it increasingly easy to obtain new investment alternatives offering higher yields. Table 6.7 shows the expected impact on profitability resulting from the adoption of new technologies.

Table 6.7 Medium- to long-term effects of technological developments on the profitability of different banking activities expected by EU banks*

Retail payment transactions	+2.58
Retail securities business	+2.02
Retail lending business	+1.67
Wholesale payments transactions	+1.57
Money/asset management	+1.50
Off-balance-sheet business	+1.08
Wholesale securities business	+1.05
Retail deposits business	+0.95
Wholesale deposit business	+0.65
Wholesale lending business	+0.63
Total (unweighted average)	+2.06

Source: EU supervisory authorities represented in the Banking Supervision Committee (European Central Bank, 1999, p.12).

* Includes the average mean value derived from the responses of banks in Germany, Greece, Spain, France, Ireland, Italy, Austria, Portugal, Finland, Sweden and the UK. Estimates were given on the following scale: (+ cost increase expected, – cost reduction expected): +/– 4, very significant; +/–3, significant; +/–2, moderately significant; +/–1, slightly significant; 0, neutral.

Although the embrace of Internet banking and the development of e-commerce business appear to offer substantial opportunities to earn increased profit, there are a number of factors that might qualify this expectation to a greater or lesser extent. Competition may increase to such an extent that banks are forced to pass a greater proportion of their cost savings on to consumers than is currently anticipated. The extent to which customers may choose to switch to non-bank providers offering substitute products is also uncertain. Deposits businesses, for example, may tend to switch to mutual funds or other investment providers. Technology leaders may not be the most profitable in the short run because of high set-up costs.

As developments in Internet banking and e-commerce change the economics of banking, so the structural characteristics of the industry will alter. The number of branches will decline, so as to achieve a balance between physical and remote distribution channels. In addition, there will also be a growth in strategic alliances and cooperation agreements between banks on both the production (e.g. development of common standards, sharing of development costs, processing of payments) and distribution (e.g. compatible e-commerce transactions) sides. These will enable banks to obtain efficiency advantages and provide consumer benefits through widely acceptable payments media. In addition, alliances and joint ventures between European banks and IT firms, as well as telecommunication companies, are also becoming increasingly common. These facilitate the more effective application of up-to-date technology, as well as cooperation in research and development leading to lower implementation costs. Internet banking business is likely to shift the emphasis in terms of the services that banks require from their staff towards areas such as marketing, complementing IT developments, and selling increasingly sophisticated value-added services.

Despite the apparent potential, at the start of 2000 most European banks used the Internet primarily as an additional delivery channel in order to meet the requirements of more sophisticated customers. As yet, the size of the Internet banking market in Europe remains relatively small. 'Only MeritaNordbanken in Finland states that it has significant Internet penetration among its total customer base, of some 18%, whereas other banks' rates are in the very low single digits' (Morgan Stanley Dean Witter, 1999, p.1).

Figure 6.3 shows the extent of Internet banking penetration in a handful of countries. It suggests that the main European banking markets are lagging some way behind the USA. Perhaps surprisingly, Internet banking development in the UK appears to be behind that in Germany. This finding is confirmed by the results of an extensive survey on Internet banking in the UK reported in *Financial IT* (1999), which lists the range and functionality of Internet services provided by the main banks, building societies and insurance companies:

Two years after the launch of the UK's first true on-line bank the finance industry has failed to make any significant advances on the Internet. Nationwide [Building Society] rolled out its Internet bank in May 1997, yet since then only a handful of its UK based competitors have followed suit, while other countries – most notably Scandinavian countries, Germany and the US – have stolen the march and are claiming the delivery channel is their own. According to the latest research from Unisys, Germany currently has twice the number of companies offering some form of banking on the Internet than the UK, while the US easily outstrips its British contemporaries. Surfing various Web sites it is clear the vast majority of the UK's finance companies regard Internet as little more than a means to a marketing end. Most banks, building societies and insurers have some kind of Web presence but this is mainly used simply as brochureware.

Financial IT (1999, p.10)

According to data from the On-Line Banking Report (1999) the US is light years ahead of the UK in terms of Internet delivery. By March 1999 there were 297 banks in the US that met the definition of a 'true Internet bank' set up by the report . . . there is no doubting that American banks easily outstrip home grown offerings.

Financial IT (1999, p.12)

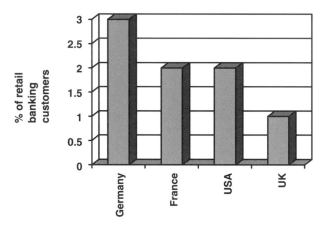

Figure 6.3 Current consumer use of online banking.
Source: Business Intelligence Report (1998, p.15).

Table 6.8 shows the number of Internet banking customers for the main providers in the UK. Barclays has established an Internet platform that replicates the full range of retail financial services (including payments, savings and credit cards) provided by its telephone banking service, as this is the operating infrastructure into which Internet banking is linked. The majority of Barclay's Internet banking clients are existing customers, probably because users have to provide some form of physical verification to open an account. Egg, the banking subsidiary of Prudential, also has a reasonable number of online customers. Customers can

Table 6.8   Number of Internet banking customers in the UK

	Number of Internet banking customers
Barclays	380 000
First Direct	120 000 (*source:* First Direct)
Nationwide	90 000 (*source:* Nationwide)
Lloyds/TSB	67 000 (*source:* Report and Accounts)
Egg	60 000 (*source:* Prudential interim figures)
Royal Bank of Scotland	45 000 (*source:* Royal Bank of Scotland)

Source: Financial World (1999, p.22).

sign up for Egg's deposit account on the Internet, but the process cannot be completed without physical documentary verification of the customer's identity. In addition, transactions have to be effected using paper-based systems.

The Internet will inevitably create more competition between bank and non-bank financial service providers. While much is made about the threat of non-bank providers, in most European countries banks still have two major advantages over their non-bank competitors: general public confidence and trust, and a monopoly position in deposit taking from the public. Potential non-bank competitors, such as securities brokers, finance companies, insurance firms, IT companies, telecommunications firms, retailers and media enterprises, are not entitled to take deposits from the public. Banks, therefore, could possibly exploit this position through cooperation agreements with the commercial sector, as well as between banks and credit-card companies. In general, the securities and investment business (mutual funds, investment accounts and securities intermediaries), payment transfers and advice services are among those that appear likely to face the fiercest competition from remote banking channels offered by non-bank providers. Over the longer term, competition may also be expected from software firms managing companies' payments via electronic means, telecommunications carriers, mailing firms (e.g. electronic bill presentation via the Internet), credit-card firms, and retailers.

The new competitive environment brought about by the Internet and development of e-commerce is likely to revolutionise the global provision of financial services. Customers benefit because they can access financial services more conveniently. Products can be tailored to meet their specific needs, and they will have greater access to price and product information, making it easier to shop around. Global banks benefit from lower transaction costs, increased information on customer attributes and preferences, and the consequent ability to tailor products and services. In addition, global banks will be able to access larger markets and offer a wider range of products and services. Despite the risks, such as the potential decline in customer loyalty, the cost of establishing an e-brand, and the effects of pan-European and global competition, these factors should create the potential for improved efficiency and enhanced quality of service to customers. This in turn should ultimately boost the returns earned by banks and their shareholders.

BANK SERVICE DELIVERY CHANNELS

The desire by many European banks to deliver their services through a broader array of distribution channels is reflected in many of the features discussed earlier in this chapter. A 1999 survey by the UK's Chartered Institute of Bankers provides an interesting insight (Financial World, 1999). A summary of the findings is shown in Figures 6.4–6.7. Taken together, these figures show that UK banks expected the role of branches to decline in favour of alternative delivery systems (Figure 6.4). New retail entrants (such as Virgin Direct, Egg, Charles Schwab, MBNA) are also more heavily dependent than traditional providers on PC or Internet services (Figure 6.6). The traditional providers expected their customers to migrate mainly from branches to the telephone, despite the rapid growth forecast for the Internet and interactive television. In contrast, the new operators expected their customers to migrate from telephone-based delivery channels to the Internet and interactive television.

The same survey also found that 70% of respondents from established financial services providers believed that they were losing market share to providers that only use the new direct

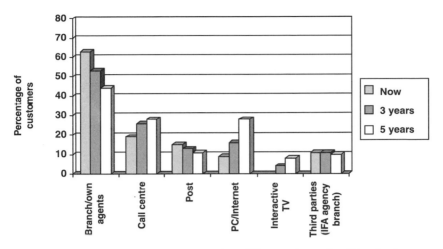

Figure 6.4 Percentage of customers using different channels: all institutions.
IFA, independent financial advisor
Source: Financial World (1999, p.22).

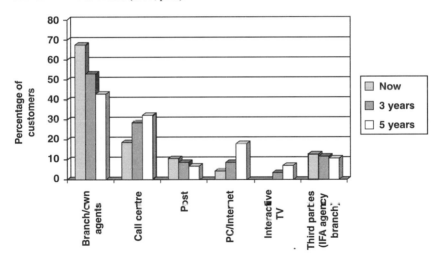

Figure 6.5 Percentage of customers using different delivery channels: established institutions.
IFA, independent financial advisor
Source: Financial World (1999, p.23).

channels. In addition, nearly all respondents believed that electronic delivery, especially Internet and interactive television banking, would become at least as popular as telephone banking within five years. HSBC, for instance, launched an interactive TV

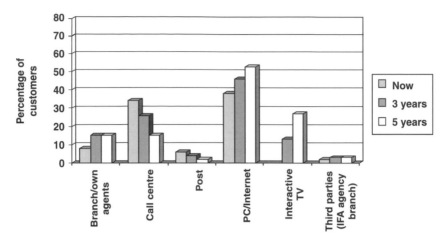

Figure 6.6   Percentage of customers using different delivery channels: new retail entrants.
IFA, independent financial advisor
Source: Financial World (1999, p.23).

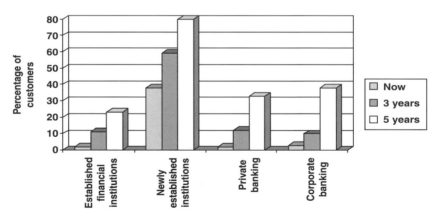

Figure 6.7   Customers expected to make significant use of Internet and interactive TV services.
Source: Financial World (1999, p.24).

banking service in anticipation of the eventual switch from ana-
logue to digital television in the UK. In the USA, there appears to
be less interest in developing interactive TV banking services,
given the wider use and greater current acceptance of Internet

technology. In Germany, where cable television currently feeds 60% of households compared with 8% in the UK, and where satellite television has greater penetration (22% of households compared with 16% in the UK), there may be more opportunity to develop such services in the short term.

CUSTOMER RELATIONSHIP MANAGEMENT SYSTEMS

The development and integration of effective CRM systems has been, and continues to be, an important feature of many banks' IT development strategies. These aim to provide banks with information on the lifetime value of a customer, and create the ability to segment actual and prospective customers by needs, behaviour, propensity to buy, and other characteristics. In general, they provide banks with the ability to price and cost customer relationships across a broad range of market segments: product, customer, geographical, and so on. A better understanding of customer requirements can help sell more products, acquire new customers, and retain established customers. Ultimately, this should result in improved profitability.

In principle, the aim of CRM is straightforward. New systems, however, cannot simply be added on to the multichannel, multiproduct organisation of most banks. Organising a multiproduct (usually business unit oriented) bank around customer segments at the same time as building data-driven marketing and customer-management capabilities creates extraordinary complexities for systems and staff. The implementation of successful CRM systems is therefore relatively slow.

To a certain extent, the motivation for implementing such systems has been driven by the success of US monoline financial service providers, such as MBNA and Charles Schwab. These firms tend to have a narrower product focus compared with traditional banks, and tend to use more advanced CRM systems to compete effectively. The success of these and other new entrants illustrates the competitive advantage that advanced CRM (as well as other) systems can provide.

Unfortunately, there is little empirical evidence to indicate the extent of development of CRM systems in European banking. Anecdotal evidence suggests that US banks such as BancOne, Wells Fargo and Citibank are further advanced than the biggest European banks in implementing successful CRM strategies. One explanation is that, on average, US banks do not have the same level of complexity in product offerings because universal banking has not been permitted (although following the abandonment of the Glass–Steagall Act in November 1999, this situation may change). The smaller and less complex the bank, the easier it is to implement CRM systems. New entrants or new start-ups by established banks are likely to have more advanced CRM systems.

BUSINESS-MANAGEMENT TECHNOLOGIES

Business-management technologies include systems that aim to enhance the organisation and flow of information within banks (and other firms) in order to enhance managerial decision making. Such technologies include data warehousing, data mining, middleware and credit and risk management systems.

According to Gandy (1999a, p.96), 'Data warehousing is the name given to a group of technologies that aim to draw together an organisation's diverse sources of information, allowing it to understand and successfully mobilise that information.' Data mining technologies are the systems that analyse (statistically or otherwise) information flows and databases related to banks' business activities. Middleware refers to a broad array of software solutions that allow elements of applications to interact across networks, despite differences in the underlying business definitions, communications protocols, system architectures, operating systems, databases and other application services.

The successful implementation of business-management technologies for the main European banks is linked inextricably to how new systems can be integrated with existing, and perhaps outdated, systems or legacy systems. The extent and success to which new technologies can be integrated with legacy systems, of

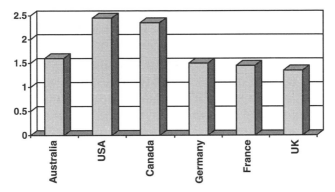

Figure 6.8 Implementation of new business-management technology in retail banking, 1999.
0 = low, 5 = high
Source: TCA Consulting (1999).

course, is also related inversely to bank size and complexity. Again, this is a topic on which it is difficult to find empirical evidence. Figure 6.8 provides an assessment of the extent to which European and other banks are implementing new business-management technologies.

The desire to benefit from scope economies through cross-selling financial services is often quoted as a major motivating factor for European banks to develop their business-management systems. The evidence suggests, however, that this is not happening on the scale required to justify large IT expenditure in this area. In addition, new technologies are coming on to the market on a monthly basis (at least), so decisions to spend on such technology tend to be deferred pending the next technology advance. Overall, it seems that while many large European banks have made advances in the development of their internal credit and other risk-management systems, they are still constrained by their legacy systems in using new middleware and data-warehousing technology to its maximum potential. As in the case of other areas of technology implementation, established financial service firms consider the US monoline providers (such as MBNA) and retail banks (such as BancOne and Wells Fargo) to be the market leaders in using sophisticated technologies for database marketing and risk assessment.

CORE PROCESSING TECHNOLOGIES

Core processing technologies relate to systems such as those involved with cheque processing, statement issuance, interest and charging systems. In most large banks, mainframe computers run the core banking processes that provide information resources for the large branch networks and customer bases (Gandy 1999b). While these systems are well developed in European banks, in recent years they have not evolved as rapidly as expected given the demands imposed by Y2K compliance and euro conversion.

A major constraint faced by large European banks in developing their core processing technologies arises from the sheer size of customer bases. For example, there are no technology providers that currently supply systems that can work effectively at the scale of the main European banks in terms of volumes of business and numbers of customers. Consequently, these banks cannot easily replace outdated systems, and instead have to adapt their existing systems. Considerable efforts, however, have been made in this area within the given constraints. The use of processing centres has grown, although industry analysts suggest that the process of centralisation still has a long way to go. Some banks have introduced innovative workflow call centres and document-management and cheque-processing systems, and there have been specific applications in niche product areas. Overall, however, the ability of large banks to innovate in the core processing area remains severely constrained by dependence on mainframe technology and the need for any new systems to be capable of processing massive volumes.

Finally, the recent trend towards the outsourcing of core processing activity is, at present, not a major option for many of Europe's largest banks. New entrants and smaller foreign banks, however, often use outsourcing providers for all of their processing.

SUPPORT AND INTEGRATION TECHNOLOGIES

The final area where banks dedicate IT investment is in the area of support and integration technologies. These typically relate to human resources systems, general ledgers, finance systems and technology support systems. Traditionally, the European banking industry has not been used to using standard processes, and has resisted implementing large integration technology solutions to deal with these somewhat disparate areas. One of the main problems has been that banks tend primarily to be product oriented. In addition, management-information tools are weak, with nearly all information being based on separately produced spreadsheets at all levels. As such, banking business tends to be managed at a very narrow level.

Recently, however, there appears to be a gradual move by banks to consider implementing much greater integration across support and other systems. Introduction of enterprise resource planning (ERP) solutions is taking place, especially in core areas relating to human resources and finance. Datamonitor (1999b) forecast that by the end of 2004, European bank IT spending will reach $10.9 billion, of which 22.4% will be on 'big' packaged or integrated systems relating to ERP, a market currently dominated by SAP, a German software/consulting firm.

Overall, technological innovation in banking has focused traditionally on banking processes rather than support processes. With an increased proportion of costs being unrelated to service delivery and staff costs, however, this is likely to change. In the area of ERP solutions, as in other areas of technology implementation, it appears that North American banks (especially new entrants) have by far the most advanced support and integration technologies.

TECHNOLOGICAL CHANGE IN EUROPEAN BANKING: EMPIRICAL EVIDENCE

Most of the preceding discussion focuses on the current impact of specific technological developments in European banking. There is relatively little empirical evidence, however, as to the extent to which technological development in general impacts on the production characteristics and cost structure of the banking industry over the long term. Although technological progress has been cited widely as one of the major sources of change in European banking (Arthur Andersen 1986; Arthur Andersen 1993; Cecchini, 1988), only a handful of academic studies have attempted to quantify its effect on the costs of providing financial services, or its impact on efficient bank size.

Most previous attempts at empirical measurement of the impact of technological change have been based on one of two methodologies: econometric estimation or index numbers (Baltagi and Griffin, 1988; see also Fox (1996) for an empirical comparison). The econometric approach involves the inclusion of a deterministic time trend in the estimation of a production, cost or profit function. The trend may be linear or non-linear, and the specification may allow for interactions between time and other explanatory variables, such as outputs and factor input prices. The coefficients on the time trend variables are interpreted as measures of the rate of technological change. The alternative index number approach involves a direct comparison between the rates of growth of indices of output and inputs, with any difference attributed to technological change.

The impact of technological change on bank costs has been investigated using US data. For example, for a sample of large US commercial banks with data covering the period 1980–86, Hunter and Timme (1991) found that technological change lowered the real cost of bank production by about 1% per year. Larger banks realised a greater percentage reduction in costs than smaller banks. Technological change affected the cost-minimising product mix for all but the smallest banks in the sample. Humphrey (1993) also found that technological change had a negative impact on bank costs in the USA following bank deregulation. For large Japanese banks, McKillop et al. (1996) identify a similar impact of technological change on total costs.

Maudos et al. (1996) provide a detailed analysis of the impact of technological change on the costs of the Spanish savings bank sector between 1985 and 1994. They conclude that technical progress reduced average costs by 0.64% and operating costs by 1.93% per annum. Total costs were reduced by 0.68% per annum. Again, larger savings banks appear to have benefited more from technological change than their smaller counterparts. Lang and Welzel (1996) investigated the impact of technological change in the German cooperative banking sector between 1987 and 1992. They found that costs fell by around 2.5% per annum, with smaller banks experiencing larger cost reductions.

In a recent study, Altunbas et al. (1999) analysed the impact on costs of technological change in 15 national banking sectors in Europe using data covering the period 1989–96. Estimations are carried out for subsamples of banks in specific countries, for banks in various size categories (measured by total assets), and for commercial, savings and cooperative banks. Summary findings are that the estimated annual rate of reduction in total cost attributable to technological change for the entire sample was 3.6%. Technological change impacted more on the costs of larger banks than their smaller counterparts, and had a greater impact on the costs of those banks operating in the larger European economies than elsewhere. This study also found little evidence of differences in the impact of technological change between banks across various ownership structures.

CONCLUSION

Technological change is currently having a major impact on the cost characteristics and distribution capabilities of the European banking industry. While there is much evidence to measure the extent to which new distribution channels are being developed, it is naturally harder to identify and quantify the extent of changes substantially altering banks' own internal systems. The rather limited empirical industrial organisation literature on technological change in banking suggests that larger banks benefit more from technological change than their smaller counterparts. The impact of technological change on costs seems to have accelerated during the 1990s. While these are hardly startling findings, they are consistent with some of the broad trends identified in Chapter 2, such as a general decline in cost : income ratios experienced recently in many European banking sectors.

Chapter 7

The law of proportionate effect: previous empirical research

INTRODUCTION

Concentration is the proportion of an industry's total assets, sales or employment that is controlled by its largest firms. Traditional industrial organisation literature suggests a number of systematic factors that can cause industries to become dominated by a handful of large firms. These include economies of scale, the existence of entry and exit barriers, and the adoption of entry-deterring strategies by incumbents. If large firms are able to gain a competitive advantage as a result of being more efficient or through exploiting their market power, they are also likely to be able to grow faster than their smaller rivals. Over time, a market structure in which a few large firms dominate is likely to emerge.

It is possible, however, that highly concentrated industry structures may develop, even if larger size does not enhance a firm's growth prospects. Gibrat (1931) investigated the implications for the evolution of industry structure if each firm's growth in any year was independent of its size and its growth in previous years. Effectively, each firm's growth rate in any year is determined randomly, in the sense that the factors that influence a firm's growth, such as growth of demand, managerial talent, innovation, organisational structure and luck, are distributed across firms in a manner that cannot be predicted from information about the firm's current size characteristics, or its previous growth performance. Gibrat showed that this non-relationship between growth and firm size, known as the law of proportionate effect (LPE), has far-reaching consequences for the development of concentration and industry structure over time. The firm size distribution within the industry concerned becomes increasingly skewed, and the industry tends to become dominated by a small number of large firms. Previous research has found that the empirical size distribution of firms in many industries accords reasonably well with the theoretical size distribution generated by simulation models in which growth rates are distributed in accordance with the LPE.

Subsequently, Gibrat's early contribution spawned a large empirical literature, which seeks to establish whether the LPE provides a suitable description of actual firm size distributions and growth patterns. Chapter 7 reviews the empirical literature on the LPE. We describe how growth in accordance with the LPE causes industry concentration to increase over time, as well as considering briefly a number of factors, other than the underlying relationship between the size and growth of incumbent firms, that also influence the evolution of industry structure. We then review previous empirical studies that have tested the LPE. First, we review studies that have tested the LPE indirectly, by comparing empirical firm size distributions with a family of theoretical skewed distributions that would be generated if the industry had evolved in accordance with the LPE. Then we review studies that have tested the LPE directly, using regression analysis to investigate the relationship between firm growth rates over a given period and firm sizes at the start of the period.

THE LAW OF PROPORTIONATE EFFECT AND OTHER INFLUENCES ON CONCENTRATION

The notion that industries tend to become increasingly concentrated over time, even if large and small firms have exactly the same chance of attaining any particular growth rate in any period, may perhaps sound counterintuitive. If growth rates are allocated randomly between firms and over time, intuition might suggest that in the long term, all firms will grow at the same rate on average, and that the firm size distribution should therefore remain unchanged. Over the years, a number of writers have sought ways of demonstrating that this intuition is in fact not correct, and of popularising Gibrat's original insight. Schwed (1965) for example, describes the analogy of the 'great coin flipping contest':

> The referee gives a signal for the first time and 400 000 coins flash in the sun as they are tossed. The scorers make their tabulations, and discover that 200 000 people are winners and 200 000 are losers. Then the second game is played. Of the original 200 000 winners, about half of them win again. The third game is played, and of the 100 000 who have won both games half of them are again successful. These 50 000 in the fourth game are reduced to 25 000, and in the fifth to 12 500. These 12 500 have now won five straight without loss and are no doubt beginning to fancy themselves as coin flippers. They feel they have an 'instinct' for it. However in the sixth game, 6250 are disappointed and amazed they have finally lost, and perhaps some of them start a Congressional investigation. But the victorious 6250 play on and are successively reduced in number until less than a thousand are left. This little band have won nine straight without a loss, and by this time most of them have at least a local reputation for their ability. People come from some distance to consult them about their method of calling heads and tails, and they modestly give explanations of how they have achieved their success. Eventually there are about a dozen men who have won every single time for about 15 games. These are regarded as the experts, the greatest coin flippers in history, the men who never lose, and they have their biographies written.
>
> Schwed (1965, pp. 160–161)

According to this analogy, the dozen individuals who are fortunate to have survived after 15 rounds are equivalent to the small number of firms that come to achieve a dominant position within the industry over time, through processes that could not have

been predicted from observable characteristics of the firms concerned at the time when they were first established, and that
might therefore be described as 'good luck'. Regarding the
owners or managers of such firms as inherently superior in terms
of skill or efficiency, however, simply because they have
achieved high growth, would be a mistake. This would be
equivalent to judging the successful coin flippers as being highly
skilled simply because they were successful. Hannah and Kay
(1977, p. 103) develop a similar gambling analogy to make the
same point:

> ... if a group of rich men and a group of poor men visit Monte Carlo,
> it is likely that some of the rich will become poor and some of the poor
> become rich: but it is also probable that some of the rich will get richer
> and some of the poor will get poorer, so that the extent of inequality
> within each group and over the two groups taken together is likely to
> increase. The process works to increase industrial concentration in
> much the same way.

Prais (1976) constructs a simple numerical example to compare
the implications for the development of industry concentration
over time of two growth processes. In the first, all firms have an
identical chance of achieving any given amount of absolute
growth in any period. In the second, all firms have an equal
chance of achieving any given proportionate growth rate in any
period. The second case corresponds to the LPE.

The numerical example involves a hypothetical industry that
consists of 128 firms, each employing 100 employees. Under the
equal-absolute-growth model, 50% of the firms remain the same
size, 25% increase in size by ten workers, and 25% decrease in
size by ten workers. Under the equal-proportionate-growth
model, 50% of firms in any period stay the same size, while 25%
grow by 10% and 25% decline by 10%. In both cases, concentration tends to increase. From an initial value of 7.8% in year zero,
concentration levels of around 9.5% or 9.6% are reached by the
end of year three. 'The dispersion of the distribution thus grows
inexorably as time proceeds as a result of spontaneous drift (the
sizes of firms follow a random walk, as sheep which have no
shepherd)' (Prais, 1976, p.26). In the long term, however, the
equal-proportionate-growth model leads to a faster increase in
industry concentration than the equal-absolute-growth model.

After a sufficiently large number of time periods, the firm size distribution under the equal-proportionate-growth model eventually approximates to the log-normal distribution.

The LPE refers to the distribution of growth rates over a cohort or population of incumbent firms. There are, however, a number of other factors at work that may affect the evolution of the size distribution of firms within an industry. These factors include the actual or potential entry of new firms, the exit of incumbent firms, and mergers and acquisitions. In addition, it is possible to introduce a number of qualifications or modifications to the LPE in its strongest form as described above, which will also influence the way in which industry structure evolves.

Most of the empirical studies described in this chapter report results derived from analyses of samples of firms that were members of the population for the entire period of the investigation. They therefore say little or nothing about the relationship between size and growth for firms that entered during the observation period, for firms that failed to survive, and possibly (depending on the sample selection criteria) for firms involved in mergers or take-overs. This introduces possibilities of selection bias (Mansfield, 1962) if, for example, the probability of survival is related to initial size and subsequent growth. It seems likely that entry rates into the smallest firm size categories may be higher than rates into the larger size categories (Simon and Bonnini, 1958). If so, the tendency for concentration to increase over time as a result of proportionate growth among incumbents may be checked. On the other hand, entry can also be a consequence of diversification strategies by larger firms in other industries, in which case entrants may be operating on a large scale, and concentration may increase (Davies, 1989). Potential or unobservable entry as discussed in the literature on contestable markets (Baumol, 1982), in which incumbent firm behaviour is constrained by actions of potential entrants, may also have implications for the growth performance of incumbent firms. Finally, there is some empirical evidence that the probability of involvement in a merger or take-over is also related to current size (Dunne and Hughes, 1994).

Possible qualifications or modifications to the LPE in its strongest form arise in the cases where there is persistence of growth, where there is heteroscedasticity in growth rates, or where the LPE applies only to firms that are operating above the minimum efficient scale (MES). Under the LPE in its strongest form, it is assumed that each firm's growth rate in any period is independent of its growth in previous periods. It is quite possible, however, that factors that influence growth, such as the motives of owners or the efficiency of managers, tend to exert a similar influence on growth over several successive time periods. If there is positive persistence in growth rates between successive periods, then concentration will tend to increase at a faster rate than if there is zero persistence. Alternatively, negative persistence is also a theoretical possibility. It may be that rapid growth in one period tends to be followed by a period of consolidation in the next period, during which the firm grows more slowly. If there is negative persistence, concentration will tend to increase more slowly than if there is zero persistence. The effects of positive and negative persistence on trends in concentration are investigated using numerical simulations in Chapter 8.

Under the LPE in its strongest form, it is also assumed that growth rates are homoscedastic. In other words, the variance of the distribution from which each firm's growth rate is drawn randomly (in the sense described above) is assumed to be the same for firms of all sizes in all time periods. This assumption may be unrealistic, however, if larger firms tend to pursue strategies of diversification, enabling them to spread risk over a larger number of products than is possible for their smaller counterparts. Successful diversification is likely to lead to greater stability in growth over time (Singh and Whittington, 1968). Larger firms are also likely to be older than smaller firms, and may therefore benefit from learning economies of scale, enabling them to avoid making costly mistakes (Jovanovic, 1982). Again, this may imply that large firms' growth is subject to less variation than that of smaller firms. It is also possible that competitive conditions in different industries influence the variability of the growth rates of the firms concerned. In industries that are characterised by a high degree of non-price competition, for example, profits may be subject to high variability because the outcomes of product and process innovations are uncertain (Weiss, 1963). High variation in profit may feed through into equivalent variation in growth. The effects of heteroscedasticity in growth rates on trends in concentration are also explored in Chapter 8.

Finally, it appears that implicit in the LPE is an assumption that average cost is invariant to changes in output, or in other words, average cost curves are horizontal. In microeconomic theory, however, it is normally assumed that average cost curves are U-shaped or L-shaped. In either case, firms must reach the industry MES in order to produce competitively, and perhaps in order to survive (Stigler, 1958). It is possible, therefore, that the validity of the LPE is limited to firms that are already operating above the MES. Small firms must pursue rapid growth to reach the MES, or exit as a result of bankruptcy or take-over. Large firms that have already attained the MES are under less pressure to grow rapidly, and may exhibit growth patterns in accordance with the LPE. In other words, there may be a threshold for firm size, below which the LPE does not hold (Simon and Bonnini, 1958; Davies and Lyons, 1982).

Several authors have argued in favour of a methodological approach to modelling growth that can incorporate both systematic and non-systematic influences. Davies and Lyons (1982), for example, developed a model that enabled them to distinguish between what they term 'technological' and 'stochastic' explanations for observed patterns of concentration. The technological explanations focus on firm numbers, economies of scale, and barriers to entry. The empirical model succeeds in explaining a high proportion of the variation between UK industries in the 1968 Census of Production concentration data.

More recently, Sutton (1991, 1997, 1998) also argues the need for an integrated theory capable of explaining variations between industries in concentration and in the shape of their firm size distributions. In Sutton's most recent contribution, the extent to which successful product or process innovation causes an industry to fragment into separate submarkets, or conversely the extent to which a successful innovation affects the entire market in a homogeneous fashion, is a major determinant of concentration. Markets that tend to fragment remain less concentrated than those that tend to remain homogeneous. For any given overall concentration ratio, firm size distributions are modelled as the outcome of a dynamic process in which there is a fixed probability that any submarket will be contested by an entrant, which may be either an established firm already operating in other submarkets or a new firm. It is possible to derive a theoretical firm size distribution that would apply if the probability of successfully contesting a new submarket were the same for established firms already operating in other submarkets and for new firms. In Sutton's framework, this case is analogous to the LPE. Departures from this theoretical size distribution (in the direction of greater skewness) would occur if established firms enjoyed advantages over new firms, affording a higher probabability of successfully contesting new submarkets as they arise. For Sutton, the development of a probabalistic model that predicts the development of theoretical firm size distributions conditional on the technological characteristics of the industry is only the beginning of the story. Subsequently, extensive industry case studies are used to add substance and detail to the more abstract theoretical and stochastic framework. In a review article, Scherer (2000) discusses the merits and demerits of Sutton's approach, and considers the extent to which it is complementary to traditional paradigms, including the LPE.

EMPIRICAL TESTS OF THE LAW OF PROPORTIONATE EFFECT BASED ON ANALYSIS OF FIRM SIZE DISTRIBUTIONS

Previous empirical studies that test the LPE can be grouped into two main categories. The first category involves the analysis of empirical firm size distributions. Using goodness-of-fit tests, it is possible to establish how closely the observed, often skewed firm size distributions approximate to a family of theoretical skewed distributions that would be generated if the industry had evolved in accordance with the LPE. The relevant theoretical distributions include the log-normal, Pareto and Yule distributions. Studies that have adopted this approach use data from the USA, the UK, Sweden and a number of formerly socialist countries. This research is reviewed in the current section. The second category of empirical research tests directly the relationship between the initial size and the subsequent growth of a cohort of firms over a specified time period, using regression analysis. These studies are reviewed later in this chapter.

Using a sample of firms quoted on the UK Stock Exchange, which varies in number from 60 firms in 1885 to 2103 in 1956, Hart and Prais (1956) examine the extent to which their sample firm size distributions approximates to the log-normal distribution. Size is measured using stock market capitalisation. Hart and Prais carried out goodness-of-fit tests for skewness and kurtosis of the distribution of the logarithmic firm size distributions in 1885, 1896, 1907, 1924, 1939 and 1950. They found no departures from log-normality for the period up to 1907, but from 1907 onwards departures from log-normality become significant.

As noted above, Simon and Bonnini (1958) argue that LPE applies only to firms that are operating above the MES. Firms operating below this scale must either grow rapidly in order to achieve the MES, or perish. Consequently, most established firms will be operating at or above the MES, and will have exhausted economies of scale. Any subsequent growth is therefore likely to be independent of size. Simon and Bonnini assume there is a constant entry rate into the lowest size class of firms. If this assumption holds, firm sizes will approximate the Yule distribution. Simon and Bonnini test these arguments by fitting straight lines to the logarithms of cumulative distributions using UK and US data. The UK data are the same as those used by Hart and Prais (1956), while the US data cover the top 500 firms between 1954 and 1956. They find that the empirical logarithmic size distributions conform closely with the theoretical distributions that are implied by the LPE.

> Whether sales, assets, number of employees, value added, or profits are used as a size measure, the observed distributions always belong to the class of highly skewed distributions that include the lognormal and the Yule. This is true of the data on individual industries and for all industries taken together. It holds for sizes of plants as well as firms.
> Simon and Bonnini (1958, p.611)

Quandt (1966) uses data on 30 US industries to test how well the observed firm size distributions comply with variants of the Pareto distribution, and the log-normal distribution. In 66% of the cases analysed, the null hypothesis that the empirical distribution of firm sizes fits with one of the theoretical distributions can be accepted. Quandt finds, however, that it is difficult or impossible to discriminate between the alternative theoretical distributions as to which one best fits the data.

Silberman (1967) analyses plant and firm level data for a sample of 90 (four-digit) industries observed in 1947 and 1958. A goodness-of-fit test is used to test the empirical size distributions for consistency with the log-normal distribution, and actual concentration measures are compared with those that would be expected if the true distributions were log-normal. The results are mixed. For firms, the log-normal null can be accepted in about half of the cases tested. For plants, the log-normal null can be accepted in only 17 out of 79 cases.

Engwell (1973) found support for the log-normal hypothesis when applied to Swedish car and shoe manufacturing establishments using data covering the period 1952–66. Using an approach similar to the one adopted by Silberman, Engwell accepted that the log-normal distribution provided a good description of the firm size distributions in these two industries. Engwell also carried out similar tests at establishment level using data for Poland, Yugoslavia, Romania and Czechoslovakia. Again, a log-normal null hypothesis was generally found to be acceptable. On the basis of these results, Engwell argued in favour of acceptance of the LPE in the case of mature and stable industries that have undergone relatively little change in patterns of demand and firm numbers. When systematic influences on growth are absent, random influences naturally tend to predominate.

Clarke (1979) also tested the accuracy of the log-normal distribution in characterising firm and plant size distributions, using data on 147 UK (three-digit) manufacturing industries observed in 1968. Each industry's firm and plant size distribution was tested for log-normality using tests for skewness and kurtosis. At the firm level, the log-normal null was accepted in only nine of the 133 tests. At the plant level, the log-normal null was accepted in around one-quarter of the tests. Clarke found that the numbers of firms and plants at upper ends of the size distributions tended to suggest that there may be systematic factors favouring the growth of large firms.

Kwoka (1983) tested the goodness of fit of the Pareto distribution using data for 308 US manufacturing industries observed in

1980. Kwoka attempted to fit data on the market shares of the top ten firms in each industry to the Pareto distribution. Although the latter failed to provide an adequate description of the empirical firm size distributions, Kwoka (1983, p. 395) did find some regularity in the empirical distributions:

> While stochastic growth processes may be at work in these data, many other factors play decisive roles in determining firm size distributions. Those factors – like serially correlated growth rates, mergers and acquisition, and other firm behaviour – deserve close examination in light of the particular empirical findings in this paper.

Analysis of empirical firm size distributions is evidently capable of providing a number of useful insights. As a method of testing the LPE, however, this approach is rather indirect. If the empirical size distributions are consistent with those that we know would tend to develop over time if the LPE were valid, then this does constitute evidence in favour of the LPE, but it is only circumstantial evidence. The approach adopted in the papers described above is also fundamentally static, and consequently is unable to say much about influences on firm size distributions, such as persistence of growth or heteroscedasticity in growth rates. As a result of these limitations, the analysis of empirical firm size distributions has now been largely superseded as a means of testing the LPE by more direct methods, based on regression analysis of the relationship between firm size and growth. Previous studies that have adopted this latter approach will now be reviewed.

REGRESSION-BASED TESTS OF THE LAW OF PROPORTIONATE EFFECT: VARIOUS INDUSTRIES

This section outlines studies that have used regression analysis to test directly the relationship between the initial size and the subsequent growth of a cohort of firms over a specified time period. The test in its simplest form focuses on the value of the parameter β in the following regression:

$$s_{it+T} = \alpha + \beta \, s_{it} + u_{it+T} \qquad [7.1]$$

where s_{it} and s_{it+T} are the values of a suitable measure of firm size expressed in natural logarithms, observed at the start and end of the period t to t + T. Size measures based on assets or employees are commonly used. If $\beta = 1$, then equation 7.1 implies that closing size is equal to opening size plus a systematic component denoted by the parameter α, which allows for any trend component in firm sizes that is common to all firms, plus a non-systematic component denoted by the stochastic error term, u_{it+T}. In other words, after allowing for any trend component, the change in size is non-systematic, as in the case described by the LPE. Departures from $\beta = 1$ imply departures from the LPE, because growth is partly dependent on opening size. If $\beta > 1$, then large firms tend to grow faster than small firms, and if $\beta < 1$, small firms tend to grow faster than large firms. Some researchers have employed an adapted version of equation 7.1 as follows:

$$s_{it+T} - s_{it} = \alpha + (\beta - 1) s_{it} + u_{it+T} \qquad [7.2]$$

Equation 7.2 is derived simply by subtracting s_{it} from both sides of equation 7.1. Remembering that s_{it+T} and s_{it} are both in natural logarithms, then the left-hand side of equation 7.2 is simply the (logarithmic) growth rate of firm i over the period t to t + T. In terms of equation 7.2, the condition for the LPE to hold is that growth should be unrelated to opening size, or $\beta - 1 = 0$, which is the same as $\beta = 1$. The LPE does not hold if $\beta - 1 > 0$ (growth is related positively to opening size) or if $\beta - 1 < 0$ (growth is related inversely to opening size).

As well as investigating the shape of their empirical firm size distributions at specific points in time (see earlier), Hart and Prais (1956) used regression analysis and other methods to investigate the nature of change in these distributions over time. Transition matrices are calculated in order to examine the mobility of firms between various size categories over time. For this purpose, the sample period (1885–1956) is split into five subperiods of approximately equal duration. The analysis shows that among firms that were 'live' at both the start and end of each subperiod, the dispersion of firm sizes increased. This implies that there was a tendency for concentration to increase. Hart and Prais also carried out a regression analysis of opening firm size on closing firm size for the subperiods 1885–96, 1896–1907, 1907–24, 1924–39 and 1939–50.

For all except the last of these subperiods, $\hat{\beta}$ is close to 1, but for 1939–50, a $\hat{\beta}$ value significantly smaller than 1 is obtained.

To provide a basis for various empirical tests, Hart (1962) identified the following implications of the LPE: (1) large, medium and small firms should have the same average proportionate growth; (2) the dispersion of growth rates around the mean should be the same for firms of all sizes; (3) the distribution of firm sizes should be log-normal; and (4) the relative dispersion of firm sizes should increase over time. Hart's sample contains data from the 1930s, 1940s and 1950s for the UK brewing, cotton and drinks manufacturing industries, as well as data on unquoted firms from various industries. Using gross profits minus depreciation as a measure of firm size, Hart found no evidence of differences between the mean growth of small and large firms. In the case of the brewing firms, however, large firms were found to experience more variable growth. For the unquoted firms, departures from log-normality in the size distributions in 1950 and 1955 were modest, and the variance of the size distribution increased over this period.

Mansfield (1962) tested the LPE using US data on firms in the tyre industry (for the period 1937–52), the petroleum industry (1921–57) and the steel industry (1916–57). Size was measured in terms of employees for the tyre industry, and in units of output for the petroleum and steel industries. The role of exit in influencing the relationship between size and growth was analysed in three sets of tests of the LPE. The first set used data on all firms in existence at the start of each subperiod, including those that failed to survive until the end of the subperiod. The LPE was rejected in seven out of ten tests based on subsamples constructed by classifying firms into size bands, partly because the probability of exit varies with firm size. The second set used data on those firms that survived for the entire subperiod. The LPE was accepted in four out of the ten tests. The third set used data on those firms whose size was greater than or equal to an estimate of each industry's MES. The LPE was accepted in six out of the ten tests, but the dispersion of individual growth rates was found to be greater for smaller firms than for their larger counterparts.

Samuals (1965) analysed a sample of 400 UK manufacturing firms with data for the period 1951–60. Net assets, defined as total assets minus current liabilities, was the chosen firm size measure. Samuals found a significant difference between the mean growth rates of firms in four size bands. The LPE was tested by examining the relationship between firm sizes at the start and end of the 1950s. The LPE was rejected, with $\hat{\beta} = 1.07$. The standard deviation of growth rates was interpreted as a measure of the mobility of firms. The standard deviation of 1.38 exceeds the values reported by Hart and Prais (1956) and Hart (1962) of 0.99 and 1.24, respectively. Samuals' results differ from those of Hart (1962), who found support for the LPE using data covering the period 1950–55. The findings of the two studies might be reconciled, however, if the tendency for larger firms to grow faster than small firms was more pronounced in the second half of the 1950s. Samuals also examined the extent to which mergers contributed to the larger firms exhibiting faster growth. Mergers were found to have increased the average growth of medium and large firms, but even after allowing for merger, the larger firms still grew faster than their smaller counterparts. Samuals sounded a note of caution, however, with respect to this finding. It could be an artefact of the data if there was a tendency for large firms to revalue their assets more regularly than small firms.

Singh and Whittington (1968) analysed a UK data set for the period 1948–60 covering firms in four industries: shipbuilding and non-electrical engineering, food, clothing and footwear, and tobacco. Regressions of closing size on initial size are used to test the LPE. Values of $\hat{\beta}$ significantly greater than 1 are obtained for all four industries, both for the full sample period and for the two subperiods (1948–54 and 1954–60). In accordance with the earlier findings of Samuals (1965), the extent of departure from LPE appears to be more pronounced in the second subperiod than in the first. Singh and Whittington (1975) reported results for an extended sample comprising 2000 firms in 21 industry groups, with data for the same period. As in the earlier study, a positive relationship between size and growth was obtained. In addition, the standard deviation of growth was found to be related inversely to size. The highest values of $\hat{\beta}$ tended to be obtained for the industries with the slowest overall growth rates. This finding is interpreted as being consistent with neoclassical oligopoly theory: large firms grow faster in industries that are protected by entry barriers, or in which there is implicit or explicit collusion and in which overall industry growth consequently tends to be rather sluggish. Finally, from a regression of growth for 1954–60 on growth for 1948–54, Singh and Whittington (1975, p.22) reported evidence of positive persistence in individual firms' growth rates over time:

> A large proportion of the positive relationship between size and growth is due to the positive serial correlation of growth rates. This does not affect our conclusion that the Law of Proportionate Effect is contradicted by the observed relationship between growth and opening size, but it does draw attention to the probability that serial correlation of growth rates is the main cause for this result.

Utton (1972) analysed a UK data set for the period 1954–65 covering 1527 manufacturing firms in 13 industrial groups. In regressions of firm sizes in 1965 against those in 1954, the LPE was accepted for seven industrial groups but rejected in favour of an alternative in which large firms grow faster than small firms for five groups. This was the case when the data for all sample firms were pooled. In the remaining group, small firms grew faster than their larger counterparts.

Utton also investigated whether the tendency for large firms to grow faster reflected internally or externally generated growth. When the tests were repeated using only the data for firms that were not involved in mergers, the LPE was accepted for several of the industry groups for which it was rejected previously, and was accepted for the pooled sample. These results suggest that involvement in merger activity was an important contributory factor in enabling large firms to grow faster than small firms. Utton argues there is a role for the Monopolies and Mergers Commission to intervene in the industries where external growth has led to increasing concentration.

Samuals and Chesher (1972) analysed a data set comprising 183 UK commercial and manufacturing firms covering the period 1960–69. In regressions of closing size on opening size, a value of β significantly smaller than one was obtained for the entire sample, and for five out of 11 industrial subgroups, implying that small firms grew faster than large firms in these cases. In contrast, Aaronovitch and Sawyer (1975) found no evidence to reject the

LPE using a data set comprising 233 large UK manufacturing firms observed over a similar sample period, 1958–67.

Chesher (1979) argued that the model used to test the LPE should incorporate a term allowing for persistence of growth from period to period. Chesher's tests of the LPE were based on a sample of 183 UK manufacturing firms for the period 1960–69. Experimentation with the model specification resulted in the adoption of a version that included one lagged value of firm size. The null hypothesis $\beta = 1$ was accepted, but there was also evidence of persistence of growth from one period to the next.

Kumar (1985) analysed a UK data set for the period 1960–76 covering 2000 quoted firms. An attempt was made to subdivide growth into internally and externally generated components. Five alternative measures of firm size were employed: net assets, physical assets, equity, employees and sales. The LPE was tested by regressing current size on initial size over three subperiods. Using the net assets size measure, there was a significant negative relationship between size and growth for 1960–65 and 1972–76, but the LPE could not be rejected for 1966–71. Kumar tested whether the results for 1966–71 were robust with respect to the size measure used. With the alternatives, a significant negative relationship between size and growth was obtained with the physical assets and equity size measures, but not with the employees and sales measures. Kumar also tested for persistence in growth rates between two subperiods, 1960–71 and 1966–76, and obtained estimated persistence coefficients that are positive and significant but smaller than the earlier estimates of Singh and Whittington (1975). An increase in the level of competition could account for the decline in the persistence coefficient. An analysis of externally generated growth found a positive relationship between size and growth by merger and acquisition for the period 1960–71, but a negative relationship for 1966–76. Mergers and acquisitions also tend to cause larger firms to have less variable growth than their smaller counterparts.

Evans' (1987a) data set comprised 42 339 small US firms classified into 100 manufacturing industry subgroups for the period 1976–82. An employment size measure was adopted. The tests of the LPE controlled for the firm's age and for heteroscedasticity in growth rates, and allowed for selection bias arising from attrition.

A three-equation model was specified to explain the determinants of survival, growth and the variability of firm growth. Separate analyses were carried out for both young (aged six years or less) and old (aged seven years or more) firms. In general, it was found that the probability of failure decreased with the firm's age, as did both average growth and the variability of growth. The LPE was rejected for both smaller and larger firms, although the rejection was quite marginal for the larger size group. This could suggest that there is a threshold size level (or MES) above which the LPE holds. Evans (1987b) reports further results obtained from the same data set.

Hall (1987) analysed a sample of US manufacturing firms using data covering the period 1972–83. The sample period was split into two subperiods: 1972–79, for which data on 1349 firms were available, and 1976 83, for which data on 1098 firms were available. An important feature of the paper was an investigation of ways in which measurement error may affect the empirical relationship between size and growth. In most of the tests reported, the relationship between firm size and growth was found to be negative. It was estimated that uncorrelated measurement errors could not account for more than about 10% of the observed relationship between size and growth. Hall examined the extent to which the observed results may be affected by attrition bias caused by exit. The probability of survival was found to vary with firm size, but growth did not seem to be correlated with survival. Hall concluded that neither measurement error nor sample attrition could account for the negative empirical relationship between firm size and growth. The LPE was consequently rejected.

Dunne et al. (1989) investigated post-entry employment growth and failure using data on more than 200 000 US manufacturing plants, covering the period 1967–77. The plants were assigned to size classes based on age, size (measured by employment), industry group and ownership structure. For the sample as a whole, mean growth was found to be related inversely to plant size. Mean growth tends to decline with age for plants that are part of a multiplant firm, but not for those that are single-plant firms. Differences in the variability of growth rates between size classes become smaller as plants become older. Failure rates decline with both age and size. Consequently, 'Policies designed to encourage the establishment of new plants may simply elevate the level of small plant failure if the policy-induced entrants are candidates who are less likely to succeed than their older competitors' (Dunne et al., 1989, p.697).

Contini and Revelli (1989) analysed a sample of 467 Italian firms using data covering the period 1973–86. When the sample was disaggregated by firm size and industry group, the LPE was found to hold for large firms in most cases, but tended to be rejected for small firms.

Tests for persistence in growth rates, based on regressions of growth for the period 1983–86 on growth in 1977–80 and 1980–83, produced negative estimated persistence coefficients, in contrast to the results of several earlier studies. This implies that firms with above-average growth in one period tend to experience below-average growth in the next.

Acs and Audretsch (1990) presented evidence at the industry level for US manufacturing for the period 1976–80, using an employment size measure. A simple accounting framework was used to decompose the change in industry employment over the period into components resulting from the expansion and contraction of surviving firms, and from exit. Firms that entered during the period were excluded from the analysis. Firms in each of the 408 four-digit industries included in the sample were classified into four size bands. Tests for differences in average growth rates between the four size bands led to acceptance of the LPE in 245 of the 408 cases.

Wagner (1992) analysed a sample of 7000 small German firms using data covering the period 1978–89. There are four industry subgroups: capital goods, consumer goods, food and drink, and tobacco. An employment size measure was used, and only surviving firms were included in the estimations. To minimise survivorship bias, the tests were repeated over a sequence of overlapping three-year periods (1978–80, 1979–81 and 1987–89). Wagner tested the LPE for ten three-year periods for two types of firm (manufacturers of consumer and producer products) and three different size groups by regressing closing size (in the three-year period) on size in the previous two periods. Wagner carried out 80 separate regressions, and found that the LPE was rejected in 63 cases. $\hat{\beta}$ is close to one in nearly all cases, but there is strong evidence of persistence of growth, which causes the LPE to be rejected.

Dunne and Hughes (1994) investigated the relationship between size and growth using a UK data set observed over the period 1975–85. A net assets size measure was adopted. For firms that survived between 1975 and 1980, patterns of survival and growth over the period 1980–85 were examined. Of 2149 sample firms that were live in 1980, 1709 firms survived to 1985, while 440 exited. The smallest and largest size classes had the lowest and highest survival rates, respectively. The smallest firms not only had the highest liquidation rates, but were also more susceptible to exit as a result of take-over than their larger counterparts. The probability of exit is related inversely to the rate of growth across the sample as a whole, but this relationship does not hold within the largest size class.

Among the firms that survived, both the mean and variance of growth are found to decline with size. It is acknowledged, however, that this result could be a consequence of aggregation bias. If some industries are characterised by large numbers of small but rapidly expanding firms, then an analysis of data pooled across industries may produce an apparently negative relationship between size and growth, while within each industry either a positive relationship or no relationship may exist.

A regression of growth over the period 1980–85 on growth for 1975–80 for 935 surviving firms fails to find strong evidence of persistence, in contrast to the earlier findings of Singh and Whittington (1975) and Kumar (1985). This might be attributed to an increase in competitive pressure emanating from trends such as increased merger and take-over activity and globalisation, making it difficult for firms to sustain persistently high growth rates. The variance of growth is found to be related inversely to firm size. This is attributed to the greater stability of the growth rates of large diversified firms, as suggested by Prais (1976).

Dunne and Hughes (1994) re-estimated their model including and excluding an age variable. They found an inverse relationship between firm growth and age for the sample as a whole, and for small, medium and large firms. They found a similar relationship for 15 out of the 19 industry groups, although the estimated coefficients were significant in only three of these cases. While small firms tended to grow faster than large firms, there also seems to be a lifecycle effect: younger companies tend to experience faster growth, but their growth is also more variable. Dunne and Hughes argue that the empirical growth–age relationship is consistent with the model of Jovanovic (1982).

Finally, Dunne and Hughes examined the possibility that the tests of the LPE are affected by attrition bias, by re-estimating the model using data for both survivors and non-survivors, and including a dummy variable to distinguish between the two groups. The results were found to be quite consistent with previous estimates, implying that there is little or no evidence of attrition bias.

Hart and Oulton (1996) analysed a sample of 87 109 independent UK firms, using data for the period 1989–93. In tests of the LPE for the sample as a whole, a value of $\hat{\beta}$ significantly smaller than one was obtained. In tests for firms within each of nine size classes, $\hat{\beta}$ was found to decline monotonically from largest to smallest size class. The possibility of attrition bias is acknowledged, however. If the smallest firms are the most likely to exit, then the growth rates observed for the survivors among the smallest group are likely to be inflated. Hart and Oulton (1999) presented some further results for a smaller sample with data covering the same period.

REGRESSION-BASED TESTS OF THE LAW OF PROPORTIONATE EFFECT: BANKING

In contrast to the voluminous empirical literature on testing the LPE using (mainly) manufacturing data, there are relatively few papers that examine the same topic specifically for the banking sector. Over the years, however, this topic has attracted sporadic attention in the banking literature, and very recently it has been the subject of renewed interest.

As far as we are aware, Alhadeff and Alhadeff (1964) were the first researchers to investigate patterns of firm growth within the US banking sector. The growth of the 200 largest US banks over the period 1930–60 was compared with the growth of total banking sector assets. During each of the three ten-year subperiods within the 30-year sample period, Alhadeff and Alhadeff found that the largest banks tended to grow more slowly than the average for the sample as a whole. Rhoades and Yeats (1974) examined growth, concentration and merger activity in the US commercial banking sector using a sample of 600 banks with data covering the period 1960–71. In order to distinguish between internally generated growth and external growth by merger, the latter was isolated by removing the deposits of acquired banks from the assets of the acquirer. It was found that banks in the smallest and largest size bands experienced the slowest growth. In a regression of closing size on opening size, a value of $\hat{\beta}$ significantly less than one was obtained. Merger was found to be the most important source of growth for banks in the largest size group. When growth through merger was removed, however, the internal growth of the largest banks was significantly below that of the smallest banks. Medium-sized banks experienced the fastest average rate of internal growth.

Yeats et al. (1975) examined the growth over a ten-year period of a sample of 48 new banks established in the USA between 1960 and 1963. Similarities between the growth patterns of these banks might be expected for three reasons: banking services tend to be homogeneous, so banks should charge similar prices and grow at similar rates; competition between banks is tightly regulated; and if banks are uniformly distributed geographically, they will tend to capture similar shares of any existing or new business. Age, average changes in disposable income for each bank's market, and the number of entrants are included as explanatory variables in the estimated growth equation. In the estimations, there is a positive relationship between age and growth, and between changes in disposable income and growth. Entry is found to have a negative effect on growth. Yeats et al. suggested that the model could be used by managers and regulators to examine deviations of actual from expected growth rates.

In a follow-up study, Alhadeff and Alhadeff (1976) examined the growth up to 1970 of 986 new banks that entered the US banking industry between 1948 and 1966. Size in 1970 was modelled using environmental factors common to all banks, internal factors specific to a bank, and the number of years since entry as explanatory variables. In banking, internal factors are likely to be relatively unimportant because tight regulation constrains the activities of management. External factors, including restrictions on entry of new banks, branch expansion and the size and structure of banks' assets and liabilities, tend to determine the growth and performance of banks. Consequently, banks that are successful in identifying areas where regulation is conducive to growth will be successful. Variables capturing entry restrictions, restrictions on branch expansion, market growth, the size of local markets, and a time trend (to control for learning effects) are found to be significant in explaining bank growth. Restrictions on branching and market growth did most to explain the positive growth enjoyed by new banks in branch banking states, while market growth did most to explain the growth of new banks in unit bank states. The size of branch banks at the end of the period was found to be around 10% cent higher than that of unit banks, perhaps because the former can open branches. Unit banks were four times more likely to survive, however, than banks operating in branching states.

Tschoegl (1983) investigated the relationship between size and growth for a sample of large international banks using data from the 1970s. Three hypotheses relating to the LPE were tested: growth is independent of size; variability of growth between banks is independent of initial size; and growth does not persist from one period to the next. If these propositions held, then concentration would increase over time. 'This result is due strictly to the workings of chance and requires no assumptions about the behaviour of firms or managers, economies of scale, or monopoly advantage' (Tschoegl, 1983, p.189).

Total assets was Tschoegl's chosen size measure. An alternative equity size measure was also used in some estimations. Problems with the assets measure may arise from differences in accounting practices across countries: in some cases, the regulations allow banks to keep hidden reserves, enabling them to smooth performance from year to year. In estimations of equations 7.1 or 7.2, this may introduce bias towards acceptance of the LPE. The model specification allows for persistence in growth rates, and for national differences in the size–growth relationship using dummy variables. Tschoegl found that initial size was unrelated to final size. The variability of growth declined with size in all equations, so smaller banks tended to exhibit more variable growth rates than large banks. The growth persistence coefficient was positive but insignificant. Growth in one period is therefore not a good predictor of growth in subsequent periods, and banks find it difficult to sustain above-average growth over successive periods.

Tschoegl found a positive relationship between bank size and the extent of transnationality, but also found that growth and transnationality are unrelated. It may be that if banks become more transnational as they grow, they will tend to become subject to a larger number of random shocks. This would lead towards acceptance of the LPE for transnational banks. The variability of growth is related positively to transnationality, so banks engaging in foreign activities tend to experience more variable growth than banks specialising in domestic business. Transnational banks therefore do not appear to benefit by pooling risk across several markets. An implication is that regulation should take account of differences between the risk profiles of banks of different sizes, and of banks with different (domestic or transnational) portfolios of business.

Vander Vennet (1999) examined the growth of banks located in 23 Organization for Economic Cooperation and Development (OECD) countries using industry-level data covering the period 1985–94. The total assets of each country's banking sector were the chosen size measures adopted. Macroeconomic, market structure and bank performance variables were included in the growth equation. For the period 1985–89, $\hat{\beta}$ was significantly less than one, implying that smaller banking sectors grew faster than their larger counterparts. For the period 1990–94, however, $\hat{\beta}$ was not significantly different from one. There is some evidence of negative persistence in growth rates, while efficiency, the average capital to assets ratio, the quality of credit and macroeconomic growth are all significant in the growth equation.

Wilson and Williams (2000) investigated the relationship between size and growth for a sample of French, German, Italian and UK banks, using data covering the period 1990–96. Total assets, equity and value of off-balance-sheet business size measures were adopted. Lagged growth, bank type and country of origin dummies were included as additional explanatory variables in the growth equation. No relationship was found between bank size and growth for France, Germany and the UK, but in Italy small banks grew faster than large banks. Growth rates for 1993–96 were correlated with those for 1990–93 for France and Germany, but were uncorrelated for Italy and the UK. Large banks were found to have less variable growth rates than their smaller counterparts. This suggests that large banks may enjoy diversification advantages, which makes them less susceptible to large fluctuations in growth.

Scholtens (2000) examined the relationship between growth in profit and size, using a sample of Europe's 100 largest banks covering the period 1988–98. Pretax profit, and total assets and total tier one capital were the profit and size measures adopted. The profits of banks classed as small in terms of assets grew faster than the largest banks. The opposite was found, however, when banks were classified according to a total tier one capital measure.

CONCLUSION

This chapter has described previous empirical research that has explored the relationship between firm size and growth, and its consequences for industry structure. In general, early research based on the analysis of empirical firm size distributions indicates that many observed industry structures could have been generated by the type of growth process described by the LPE, in which growth is independent of size. In research based on regression analysis of the relationship between the initial size and subsequent growth of cohorts of firms, the results have been rather more mixed. Most early studies that used data from the 1960s and before found either no relationship or a positive relationship between firm size and growth. Many studies that used more recent data from the 1970s onwards found that small firms tend to grow faster and have more variable growth rates than their larger counterparts. For banking specifically, the evidence concerning the LPE is somewhat mixed. On the whole, however, there is little evidence to suggest either a strong or a consistent relationship between size and growth in banking. This suggests that the LPE may indeed offer a reasonable description of the growth process.

Both the theoretical models and the econometric methodology employed have become progressively more sophisticated over time. Some researchers have allowed for the effects on the growth model of persistence and heteroscedasticity in growth rates. Others have attempted to control for problems such as survivorship or attrition bias. Some authors have drawn links between evolutionary learning models (where younger, less experienced firms enjoy less stable growth than their larger counterparts) and more traditional arguments based on economies of scale and strategic behaviour.

Drawing on the literature reviewed in Chapter 7, Chapter 9 will attempt to assess the extent to which the recent growth patterns exhibited by European banks are in accordance with the LPE. Prior to this, however, Chapter 8 will use simulation methods to quantify the implications of variations in the parameters of a simple stochastic growth model for the evolution of industry structure for a hypothetical cohort of firms over time.

Chapter 8

Stochastic models of the growth of banks

INTRODUCTION

Chapter 8 uses simulation methods to investigate the implications of variations in the assumptions of a simple stochastic growth model, on the evolution over time of the size distribution of a group of banks. Stochastic simulation is a flexible approach that uses randomly generated numbers to explore the properties of an underlying structural model. First, we review previous work in the industrial organisation literature that has used stochastic simulation in order to model the growth of firms. Then we describe the construction of a simulation model for a constant population of banks, and consider the implications for the size distribution of the banks of various assumptions regarding the relationship between size and growth. We then repeat this exercise, but in addition allow the population of banks to vary as a result of entry, exit and merger. Finally, we attempt to characterise the five largest European banking sectors in terms of their recent rates of entry, exit and merger. The technical analysis in this chapter, however, is purely theoretical; all simulations refer to a hypothetical population of banks. Chapter 9 presents empirical evidence for a sample of banks from a number of European countries, which allows us to calibrate the theoretical models that are presented in Chapter 8.

PREVIOUS EVIDENCE

A number of researchers have studied the use of simple parametric models of growth to generate simulated populations of firms, whose size distributions are capable of replicating those that are observed empirically.

Ijiri and Simon (1964) carried out Monte Carlo simulations to investigate the properties of various stochastic models of firm growth that lead to skewed firm size distributions. They developed a model in which the growth of a firm was influenced partly by random factors, and partly by previous growth, the influence of which declines as time proceeds. Allowance was made for the entry of new firms into the lowest size category only. To generate a distribution of firm sizes, they began with an industry consisting of a collection of firms of approximately equal size. They simulated the model over 1000 time periods, and found that 75% of growth was attributed to existing firms and 25% to new entrants. A positive association was found between firm size and age: older firms tended to become (and remain) larger than their younger counterparts. The larger firms' advantages were greater when there was positive serial correlation in growth rates, and when the rate of entry was low. Ijiri and Simon showed that their simulations generate a log-normal distribution of firm sizes.

> We can now confidently predict that many other processes, incorporating comparably weak forms of the law of proportionate effects, will lead to a highly similar distribution. Thus our analysis greatly increases the plausibility of a stochastic explanation of firm sizes.
>
> (Ijiri and Simon, 1964, p. 89)

Engwell (1973) used simulations to examine the size distribution of firms in Sweden, using a model calibrated with data for the car and shoe industries. A model was developed that allowed for growth of existing firms, as well as entry and exit. Entry and exit were modelled using a simple two-step procedure. First, a random draw was made from a suitable probability distribution to establish whether a new firm enters or an established firm exits from the market. Second, a random draw was made from another distribution to establish the size of the entering or exiting firm. Making reasonable theoretical assumptions regarding growth rates, and accounting for empirical facts on previous entry to and exit from the two industries, Engwell found that the size distributions of firms generated by the simulation model fit reasonably well with the actual distribution of firm sizes in both cases.

Scherer (1980) tested the LPE by constructing a hypothetical industry made up of 50 equal-sized firms. Each firm's growth rate in each year was drawn from an identical normal probability distribution whose parameters (mean and variance) were calibrated using a sample of 369 firms drawn from the 500 largest US firms over the period 1954–60. Scherer ran the growth process 16 times over a 140-year time period, and calculated the average concentration ratio. He found that CR_4 increased from 8% in year one to approximately 58% in year 140.

McCloughan (1995) developed a stochastic model of growth that also incorporated entry and exit. Five versions of the model were specified, which mimic the findings of previous studies, in which (i) the LPE holds; (ii) small firms grow faster than large firms; (iii) large firms grow faster than small firms; (iv) there is serial correlation in growth rates; and (v) there is heteroscedasticity, with the growth of small firms more variable than that of large firms. To allow for entry, McCloughan assumed that entrants were smaller than incumbent firms, and that the probability of exit was the same for all firm sizes.

McCloughan examined 14 hypothetical industry types, each based on different assumptions about entry, exit, serial correlation and heteroscedasticity. In industries in which larger firms grew faster than small firms, a high rate of entry had no effect on concentration, while in industries in which smaller firms grew faster, a high rate of entry led to deconcentration. Overall, differences in average growth between firms in different size categories tended to play a more important part in determining industry concentration than entry, exit or heteroscedasticity in growth rates. There are, however, some limitations with the stochastic simulation approach:

> Stochastic simulation lacks the generality of asymptotic theory and the results generated are much less robust than those from analytical techniques, in that they tend to be sensitive to the way in which the underlying parameters are calibrated.
>
> (McCloughan, 1995, p. 431)

A STOCHASTIC MODEL OF GROWTH FOR A FIXED POPULATION OF BANKS

This section outlines the assumptions underlying the simulation model of bank growth. The exercise seeks to examine the sensitivity of industry structure to changes in assumptions regarding the relationship between the size and the rates of growth of banks. The key indicators used to reflect outcomes in terms of industry structure are: the evolution of market concentration, changes in the distribution of bank sizes, and the persistence of dominance, measured by the extent to which one bank retains the largest market share through time.

The assumptions that determine the evolution of market concentration for a fixed population of banks concern the relationship between a bank's current size and its growth rate, the relationship (if any) between a bank's growth rates in successive periods (serial correlation or persistence in growth rates), and the relationship (if any) between a bank's current size and the variance or standard deviation of the probability distribution from which its growth rate is drawn (heteroscedasticity in growth rates).

For the purposes of this exercise, it is assumed that there is no deterministic trend in the evolution of bank sizes through time. The possibility of such a trend is ignored because its inclusion would not affect the results concerning the relative distribution of bank sizes, the evolution of concentration, or the persistence of dominance.

Defining s_{it} as the natural logarithm of the size of bank i at time t as before, a general form that the model specifying the evolution of bank size over time could take is:

$$s_{it} - s_{it-1} = \alpha_i + vt + (\beta - 1)s_{it-1} + u_{it}; \qquad u_{it} = \rho u_{it-1} + \varepsilon_{it} \qquad [8.1]$$

where $E(\varepsilon_{it}) = 0$, $var(\varepsilon_{it}) = \sigma_{it}^2$ and ε_{it} are distributed normally. A deterministic trend component would be incorporated by assuming that $v \neq 0$ if $\beta < 1$, or $\alpha_i \neq 0$ and $v = 0$ if $\beta \geq 1$. In order to exclude the deterministic trend, in the simulations it is assumed that $\alpha_i = v = 0$ for all i. $\alpha_i = 0$ ensures that the long-term values to which logarithmic sizes are mean-reverting are zero whenever $\beta < 1$. By setting initial logarithmic size, s_{i0}, to zero in all simulations, a zero mean logarithmic size is also ensured for the case $\beta = 1$. The simulation model can then be simplified as follows:

$$s_{it} - s_{it-1} = (\beta - 1)s_{it-1} + \rho(s_{it-1} - s_{it-2}) + \eta_{it} \qquad [8.2]$$

where $\eta_{it} = \varepsilon_{it} + \rho(1 - \beta)s_{it-2}$. If $\beta = 1$, then $\eta_{it} = \varepsilon_{it}$, so $E(\eta_{it}) = 0$, $var(\eta_{it}) = \sigma_{it}^2$ and η_{it} are distributed normally. The relationship between current size and growth is controlled by the parameter β, serial correlation in growth rates by the parameter ρ, and heteroscedasticity in growth rates by assumptions governing variation in σ_{it} over i and t.

The simulations will be used to examine the implications for the evolution of the size distribution of banks of seven alternative sets of assumptions concerning these parameters. These are as follows:

- *Industry 1 (I1)*: All banks grow at the same rate on average, and there is no serial correlation or heteroscedasticity, therefore the LPE holds. The parameter assumptions are $\beta = 1$, $\rho = 0$, and $\sigma_{it} = \sigma$.
- *Industry 2 (I2)*: Small banks tend to grow faster than large banks, and there is no serial correlation or heteroscedasticity. The parameter assumptions are $\beta < 1$, $\rho = 0$, and $\sigma_{it} = \sigma$.
- *Industry 3 (I3)*: Large banks tend to grow faster than small banks, and there is no serial correlation or heteroscedasticity. The parameter assumptions are $\beta > 1$, $\rho = 0$, and $\sigma_{it} = \sigma$.
- *Industry 4 (I4)*: Large banks have more variable growth rates than small banks. There is heteroscedasticity, but no serial correlation. The parameter assumptions are $\beta = 1$, $\rho = 0$, and $\sigma_{it} = f(s_{it-1})$, where $f' > 0$.
- *Industry 5 (I5)*: Small banks have more variable growth rates than large banks. There is heteroscedasticity, but no serial correlation. The parameter assumptions are $\beta = 1$, $\rho = 0$, and $\sigma_{it} = g(s_{it-1})$, where $g' < 0$.

- *Industry 6 (I6):* Banks that enjoyed above-average or below-average growth in the previous period tend to do so again in the current period. There is positive serial correlation, but no heteroscedasticity. The parameter assumptions are $\beta = 1$, $\rho > 0$, and $\sigma_{it} = \sigma$.
- *Industry 7 (I7):* Banks that experienced above-average or below-average growth in the previous period tend to experience below-average or above-average growth, respectively, in the current period. There is negative serial correlation, but no heteroscedasticity. The parameter assumptions are $\beta = 1$, $\rho < 0$, and $\sigma_{it} = \sigma$.

The simulation results are reported using three sets of measures reflecting the evolution of the size distribution of banks: the mean and standard deviation of bank size; the one-, two- and five-bank concentration ratios (CR_1, CR_2 and CR_5) and the numbers equivalent of the Herfindahl–Hirschman (H–H) index (see Chapter 3); and the persistence of dominance, measured by the average number of time periods as market leader that were achieved by the bank with the most periods as market leader in each replication.

Table 8.1 reports the average results across 20 simulations of the evolution over 50 time periods of the sizes of a hypothetical group of 20 banks for industries 1–7 (I1–I7). The banks begin equal in size at time t = 0, and their subsequent evolution is driven by equation 8.2. The assumption that all banks are equal in size at the outset is not intended to represent even a stylised approximation to conditions existing in any actual banking sector. Rather, the objective is to compare the speed at which industry structure departs from this hypothetical structure of size equality under various sets of parameter assumptions.

For I1, the LPE holds in its strictest form. I1 therefore represents a benchmark against which to compare the other industries, each of which represents some form of departure from the LPE. In I1, s_{it} (for each bank i) follows a random walk, with a homoscedastic disturbance term. Lower-case symbols are used to denote the natural logarithm of bank size, so s_{it} = log size of bank i

at time t and $\quad \bar{s}_t = \sum_{i=1}^{N} s_{it}/N$ = arithmetic mean of s_{it}. Upper-case

Table 8.1 Evolution of market structure: no entry, exit or merger

	Mean	Standard deviation	CR_1	CR_2	CR_5	Numbers equivalent
I1: $\beta = 1$, $\rho = 0$, $\sigma_{it} = 0.1$			Top = 26.7			
$t = 10$	1.03	0.33	8.7	16.1	35.4	18.2
$t = 20$	1.10	0.49	10.5	19.1	40.0	16.7
$t = 50$	1.26	0.91	15.1	25.7	49.0	13.2
I2: $\beta = 0.95$, $\rho = 0$, $\sigma_{it} = 0.1$			Top = 18.4			
$t = 10$	1.05	0.27	8.2	15.1	33.4	18.9
$t = 20$	1.09	0.34	8.6	16.0	35.3	18.2
$t = 50$	1.05	0.33	8.8	16.2	35.4	18.2
I3: $\beta = 1.02$, $\rho = 0$, $\sigma_{it} = 0.1$			Top = 30.5			
$t = 10$	1.08	0.37	9.0	16.8	36.4	17.9
$t = 20$	1.19	0.64	11.6	21.1	43.0	15.6
$t = 50$	2.10	2.83	27.2	40.0	64.8	7.3
I4: $\beta = 1$, $\rho = 0$, $\sigma_{it} = 0.1+0.02\,s_{it-1}$			Top = 25.2			
$t = 10$	1.07	0.35	9.0	16.5	34.2	18.2
$t = 20$	1.15	0.59	11.7	20.8	42.0	15.9
$t = 50$	1.38	1.20	18.2	29.1	51.7	11.5
I5: $\beta = 1$, $\rho = 0$, $\sigma_{it} = 0.1-0.02\,s_{it-1}$			Top = 26.5			
$t = 10$	1.05	0.34	8.6	16.0	35.6	18.2
$t = 20$	1.09	0.48	10.1	18.8	39.3	16.7
$t = 50$	1.28	0.86	13.2	23.2	47.5	13.9
I6: $\beta = 1$, $\rho = 0.1$, $\sigma_{it} = 0.1$			Top = 26.3			
$t = 10$	1.07	0.39	9.5	17.3	36.9	17.9
$t = 20$	1.12	0.56	11.3	20.0	41.6	16.1
$t = 50$	1.30	1.03	16.3	27.0	50.8	12.5
I7: $\beta = 1$, $\rho = -0.1$, $\sigma_{it} = 0.1$			Top = 23.6			
$t = 10$	1.04	0.31	8.4	15.7	34.8	18.5
$t = 20$	1.08	0.45	10.1	18.3	39.1	16.9
$t = 50$	1.23	0.83	14.2	24.8	47.6	13.7

In each panel, the results are generated from 20 replications of the development over 10, 20 and 50 time periods of a sector comprising 20 banks, each of which starts from an initial size $S_{it} = 1$ or $s_{it} = \ln(S_{it}) = 0$, and whose subsequent evolution is driven by the model:
$\Delta s_{it} = (\beta - 1)s_{it-1} + \rho \Delta s_{it-1} + \eta_{it}$, $\eta_{it} \sim N(0, \sigma_{it}^2)$.
Mean and Standard deviation ($\bar{s}_t$) denote the mean and standard deviation of bank size.
CR_1, CR_2 and CR_5 are concentration ratios measuring the market share of the top one, two and five banks, respectively.
Numbers equivalent is the numbers equivalent version of the Herfindahl–Hirschman index.
Top denotes the number of periods (out of 50) for which the bank with the most periods as the largest bank held the position as the largest bank.

symbols are used to denote actual bank size, so $S_{it} = e^{s_{it}}$, and

$$\bar{S}_t = \sum_{i=1}^{N} S_{it}/N = \text{arithmetic mean of } S_{it}.$$ While $\bar{s}_t$ (not shown in Table

8.1) remains zero over all time periods, Table 8.1 shows that $\bar{S}_t$ tends to increase over time starting at 1.0 at t = 0, reaching 1.03 by t = 10, 1.10 by t = 20, and 1.26 by t = 50. The upward drift in the value of $\bar{S}_t$ is attributable to the increase in dispersion of s_{it} around $\bar{s}_t$, when s_{it} follows random walks as in I1 (Prais, 1976).

This phenomenon is explained as follows: Suppose there are two banks, each with $s_{i0} = 0$, so $S_{i0} = 1$ for i = 1, 2, and $\bar{s}_0 = 0$, $\bar{S}_0 = 1$. Suppose in period 1 that $\eta_{11} = s_{11} = 0.2$ and $\eta_{21} = s_{21} = -0.2$, so $S_{11} = 1.2214$ and $S_{21} = 0.8187$. Then $\bar{s}_1 = 0$, but $\bar{S}_1 = 1.0201$. Average size has increased, due to the dispersion of s_{11} and s_{21} around the logarithmic mean of $\bar{s}_1 = 0$. Banks with $s_{tt} > 0$ ($S_{it} > 1$) contribute more to $\bar{S}_t$ than banks with $s_{it} < 0$ ($S_{it} < 1$) when the exponential function is applied to s_{it} in order to obtain S_{it}. A similar phenomenon also explains the progressive increases in the concentration ratios, CR_1, CR_2 and CR_5, reported in Table 8.1. For I1, these start at 5.0, 10.0 and 25.0, respectively, at t = 0. They increase to 15.1, 25.7 and 49.0, respectively, by t = 50. Likewise, the H–H numbers equivalent falls from 20.0 at t = 0 to 13.2 at t = 50. Finally, for I1 the average number of time periods (out of 50) over which the bank with the longest duration as the largest bank held the position as largest bank was 26.7.

I2 represents the case in which smaller banks grow faster than larger banks, so the LPE does not hold. For the purpose of the simulations reported in Table 8.1, the parameter β is set to 0.95. From an initial position in which all banks are of equal size, random fluctuations from year to year in logarithmic size around its mean size cause the average bank size and the concentration ratios to increase slightly from their initial values. Once the equilibrium level of dispersion around the logarithmic mean is achieved, however, the proportionately faster growth of small banks slows and eventually halts the rate at which average bank size and concentration increase. Consequently, there is no further tendency for average bank size or concentration to increase. As shown in the results reported in Table 8.1, market structure in I2 remains almost constant between t = 20 and t = 50.

I3 represents the case in which larger banks grow faster than smaller banks. Again, the LPE does not hold. For the purpose of the simulations reported in Table 8.1, the parameter β is set to 1.02. For values of β much greater than about 1.02, the growth of the larger banks is sufficiently explosive to produce unstable and unrealistic projections of industry structure after 50 time periods. In I3, even with $\beta = 1.02$ the pattern of growth in s_{it} leads to a wide divergence in bank sizes. Consequently, the average bank size and the dispersion of sizes both increase much faster that in I1. Levels of concentration at t = 50 in I3 ($CR_1 = 27.2\%$, $CR_2 = 40.0\%$ and $CR_5 = 64.8\%$) are much higher than in I1 ($CR_1 = 15.1\%$, $CR_2 = 25.7\%$ and $CR_5 = 49.0\%$). The average number of time periods (out of 50) over which the bank with the longest duration as the largest bank held that position is 30.5 (also higher than in I1). I3 represents a growth model that could be observed over a finite period, but that would be unlikely to provide a realistic description of the size–growth relationship over the long term.

I4 and I5 illustrate the effects of heteroscedasticity in the disturbance term, when σ_{it} is related positively to s_{it-1} (I4) and related negatively to s_{it-1} (I5). If σ_{it} increases with s_{it-1}, a bank that is fortunate to draw its growth rate (randomly) from the top end of the appropriate probability distribution in one period will become bigger, and will therefore draw its growth rate in the next period from a probability distribution with a larger variance. If the bank is fortunate again and draws from the top end of the distribution, it will have grown faster over the two time periods than a bank that experienced two 'good' draws in successive periods from distributions whose variances do not increase with bank size. In I4, this pattern of growth in s_{it} leads to larger average values of bank size than in I1. Levels of concentration at t = 50 in I4 ($CR_1 = 18.2\%$, $CR_2 = 29.1\%$ and $CR_5 = 51.7\%$) are also somewhat higher than in I1 ($CR_1 = 15.1\%$, $CR_2 = 25.7\%$ and $CR_5 = 49.0\%$).

I5 illustrates the reverse case of heteroscedasticity in the disturbance term, with σ_{it} related inversely to s_{it-1}. In this case, the long-term tendency towards increased concentration implied by the assumption of no systematic relationship between size and growth ($\beta = 1$) is offset to some extent by the effects of the heteroscedasticity. A bank that is fortunate to achieve growth rates from the top end of the distribution in two successive periods will tend to grow at a slower rate than it would if the error structure were homoscedastic. In the second period, the growth rate will be drawn from the top end of a distribution with a smaller variance, as a result of the increase in size that was achieved in the first period. Heteroscedasticity that follows this pattern does not bring about convergence in bank sizes (the tendency toward increased concentration still continues in the long term), but it does slow the rate at which divergence takes place. Levels of concentration at t = 50 in I5 (CR_1 = 13.2%, CR_2 = 23.2% and CR_5 = 47.5%) are therefore somewhat lower than in I1 (CR_1 = 15.1%, CR_2 = 25.7% and CR_5 = 49.0%).

Mansfield (1962), Singh and Whittington (1975), Evans (1987a, 1987b), Hall (1987), Dunne and Hughes (1994) and Hart and Oulton (1996) all found evidence of heteroscedasticity of the type represented by I5. This type of heteroscedasticity seems likely to be more typical than that represented by I4. This is because large banks (and large firms in other sectors) often enjoy advantages associated with diversified operations that make them less susceptible than their smaller counterparts to periods of extremely high or low growth. Smaller firms may be dependent on a narrower range of products or activities, and therefore more susceptible to large fluctuations in growth.

I6 represents the effects of positive serial correlation in rates of growth. Positive serial correlation ($\rho > 0$) tends to prolong the advantages of banks that are initially fortunate in drawing an above-average growth rate. If a bank does so in one period, it has a better-than-evens chance of repeating this performance in the following period: success tends to lead to further success (likewise, failure tends to be followed by further failure). This type of growth process tends to result in a faster rate of increase in the average bank size than the case in which there is no serial correlation. Industry concentration also tends to increase at a faster rate. Levels of concentration at t = 50 in I6 (CR_1 = 16.3%, CR_2 = 27.0% and CR_5 = 50.8%) are therefore somewhat higher than those in I1 (CR_1 = 15.1%, CR_2 = 25.7% and CR_5 = 49.0%).

For manufacturing, Singh and Whittington (1975), Kumar (1985) and Dunne and Hughes (1994) all found evidence of persistence in growth rates, or positive serial correlation as represented by I6.

Finally, I7 represents the effects of negative serial correlation in rates of growth. Negative serial correlation ($\rho < 0$), by ensuring that periods of above-average and below-average growth tend to follow one another, causes periods of 'good' and 'bad' fortune to be distributed more evenly across the population of banks than is the case when serial correlation is not present. The effect is to reduce the speed at which the size of the average bank increases. Negative serial correlation does not bring about convergence in bank sizes, but it does slow the rate at which divergence takes place. Levels of concentration at $t = 50$ in I7 ($CR_1 = 14.2\%$, $CR_2 = 24.8\%$ and $CR_5 = 47.6\%$) are lower than those in I1 ($CR_1 = 15.1\%$, $CR_2 = 25.7\%$ and $CR_5 = 49.0\%$).

Tables 8.2–8.4 present a sensitivity analysis showing the effects of variation in each of the parameters, β, ρ and σ, respectively (in the case where y_{it} is homoscedastic) while holding all other parameters constant. Table 8.5 shows the effects of variation in the functional relationship between σ_{it} and s_{it-1} (in the case where σ_{it} is heteroscedastic), again holding all other parameters constant.

Table 8.2 shows the implications for the evolution of industry structure of variation in the value of β. The rows for $\beta = 0.95$ reproduce the results for I2, while $\beta = 1$ is I1 and $\beta = 1.02$ is I3. For $\beta < 1$, the random component of bank growth ensures there is a distribution of values of s_{it} around zero (and a corresponding distribution of S_{it} around one), which opens out during the first few time periods, before settling down and eventually reaching a level of dispersion that does not increase any further. The closer to one is the value of β, the larger the variance of the equilibrium bank size distribution, and the longer it takes for the distribution to reach this equilibrium. When $\beta \geq 1$, as already seen, concentration continues to increase indefinitely, and there is no equilibrium distribution of bank sizes.

Table 8.3 shows the implications of variation in the strength of serial correlation for various values of ρ on either side of zero. The rows for $\rho = 0.1$ and $\rho = -0.1$ reproduce the results for I6 and I7 in Table 8.1, while the rows for $\rho = 0$ represent I1. Table 8.3 shows that the tendencies identified in Table 8.1 are simply accentuated if there is stronger positive or negative serial correlation. The former tends to accentuate the trend towards higher concentration over time, while the latter tends to offset (but not halt) the same trend.

Table 8.2   Sensitivity analysis for variation in β

β	Mean	Standard deviation	CR_1	CR_2	CR_5	Numbers equivalent	Top
t = 10							
0.50	1.01	0.12	6.3	11.9	28.7	19.6	n/a
0.75	1.01	0.15	6.5	12.6	29.6	19.6	
0.90	1.03	0.22	7.5	14.0	31.8	19.2	
0.95	1.05	0.27	8.2	15.1	33.4	18.9	
0.97	1.03	0.27	8.2	15.1	33.3	18.9	
0.99	1.05	0.30	8.2	15.4	34.5	18.5	
1.00	1.03	0.33	8.7	16.1	35.4	18.2	
1.02	1.08	0.37	9.0	16.8	36.4	17.9	
t = 20							
0.50	1.01	0.11	6.1	11.9	28.4	19.6	n/a
0.75	1.01	0.14	6.4	12.4	29.5	19.6	
0.90	1.01	0.24	7.9	14.6	32.8	18.9	
0.95	1.09	0.34	8.6	16.0	35.3	18.2	
0.97	1.05	0.34	8.7	16.2	35.5	18.2	
0.99	1.12	0.48	10.4	18.7	39.3	16.9	
1.00	1.10	0.49	10.5	19.1	40.0	16.7	
1.02	1.19	0.64	11.6	21.1	43.0	15.6	
t = 50							
0.50	1.00	0.12	6.2	12.1	28.8	19.6	6.7
0.75	1.01	0.14	6.5	12.5	29.5	19.6	8.8
0.90	1.01	0.23	7.4	14.2	32.3	18.9	14.1
0.95	1.05	0.33	8.8	16.2	35.4	18.2	18.4
0.97	1.10	0.43	9.8	18.0	37.6	17.2	18.9
0.99	1.21	0.67	11.5	21.3	43.7	15.4	22.8
1.00	1.26	0.91	15.1	25.7	49.0	13.2	26.6
1.02	2.10	2.83	27.2	40.0	64.8	7.3	30.2

In each panel, the results are generated from 20 replications of the development over 10, 20 and 50 time periods of a sector comprising 20 banks, each of which starts from an initial size $S_{it} = 1$ or $s_{it} = \ln(S_{it}) = 0$, and whose subsequent evolution is driven by the model $\Delta s_{it} = (\beta - 1)s_{it-1} + \rho \Delta s_{it-1} + \eta_{it}$, $\eta_{it} \sim N(0, \sigma_{it}^2)$, $\rho = 0$, $\sigma_{it} = 0.1$.
Mean and Standard deviation denote the mean ($\bar{S}_t$) and standard deviation of bank size.
CR_1, CR_2 and CR_5 are concentration ratios measuring the market share of the top one, two and five banks, respectively.
Numbers equivalent is the numbers equivalent version of the H–H index.
Top denotes the number of periods (out of 50) for which the bank with the most periods as the largest bank held the position as the largest bank.

Under an assumption of homoscedasticity, so $\sigma_{it} = \sigma$ for all i and t, Table 8.4 shows the implications of variation in the numerical value of the parameter σ. The rows for $\sigma = 0.1$ represent I1. Increasing σ impacts primarily on the dispersion of the bank size distribution, but also indirectly on mean bank size and concentration. The average number of periods for which the bank with the

Table 8.3 Sensitivity analysis for variation in ρ

ρ	Mean	Standard deviation	CR_1	CR_2	CR_5	Numbers equivalent	Top
$t = 10$							
0.4	1.13	0.52	10.6	19.8	40.6	16.4	n/a
0.2	1.08	0.44	10.2	18.3	38.6	17.2	
0.1	1.07	0.39	9.5	17.3	36.9	17.9	
0.0	1.03	0.33	8.7	16.1	35.4	18.2	
−0.1	1.04	0.31	8.4	15.7	34.8	18.5	
−0.2	1.03	0.28	8.2	15.4	33.8	18.5	
−0.4	1.02	0.22	7.4	14.0	32.0	19.2	
$t = 20$							
0.4	1.30	0.92	14.2	25.3	49.4	13.5	n/a
0.2	1.16	0.66	12.1	22.0	44.8	15.2	
0.1	1.12	0.56	11.3	20.0	41.6	16.1	
0.0	1.10	0.49	10.5	19.1	40.0	16.6	
−0.1	1.08	0.45	10.1	18.3	39.1	16.9	
−0.2	1.09	0.44	10.1	18.6	39.6	17.2	
−0.4	1.04	0.31	8.3	15.8	34.5	18.5	
$t = 50$							
0.4	1.93	2.30	23.2	38.0	63.7	8.6	25.8
0.2	1.51	1.58	20.9	32.9	57.8	9.9	27.6
0.1	1.30	1.03	16.3	27.0	50.8	12.5	26.3
0.0	1.27	0.91	15.1	25.7	49.0	13.2	26.7
−0.1	1.23	0.83	14.2	24.8	47.6	13.7	23.6
−0.2	1.20	0.78	14.0	24.8	46.3	14.1	24.7
−0.4	1.12	0.55	11.2	20.4	41.5	16.1	20.8

In each panel, the results are generated from 20 replications of the development over 10, 20 and 50 time periods of a sector comprising 20 banks, each of which starts from an initial size $S_{it} = 1$ or $s_{it} = \ln(S_{it}) = 0$, and whose subsequent evolution is driven by the model $\Delta s_{it} = (\beta - 1)s_{it-1} + \rho \Delta s_{it-1} + \eta_{it}$, $\eta_{it} \sim N(0, \sigma_{it}^2)$, $\rho = 0$, $\sigma_{it} = 0.1$.
Mean and Standard deviation denote the mean ($\bar{S}_t$) and standard deviation of bank size.
CR_1, CR_2 and CR_5 are concentration ratios measuring the market share of the top one, two and five banks, respectively.
Numbers equivalent is the numbers equivalent version of the H–H index.
Top denotes the number of periods (out of 50) for which the bank with the most periods as the largest bank held the position as the largest bank.

longest duration as the largest bank held that position, however, is unaffected by variations in σ.

Finally, under an assumption of heteroscedasticity, Table 8.5 shows the implications of variation in the parameters that express the functional relationship between σ_{it} and s_{it}. The rows for $\sigma_{it} = 0.1 + 0.02s_{it-1}$ and $\sigma_{it} = 0.1 - 0.02s_{it-1}$ reproduce the results for I4 and I5, respectively, while $\sigma_{it} = 0.1$ represents I1. An increase in the strength of the positive functional relationship between σ_{it} and $s_{it\ 1}$ leads to bigger increases in the mean and standard devia-

Table 8.4   Sensitivity analysis for variation in σ_{it}

	σ_{it}	Mean	Standard deviation	CR_1	CR_2	CR_5	Numbers equivalent	Top
t = 10								
	0.025	1.00	0.08	5.8	11.4	27.5	20.0	n/a
	0.05	1.00	0.16	6.7	12.8	30.0	19.6	
	0.10	1.03	0.33	8.7	16.1	35.4	18.2	
	0.15	1.08	0.52	11.1	19.9	41.1	16.4	
	0.20	1.17	0.76	13.9	24.0	46.8	14.3	
	0.25	1.28	1.07	17.1	28.5	52.5	12.0	
t = 20								
	0.025	1.00	0.11	6.1	11.9	28.5	19.6	n/a
	0.05	1.02	0.23	7.4	14.1	32.2	19.2	
	0.10	1.10	0.49	10.5	19.1	40.0	16.7	
	0.15	1.24	0.85	14.3	24.9	48.0	13.7	
	0.20	1.46	1.38	18.7	31.2	55.9	10.8	
	0.25	1.80	2.18	23.4	37.7	63.2	8.3	
t = 50								
	0.025	1.01	0.18	6.8	13.1	30.6	19.2	26.7
	0.05	1.06	0.37	9.1	16.8	36.5	17.9	26.7
	0.10	1.26	0.91	15.1	25.7	49.0	13.2	26.7
	0.15	1.67	1.90	22.5	35.8	60.8	8.9	26.7
	0.20	2.48	3.89	30.6	45.9	70.9	6.0	26.7
	0.25	4.01	8.01	38.4	55.0	78.8	4.3	26.7

In each panel, the results are generated from 20 replications of the development over 10, 20 and 50 time periods of a sector comprising 20 banks, each of which starts from an initial size $S_{it} = 1$ or $s_{it} = \ln(S_{it}) = 0$, and whose subsequent evolution is driven by the model $\Delta s_{it} = (\beta - 1)s_{it-1} + \rho \Delta s_{it-1} + \eta_{it}$, $\eta_{it} \sim N(0, \sigma_{it}^2)$, $\rho = 0$, $\sigma_{it} = 0.1$.
Mean and Standard deviation denote the mean $(\bar{S}_t)$ and standard deviation of bank size.
CR_1, CR_2 and CR_5 are concentration ratios measuring the market share of the top one, two and five banks, respectively.
Numbers equivalent is the numbers equivalent version of the H–H index.
Top denotes the number of periods (out of 50) for which the bank with the most periods as the largest bank held the position as the largest bank.

tion of bank size and higher concentration than in I1. Conversely, an increase in the strength of the negative functional relationship between σ_{it} and s_{it-1} tends to slow the rate at which the mean and standard deviation of size and the level of concentration increase over time. Note that the results reported in Table 8.5 contain a lot of statistical noise, making the reported relationship between the extent of heteroscedasticity and the bank size distribution appear erratic.

To summarise the results of this section, if the LPE provides an accurate description of the relationship between the size and growth of banks (I1), then an increase in the mean and standard

Table 8.5 Sensitivity analysis for variation in the relationship between σ_{it} and s_{it-1}

σ_{it}	Mean	Standard deviation	CR_1	CR_2	CR_5	Numbers equivalent	Top
t − 10							
$0.1 + 0.03\,s_{it-1}$	1.05	0.36	9.1	16.9	35.9	17.9	n/a
$0.1 + 0.02\,s_{it-1}$	1.07	0.35	9.0	16.5	34.2	18.2	
0.1	1.03	0.33	8.7	16.1	35.4	18.2	
$0.1 - 0.02\,s_{it-1}$	1.05	0.34	8.6	16.0	35.6	18.2	
$0.1 - 0.03\,s_{it-1}$	1.06	0.34	7.9	16.0	34.6	18.2	
t = 20							
$0.1 + 0.03\,s_{it-1}$	1.09	0.52	11.6	20.2	40.7	16.1	n/a
$0.1 + 0.02\,s_{it-1}$	1.15	0.59	11.7	20.8	42.0	15.9	
0.1	1.10	0.49	10.5	19.1	40.0	16.7	
$0.1 - 0.02\,s_{it-1}$	1.09	0.48	10.1	18.8	39.3	16.7	
$0.1 - 0.03\,s_{it-1}$	1.13	0.47	9.5	17.5	37.6	17.2	
t = 50							
$0.1 + 0.03\,s_{it-1}$	1.38	1.19	17.2	29.0	50.8	11.8	24.3
$0.1 + 0.02\,s_{it-1}$	1.38	1.20	18.2	29.1	51.7	11.5	25.2
0.1	1.26	0.91	15.1	25.7	49.0	13.2	26.7
$0.1 - 0.02\,s_{it-1}$	1.28	0.86	13.2	23.2	47.5	13.9	26.5
$0.1 - 0.03\,s_{it-1}$	1.24	0.80	12.6	23.1	46.2	14.3	25.9

In each panel, the results are generated from 20 replications of the development over 10, 20 and 50 time periods of a sector comprising 20 banks, each of which starts from an initial size $S_{it} = 1$ or $s_{it} = \ln(S_{it}) = 0$, and whose subsequent evolution is driven by the model
$\Delta s_{it} = (\beta - 1)s_{it-1} + \rho\Delta s_{it-1} + \eta_{it}$, $\eta_{it} \sim N(0, \sigma_{it}^2)$, $\rho = 0$, $\sigma_{it} = 0.1$.
Mean and Standard deviation denote the mean $(\bar{S}_t)$ and standard deviation of bank size.
CR_1, CR_2 and CR_5 are concentration ratios measuring the market share of the top one, two and five banks, respectively.
Numbers equivalent is the numbers equivalent version of the H–H index.
Top denotes the number of periods (out of 50) for which the bank with the most periods as the largest bank held the position as the largest bank.

deviation of bank sizes can be expected over time. Industry concentration can also be expected to increase. The tendency towards increased concentration develops more quickly if large banks grow proportionately faster than small banks, or if large banks experience more variable growth rates than their smaller counterparts, or if there is positive serial correlation in growth rates (I3, I4 and I6). The same tendency develops more slowly if small banks have more variable growth rates than their larger counterparts, or if there is negative serial correlation in growth rates (I5 and I7). Finally, there is no long-term tendency for the mean and standard deviation of bank sizes to increase, or for industry concentration to increase, if small banks tend to grow faster than larger banks (I2).

A STOCHASTIC MODEL OF GROWTH FOR A POPULATION OF BANKS THAT CHANGES OVER TIME

This section extends the models developed in the previous section, by allowing the population of banks to vary. Processes allowing for entry, exit and merger are each introduced in turn, and superimposed onto each of the seven industry types introduced earlier. The results show how the tendencies towards increased concentration identified in Table 8.1 for most of the industry types are affected by different assumptions concerning entry, exit and merger.

Entry

Empirical evidence on the determinants of entry for manufacturing industries now forms a substantial literature. Siegfried and Evans (1994) provide a recent survey. Most research suggests that entry is higher in profitable industries or in industries experiencing rapid growth (Geroski, 1991; Baldwin and Gorecki, 1987). In contrast, entry is slower into industries in which incumbents hold absolute cost advantages over potential entrants, or where capital requirements for entrants are substantial (Orr, 1974a). The evidence with regard to scale economies, excess capacity and restrictive pricing practices (such as limit and predatory pricing) is both limited and inconclusive (Baldwin and Gorecki, 1987; Geroski, 1991).

In banking, empirical evidence on the determinants of entry is also rather limited. Orr (1974b), using Canadian data covering the period 1963–67, estimated a model to explain the entry process in manufacturing, and then applied the estimated coefficients to predict the likely rate of entry into banking. Entry is determined by profit levels, market growth, market size, capital requirements, advertising and industry concentration. High capital requirements, heavy advertising expenditure and high existing concentration were all found to deter entry, while a large market size encourages entry. The model predicts an entry rate of 2.27 banks per year, but the actual entry rate was only 0.5 banks per year. Orr concluded that factors peculiar to banking must explain the rate of entry into this sector.

Hannan (1983) examined the relationship between market characteristics and entry decisions using US banking data for Pennsylvania covering the period 1968–70. Using a conditional logit model, entry was explained by a vector of market structure variables. Hannan found in general that entry is deterred in markets when incumbents charge low prices and invest in expanding branch networks. This suggests that limit pricing and increasing capacity are important price and non-price strategies for deterring entry.

The overall effect of entry on market concentration is dependent on two factors: the rate of entry and the sizes of entrants. Evidence from manufacturing suggests that typically, entrants tend to be smaller than established firms (Geroski, 1991). In banking, entry is regulated more heavily than in most manufacturing industries, so in general entry may be an even rarer event. Since the creation of the European Single Market in financial services, however, the rate of entry in banking has tended to increase, particularly in countries that were previously heavily regulated. This is a consequence of EU legislation introducing a single banking licence, which makes it easier for EU banks to establish a presence in other EU countries (European Commission, 1997). It has also led to increases in the numbers of foreign banks operating in the EU.

According to Berger, Bonime et al. (1999, p. 15), 'There may be an increase in the degree of contestability of financial services markets because of the removal of geographic restrictions on banking organizations allow existing institutions to enter or threaten to enter more local markets.'

In many countries, the majority of entrants have been foreign banks. During the 1980s and 1990s, the number and market shares of foreign banks increased in most EU national banking markets. This trend was especially strong in France, but was also evident to a lesser extent in Italy, Germany, Spain and the UK (European Commission, 1997). Foreign banks account for a particularly large share of banking sector assets in the UK (52.5% in

1999). In France, Germany, Italy and Spain, foreign bank influence has also increased, but at a slower rate. The assets shares of foreign banks in these four countries in 1994 were 14.1%, 4.5%, 3.5% and 10%, respectively (European Commission, 1997).

In the simulation model, the average rate of entry is denoted by the parameter λ, which is defined as the average number of new banks entering the industry per period. The probabilities that $X = 0, 1, 2 \ldots$ banks enter in each time period are assumed to follow the poisson distribution.

$$\text{prob}(X = x) = \frac{e^{-\lambda} \lambda^x}{x!} \qquad [8.3]$$

The average rate of entry is therefore the same for any two time intervals of equal length, and the rate of entry in any period is independent of the rate in any other period. It is assumed that all entrants begin with $s_{it} = 0$ ($S_{it} = 1$) when entry takes place at time t. An implication is that (except in the case of I2) entrants become smaller relative to the average size of existing banks, $\bar{S}_t$, as time proceeds.

Table 8.6 repeats the simulations for industries I1 to I3 (as introduced in Table 8.1), allowing for entry at either a low ($\lambda = 0.5$), medium ($\lambda = 1$) or high ($\lambda = 2$) rate. The entries in Table 8.6 for zero entry ($\lambda = 0$) reproduce the results for I1–I3 in Table 8.1. With an existing population of 20 banks, $\lambda = 0.5, 1$ and 2 correspond to entry rates of 2.5%, 5% and 10%, respectively. Data on entry flows into European banking markets were not available from official statistics. However, some rough estimates of entry to the Italian banking market were available from Central Bank reports. These suggest that, on average, during the early 1990s entry was approximately 3% per annum. Given that over this period the Italian market was among the most regulated in Europe, 3% is considered to be a relatively low rate of entry.

In all cases, non-zero rates of entry lead to lower mean sizes, standard deviations of bank sizes, and levels of concentration than is the case where entry is zero. Entry, even at the lowest rate, moderates quite substantially the trend towards increased concentration in I1. Concentration remains quite stable over time when $\lambda = 0.5$, while for $\lambda = 1$ or $\lambda = 2$, there is a tendency towards deconcentration over time. For an industry of 20 banks,

Table 8.6   Effect of entry on the evolution of market structure

Entry rate	Number of banks	Mean	Standard deviation	CR_1	CR_2	CR_5	Numbers equivalent	Top
I1: $\beta = 1$, $\rho = 0$, $\sigma_{it} = 0.1$								
t = 10								
Zero	20	1.03	0.33	8.7	16.1	35.4	18.2	n/a
Low	25	1.02	0.30	7.2	13.3	29.5	22.2	
Med.	30	1.02	0.29	5.8	10.9	24.3	27.8	
High	40	1.02	0.28	4.7	8.7	19.4	35.7	
t = 20								
Zero	20	1.10	0.49	10.5	19.1	40.0	16.7	n/a
Low	30	1.07	0.44	7.1	13.4	28.5	25.6	
Med.	40	1.06	0.40	5.6	9.8	21.4	35.7	
High	60	1.05	0.38	4.0	7.4	15.5	52.6	
t = 50								
Zero	20	1.26	0.91	15.1	25.7	49.0	13.2	26.7
Low	45	1.18	0.76	8.1	13.7	26.7	31.3	25.1
Med.	70	1.15	0.69	5.4	9.4	18.8	50.0	24.4
High	120	1.16	0.67	3.3	6.1	12.2	90.9	21.4
I2: $\beta = 0.95$, $\rho = 0$, $\sigma_{it} = 0.1$								
t = 10								
Zero	20	1.05	0.27	8.2	15.1	33.4	18.9	n/a
Low	25	1.04	0.25	6.7	12.3	27.2	23.3	
Med.	30	1.04	0.24	5.5	10.3	23.0	28.6	
High	40	1.03	0.22	3.9	7.4	16.6	40.0	
t = 20								
Zero	20	1.09	0.34	8.6	16.0	35.3	18.2	n/a
Low	30	1.07	0.31	5.9	10.8	24.5	27.8	
Med.	40	1.06	0.29	4.6	8.4	18.8	37.0	
High	60	1.05	0.27	3.0	5.8	13.1	55.6	
t = 50								
Zero	20	1.05	0.33	8.8	16.2	35.4	18.2	18.4
Low	45	1.05	0.31	4.3	8.0	17.6	41.7	17.8
Med.	70	1.04	0.30	2.9	5.4	11.8	66.7	14.9
High	120	1.04	0.29	1.6	3.1	7.1	111.1	15.0
I3: $\beta = 1.02$, $\rho = 0$, $\sigma_{it} = 0.1$								
t = 10								
Zero	20	1.08	0.37	9.0	16.8	36.4	17.9	n/a
Low	25	1.06	0.33	7.1	13.1	28.6	23.3	
Med.	30	1.06	0.33	6.2	11.6	25.4	27.0	
High	40	1.05	0.30	4.5	8.4	18.5	38.5	
t = 20								
Zero	20	1.19	0.64	11.6	21.1	43.0	15.6	n/a
Low	30	1.13	0.54	7.8	14.0	29.1	25.6	
Med.	40	1.12	0.51	5.9	11.2	24.0	32.3	
High	60	1.10	0.48	4.2	8.1	17.1	50.0	
t = 50								
Zero	20	2.10	2.83	27.2	40.0	64.8	7.3	30.2
Low	45	1.56	2.04	16.1	23.6	39.7	16.9	28.1
Med.	70	1.51	1.83	11.3	17.8	31.2	27.8	27.9
High	120	1.40	1.64	7.7	12.2	21.4	50.0	24.5

In each panel, the results are generated from 20 replications of the development over 10, 20 and 50 time periods of a sector comprising 20 banks, each of which starts from an initial size $S_{it} = 1$ or $s_{it} = \ln(S_{it}) = 0$, and whose subsequent evolution is driven by the model $\Delta s_{it} = (\beta - 1)s_{it-1} + \rho \Delta s_{it-1} + \eta_{it}$, $\eta_{it} \sim N(0, \sigma_{it}^2)$. Mean and Standard deviation denote the mean $(\overline{S}_t)$ and standard deviation of bank size.

CR_1, CR_2 and CR_5 are concentration ratios measuring the market share of the top one, two and five banks, respectively.

Numbers equivalent is the numbers equivalent version of the H–H index.

Top denotes the number of periods (out of 50) for which the bank with the most periods as the largest bank held the position as the largest bank.

The entry process is controlled by the expression $Pr(X=x) = \dfrac{e^{-\lambda} \lambda^x}{x!}$,

where X = the number of entrants, λ is the average number of new banks entering per period, $\lambda = 0$ represents zero entry; $\lambda = 0.5$ represents low entry; $\lambda = 1$ represents medium entry; and $\lambda = 2$ represents high entry.

an entry rate of 0.5 banks per period (2.5% of initial industry numbers) is roughly what is needed to neutralise the effect that the LPE would otherwise have on concentration. In I2, in which there is no tendency towards increased concentration in the long run with zero entry, any non-zero rate of entry gives rise to deconcentration because more banks of a size equal (on average) to those already present are joining the industry. In I3, the explosive growth pattern ensures that even when entry is at high levels, concentration still increases rapidly (albeit less so than when entry is zero). In I4, I5, I6 and I7 (not reported in Table 8.6), non-zero entry reduces the mean and standard deviation of bank sizes after any given time period, leading to lower levels of concentration than when entry is zero.

Exit

In this section, exit refers to banks leaving the industry altogether. Exit as a result of merger or take-over is considered separately below. In a theoretical sense, exit should be easy if incumbent banks have no sunk costs. In reality, this is often not the case. In Europe, regulators consider many banks to be 'too big to fail' (Gardener and Molyneux, 1997). Evidence for manufacturing suggests that exit is higher from industries in which profits are low, and in which sunk costs are insignificant (Dunne et al., 1988; see also Porter, 1980). In banking, there is some evidence to suggest that the probability of exit is related inversely to size. Using US data for the period 1946–75, Rose and Scott (1978) found that the probability of exit through failure was related inversely to bank size, market size and profitability.

It is also possible that there is an association between the entry and exit rates in any time period, if the entrants are displacing incumbent banks by capturing market share. Using US manufacturing data covering the period 1963–82, Dunne et al. (1988) found evidence of negative correlation between annual entry and exit rates. Entry and exit rates are unlikely to be correlated strongly in banking, however, given that regulators are generally unwilling to allow banks to fail in view of probable negative spill-over effects for the rest of the banking sector (Rose, 1987).

Rates of exit in banking as a result of bankruptcy (or other causes of bank failure) are generally low (Tirole, 1994; Gardener and Molyneux, 1997). According to the Bank for International Settlements (1999, p. 89), 'The banking industry is arguably characterised by an exit problem. Firms are less subject than in other sectors to the market mechanisms designed to discipline behaviour.'

Exit does, however, occur indirectly through the contraction of multinational banks' operations in selected countries, and through changes in the size of branch networks. Over the period 1980–95, the largest reductions in bank numbers were in the UK, France and Germany (where numbers fell by 24.1%, 17.6% and 18.1%, respectively), followed by Spain and Italy (13.2% and 8.9%, respectively). The numbers of branches also fell in France and the UK, but increased in Germany, Italy and Spain (European Commission 1997). These figures must be treated with some caution, however, given that reorganisation and consolidation of branch networks is often a consequence of a merger between existing banks, rather than outright closure.

In the simulation model, the pattern of exit is controlled by the parameters γ_1 and γ_2. The probability that a bank exits in period t is assumed to be governed by two factors: the size the bank has attained at the end of period $t - 1$, and the overall propensity to exit. The probability is expressed as follows:

$$\text{prob(bank i exits during period t)} = \gamma_2 \, e^{-\gamma_1 \, s_{it-1}} \qquad [8.4]$$

where γ_1 measures the strength of the relationship between s_{it-1} and the probability of exit, and γ_2 controls the overall magnitude of the probability of exit. If $\gamma_1 = 0$, then there is no relationship between bank size and the probability of exit. $\gamma_1 > 0$ implies that large banks are less likely to exit than smaller banks, while $\gamma_1 < 0$ implies the opposite. In so far as recent growth affects size, $\lambda_1 > 0$ ensures that the probability of exit is higher if the bank experienced significant negative growth during the previous year, which is in accordance with the formulation of Mansfield (1962).

Table 8.7 shows the implications of low, medium and high rates of exit in the case in which small banks are more likely to exit than large banks. In all of the simulations reported in Table 8.7, γ_1 is set equal to +1. γ_2 takes values of 0.005, 0.01 and 0.02 representing low, medium and high rates of exit, respectively. The rows of Table 8.7 for zero exit ($\gamma_2 = 0$) reproduce the results for I1–I3 in Table 8.1. In I1, exit as described above, by depleting the population of smaller banks faster than the population of large banks, tends to accelerate the tendency (evident anyway as a result of the LPE) towards increased concentration. The same is true for I3 (and for I4–I7, which are not reported in Table 8.7). Even in the case of I2, in which there is no tendency towards increased concentration when exit is zero, concentration does increase progressively when exit is included in the simulations. In this case, there is little change in average bank size in comparison with the case in which exit is zero. In I1 and I3, however, the effect of exit as described above is to increase the average size of the surviving banks after any given number of years. In all cases, exit in accordance with this pattern tends to lead to higher concentration levels.

The parameter γ_1 reflects the sensitivity of the probability of exit to bank size. Higher values of γ_1 imply a stronger inverse relationship between bank size and the exit probability. Table 8.8 shows the effects of varying γ_1 over the range of values 0 (zero sensitivity), 2 (medium sensitivity) and 4 (high sensitivity), while γ_2 is held constant at 0.01 (representing a medium exit rate). As the value of γ_1 increases, the overall exit rate tends to increase, as do the average size of the surviving banks and the level of concentration.

Mergers

As seen in Chapter 3, there are three basic types of merger: horizontal, vertical and conglomerate. For the purposes of the model, the primary interest is in simulating the effects of horizontal mergers (where two banks join together). Such merger activity can increase efficiency by reducing average costs, or by increasing average revenues by affording enhanced market power to the new merged entity. Akhavein et al. (1997)

Table 8.7 Effect of exit on the evolution of market structure (I)

	Entry rate	Number of banks	Mean	Standard deviation	CR_1	CR_2	CR_5	Numbers equivalent	Top
I1: $\beta = 1$, $\rho = 0$, $\sigma_{it} = 0.1$									
t = 10									
	Zero	20	1.03	0.33	8.7	16.1	35.4	18.2	n/a
	Low	19.2	1.03	0.33	9.0	16.7	36.6	17.5	
	Med.	17.8	1.04	0.33	9.8	18.1	39.3	16.1	
	High	16.1	1.05	0.33	10.6	19.6	42.8	14.5	
t = 20									
	Zero	20	1.10	0.49	10.5	19.1	40.0	16.7	n/a
	Low	18	1.11	0.49	11.4	20.7	42.9	15.2	
	Med.	16.1	1.11	0.50	12.8	23.0	47.3	13.3	
	High	12.9	1.17	0.51	15.0	27.3	56.0	10.6	
t = 50									
	Zero	20	1.26	0.91	15.1	25.7	49.0	13.2	26.7
	Low	15.5	1.34	0.92	17.9	30.3	56.7	10.4	26.8
	Med.	11.8	1.37	1.02	23.6	39.5	68.7	7.4	28.6
	High	6.7	1.56	0.98	32.5	53.0	88.8	4.6	27.5
I2: $\beta = 0.95$, $\rho = 0$, $\sigma_{it} = 0.1$									
t = 10									
	Zero	20	1.05	0.27	8.2	15.1	33.4	18.9	n/a
	Low	19.2	1.05	0.27	8.5	15.6	34.6	17.9	
	Med.	18.3	1.05	0.27	8.8	16.3	35.9	17.2	
	High	16.1	1.04	0.27	9.9	18.3	40.3	14.9	
t = 20									
	Zero	20	1.09	0.34	8.6	16.0	35.3	18.2	n/a
	Low	18.4	1.10	0.34	9.2	17.2	37.9	16.7	
	Med.	16.5	1.10	0.35	10.3	19.0	41.7	14.7	
	High	13.1	1.08	0.34	12.6	23.6	50.9	11.8	
t = 50									
	Zero	20	1.05	0.33	8.8	16.2	35.4	18.2	18.4
	Low	16.2	1.06	0.32	10.3	19.2	42.0	14.7	18.4
	Med.	11.8	1.09	0.34	14.0	25.7	55.0	10.5	18.8
	High	7.9	1.06	0.32	19.8	36.6	75.6	6.9	19.1
I3: $\beta = 1.02$, $\rho = 0$, $\sigma_{it} = 0.1$									
t = 10									
	Zero	20	1.08	0.37	9.0	16.8	36.4	17.9	n/a
	Low	18.8	1.08	0.37	9.4	17.7	38.3	16.7	
	Med.	18.5	1.07	0.36	9.5	17.7	38.6	16.7	
	High	15.7	1.10	0.37	11.1	20.5	44.2	13.9	
t = 20									
	Zero	20	1.19	0.64	11.6	21.1	43.0	15.6	n/a
	Low	18.1	1.20	0.64	12.6	22.9	46.6	14.1	
	Med.	16.1	1.22	0.64	14.2	24.8	50.0	12.5	
	High	13.0	1.28	0.64	15.4	28.6	57.6	10.4	
t = 50									
	Zero	20	2.10	2.83	27.2	40.0	64.8	7.3	30.2
	Low	14.8	2.42	3.10	31.5	45.7	72.5	5.9	30.5
	Med.	11.4	2.57	2.96	34.8	50.0	78.3	4.9	32.0
	High	7.3	3.00	2.87	39.0	59.4	90.7	3.8	30.3

In each panel, the results are generated from 20 replications of the development over 10, 20 and 50 time periods of a sector comprising 20 banks, each of which starts from an initial size $S_{it} = 1$ or $s_{it} = \ln(S_{it}) = 0$, and whose subsequent evolution is driven by the model $\Delta s_{it} = (\beta - 1)s_{it-1} + \rho\Delta s_{it-1} + \eta_{it}$, $\eta_{it} \sim N(0, \sigma_{it}^2)$.

Mean and Standard deviation denote the mean $(\overline{S}_t)$ and standard deviation of bank size.

CR_1, CR_2 and CR_5 are concentration ratios measuring the market share of the top one, two and five banks, respectively.

Numbers equivalent is the numbers equivalent version of the H–H index.

Top denotes the number of periods (out of 50) for which the bank with the most periods as the largest bank held the position as the largest bank.

The exit process is controlled by the expression prob(exit) = $\gamma_2 e^{-\gamma_1 s_{it-1}}$, where γ_1 controls the sensitivity of the probability of exit to s_{it-1}, and γ_2 controls the overall magnitude of the probability of exit. In Table 8.7, $\gamma_1 = 1$; $\gamma_2 = 0$ represents zero exit; $\gamma_2 = 0.005$ represents low exit; $\gamma_2 = 0.01$ represents medium exit; and $\gamma_2 = 0.02$ represents high exit.

Table 8.8　Effect of exit on the evolution of market structure (II)

	Sensitivity of exit probability to bank size	Number of banks	Mean	Standard deviation	CR_1	CR_2	CR_5	Numbers equivalent	Top
I1: $\beta = 1$, $\rho = 0$, $\sigma_{it} = 0.1$									
t = 10									
	Zero	18.7	1.02	0.32	9.2	17.1	37.4	16.9	n/a
	Med.	17.7	1.04	0.33	9.8	18.0	39.4	15.9	
	High	17.4	1.06	0.32	9.7	18.0	39.6	15.9	
t = 20									
	Zero	16.7	1.07	0.47	12.4	22.0	45.6	13.9	n/a
	Med.	15.7	1.14	0.51	12.9	23.5	48.2	12.9	
	High	14.3	1.23	0.48	13.1	23.8	49.7	12.3	
t = 50									
	Zero	12.5	1.20	0.80	20.4	35.0	65.3	8.4	26.8
	Med.	10.3	1.60	1.02	23.3	39.1	70.7	7.2	26.7
	High	9.5	1.71	0.97	23.4	39.3	73.0	6.9	27.2
I2: $\beta = 0.95$, $\rho = 0$, $\sigma_{it} = 0.1$									
t = 10									
	Zero	17.9	1.05	0.27	9.1	16.9	36.9	16.7	n/a
	Med.	17.8	1.06	0.27	9.1	16.8	36.9	16.7	
	High	17.6	1.06	0.27	9.1	16.8	37.2	16.4	
t = 20									
	Zero	15.6	1.10	0.33	10.6	19.9	43.7	14.1	n/a
	Med.	15.9	1.11	0.35	10.7	19.7	42.9	14.3	
	High	14.9	1.14	0.34	11.0	20.5	44.7	13.5	
t = 50									
	Zero	12.1	1.08	0.35	14.0	25.4	54.8	10.5	18.8
	Med.	11.3	1.09	0.33	14.7	26.9	57.9	9.7	19.3
	High	8.9	1.11	0.30	17.3	32.1	68.9	7.8	19.6
I3: $\beta = 1.02$, $\rho = 0$, $\sigma_{it} = 0.1$									
t = 10									
	Zero	18.0	1.07	0.37	9.9	18.5	39.9	16.1	n/a
	Med.	17.8	1.10	0.37	10.0	18.6	40.1	15.9	
	High	18.1	1.10	0.37	9.8	18.3	39.3	16.1	
t = 20									
	Zero	16.3	1.18	0.63	14.0	24.8	50.3	12.5	n/a
	Med.	15.6	1.26	0.65	14.1	25.2	51.2	12.3	
	High	14.7	1.32	0.63	14.2	26.0	52.1	11.6	
t = 50									
	Zero	12.2	2.05	2.75	36.1	52.3	81.2	4.5	28.8
	Med.	10.6	3.11	3.34	33.8	49.8	78.4	5.0	31.7
	High	10.0	3.34	3.35	34.5	50.8	79.2	5.0	32.3

In each panel, the results are generated from 20 replications of the development over 10, 20 and 50 time periods of a sector comprising 20 banks, each of which starts from an initial size $S_{it} = 1$ or $s_{it} = \ln(S_{it}) = 0$, and whose subsequent evolution is driven by the model $\Delta s_{it} = (\beta - 1)s_{it-1} + \rho \Delta s_{it-1} + \eta_{it}$, $\eta_{it} \sim N(0, \sigma_{it}^2)$.

Mean and Standard deviation denote the mean ($\bar{S}_t$) and standard deviation of bank size.

CR_1, CR_2 and CR_5 are concentration ratios measuring the market share of the top one, two and five banks, respectively.

Numbers equivalent is the numbers equivalent version of the H–H index.

Top denotes the number of periods (out of 50) for which the bank with the most periods as the largest bank held the position as the largest bank.

The exit process is controlled by the expression prob(exit) $= \gamma_2 \, e^{-\gamma_1} s_{it-1}$, where γ_1 controls the sensitivity of the probability of exit to s_{it-1}, and γ_2 controls the overall magnitude of the probability of exit. In Table 8.7, $\gamma_1 = 1$; $\gamma_2 = 0$ represents zero exit; $\gamma_2 = 0.005$ represents low exit; $\gamma_2 = 0.01$ represents medium exit; and $\gamma_2 = 0.02$ represents high sensitivity.

suggested that horizontal mergers lead to substantial increases in bank profitability, and in recent years there has been a marked increase in merger activity within banking (see Chapter 2, and Morgan Stanley Dean Witter, 1998b). For the period 1985–95, the highest level of merger and acquisition activity among EU banking sectors was in the UK (where 380 mergers or acquisitions in banking, insurance and other types of financial services took place), followed by France, Spain, Italy and Germany (with 77, 26, 22 and 22 mergers, respectively). In 1995, the values of merger and acquisition deals were $21.7 billion in the UK, $3.2 billion in France, $3 billion in Italy, $2.1 billion in Spain and $0.7 billion in Germany (Bank for International Settlements, 1996).

In the simulations, the probability that a merger takes place in period t is controlled by the parameter ϕ as follows:

$$\text{prob(merger)} = \frac{\phi(n_t - 1)}{n_0} \qquad [8.5]$$

where n_t is the population of banks in period t, and n_0 is the initial population of banks.

In this formulation, the probability that a merger occurs is directly proportional to the number of surviving banks in the industry. If a merger takes place, the partners are chosen randomly from the existing population of banks, with the probability of being a partner the same for all banks regardless of size or previous growth. The size of the merged bank in subsequent periods is the summation of the sizes that would have been achieved if the two banks had remained separate.

Low, medium and high rates of merger are generated by setting $\phi = 0.1, 0.2$ and 0.4, respectively. The implications for the size distribution of banks of variation between these rates of merger are reported in Table 8.9. The rows for $\phi = 0$ reproduce the results for I1–I3 in Table 8.1. As before, the results for I4–I7 are not reported. The results show that as ϕ increases, both the mean bank size and the standard deviation of bank size become higher in all cases. Overall, there is a positive relationship between the rate of merger and the level of concentration achieved after any given period, as one would expect. The extent of dominance of the top bank tends to decline as the rate of merger increases, however, because for the purposes of constructing this

Table 8.9   Effect of merger on the evolution of market structure

	Merger rate	Number of banks	Mean	Standard deviation	CR_1	CR_2	CR_5	Numbers equivalent	Top
I1: $\beta = 1$, $\rho = 0$, $\sigma_{it} = 0.1$									
t = 10									
	Zero	20	1.03	0.33	8.7	16.1	35.4	18.2	n/a
	Low	19.1	1.39	1.18	18.0	29.5	54.9	11.2	
	Med.	18.3	1.51	1.29	18.1	30.1	57.4	10.8	
	High	16.5	1.79	1.78	22.6	37.4	63.9	8.3	
t = 20									
	Zero	20	1.10	0.49	10.5	19.1	40.0	16.7	n/a
	Low	18.1	2.09	2.49	24.3	38.5	65.3	7.9	
	Med.	16.4	2.45	2.75	25.1	40.1	68.0	7.4	
	High	13.6	3.19	3.56	27.8	45.9	75.2	6.3	
t = 50									
	Zero	20	1.26	0.91	15.1	25.7	49.0	13.2	26.7
	Low	14.8	5.78	9.76	39.9	57.5	83.1	4.1	23.2
	Med.	12.7	7.09	11.06	39.7	59.6	85.2	4.0	23.1
	High	7.2	13.55	17.81	49.3	72.8	95.5	2.8	20.1
I2: $\beta = 0.95$, $\rho = 0$, $\sigma_{it} = 0.1$									
t = 10									
	Zero	20	1.05	0.27	8.2	15.1	33.4	18.9	n/a
	Low	18.9	1.40	1.08	16.8	29.3	52.4	12.0	
	Med.	17.9	1.54	1.20	17.4	30.1	54.8	11.1	
	High	16.3	1.83	1.48	18.6	32.9	61.1	9.8	
t = 20									
	Zero	20	1.09	0.34	8.6	16.0	35.3	18.2	n/a
	Low	18.3	1.74	1.62	19.5	32.5	57.7	9.8	
	Med.	16.3	2.09	1.88	21.0	34.8	61.9	8.9	
	High	13.1	2.88	2.84	26.4	40.9	70.6	6.7	
t = 50									
	Zero	20	1.05	0.33	8.8	16.2	35.4	18.2	18.4
	Low	15.5	2.12	1.86	20.1	35.6	63.6	8.7	22.3
	Med.	11.7	3.16	3.04	27.5	45.9	77.6	5.9	19.6
	High	7.4	5.98	5.62	38.4	62.2	92.0	3.8	18.0
I3: $\beta = 1.02$, $\rho = 0$, $\sigma_{it} = 0.1$									
t = 10									
	Zero	20	1.08	0.37	9.0	16.8	36.4	17.9	n/a
	Low	19	1.62	1.54	19.3	33.0	58.9	9.9	
	Med.	18	1.79	1.77	21.1	34.6	60.9	8.7	
	High	15.9	2.15	2.13	22.7	37.0	66.0	8.1	
t = 20									
	Zero	20	1.19	0.64	11.6	21.1	43.0	15.6	n/a
	Low	18.2	2.83	3.87	27.2	43.6	71.3	6.5	
	Med.	16.9	3.09	4.48	31.8	47.3	73.1	5.4	
	High	13.1	4.37	5.05	29.7	48.2	78.7	5.7	
t = 50									
	Zero	20	2.10	2.83	27.2	40.0	64.8	7.3	30.2
	Low	15.6	72.47	228.50	63.2	77.3	94.0	2.0	28.4
	Med.	12.5	82.84	241.80	64.8	80.8	95.8	1.9	28.6
	High	7.0	171.49	346.68	67.8	87.4	98.8	1.8	20.6

In each panel, the results are generated from 20 replications of the development over 10, 20 and 50 time periods of a sector comprising 20 banks, each of which starts from an initial size $S_{it} = 1$ or $s_{it} = \ln(S_{it}) = 0$, and whose subsequent evolution is driven by the model $\Delta s_{it} = (\beta - 1)s_{it-1} + \rho \Delta s_{it-1} + \eta_{it}$, $\eta_{it} \sim N(0, \sigma_{it}^2)$.

Mean and Standard deviation denote the mean $(\overline{S}_t)$ and standard deviation of bank size.

CR_1, CR_2 and CR_5 are concentration ratios measuring the market share of the top one, two and five banks, respectively.

Numbers equivalent is the numbers equivalent version of the H–H index.

Top denotes the number of periods (out of 50) for which the bank with the most periods as the largest bank held the position as the largest bank.

The probability that a merger takes place in any period is $\phi(n_t - 1)/n_0$ where n_t is the population of banks in period t and n_0 is the initial population of banks. ϕ controls the probability that a merger takes place in period t. $\phi = 0$ represents a zero merger rate; $\phi = 0.1$ represents a low merger rate; $\phi = 0.2$ represents a medium merger rate; and $\phi = 0.4$ represents a high merger rate.

measure, partner banks are assumed to acquire a new identity after the merger has taken place. With high rates of merger, the identity of the largest bank is therefore more susceptible to change than when merger activity is low.

Entry, exit and merger in the five largest European banking sectors

The overall effect of the size–growth relationship, and patterns of entry, exit and merger activity, is reflected in changes in the overall level of industry concentration. Table 8.10 shows CR_5 and CR_{10} in 1980 and 1995 for Europe's five largest banking sectors: France, Germany, Italy, Spain and the UK. Overall, concentration decreased in France and the UK, remained stable in Germany, and increased in Italy and Spain. Chapter 9 investigates the empirical size–growth relationship for existing banks in seven European countries: the five largest, plus Belgium and Denmark. As regards the other determinants of changes in concentration (entry, exit and merger) a tentative characterisation of the five largest European banking sectors can be made at this stage.

Table 8.10 Concentration in five European banking sectors, 1980 and 1995

Country	Five-bank concentration ratio (CR_5)		Ten-bank concentration ratio (CR_{10})		Change in concentration (%)	
	1980	1995	1980	1995	CR_5	CR_{10}
France	57	47	69	63	–10	–6
Germany	18	17	28	28	–1	–
Italy	26	29	42	45	+3	+3
Spain	38	49	58	62	+11	+4
UK	63	57	80	78	–6	–2

Adapted from Bank for International Settlements (1996, Table v.8, p.86).

In France, there have been relatively high levels of entry and merger activity and low levels of exit in recent years. The French banking sector is relatively concentrated. Consolidation has progressed rapidly in recent years, with decreases in branch numbers and a relatively high degree of merger and acquisition activity. In recent years, the numbers employed have fallen less than in the UK, as a consequence of relatively strict employment laws (Morgan Stanley, 1996).

The German banking sector has a relatively low level of concentration. Entry into the German market has been relatively low and exit has also been low, while the rate of merger and acquisition activity was, until recently, the lowest in Europe. Although some consolidation has taken place in commercial banking, the savings and cooperative banking sectors are still highly fragmented (Morgan Stanley Dean Witter, 1998a).

In Italy, entry, exit and merger activity have all been low in the past (Williams, 1996). Historically, the market has been tightly regulated, and is one of the most fragmented in Europe. The level of concentration is consequently relatively low. Recent research suggests that the Italian banking sector could benefit greatly from efficiency gains if substantial consolidation takes place (Morgan Stanley Dean Witter, 1998b). During 1998, the Italian banking market experienced a wave of large bank mergers (Williams, 1998).

In Spain, the rate of entry has been moderate, while exit has been low. Historically, merger and acquisition activity has been low. In recent years, however, some degree of consolidation through merger and acquisition has taken place, leading to increased levels of concentration (de la Fuente, 1998). Some research argues that since the Spanish banking sector is one of the most profitable, there may be little pressure for further consolidation (Morgan Stanley Dean Witter, 1998c). However, this feature appears to be changing as the integration of European banking markets increases competitive pressure. In February 1999, a merger took place between Spain's two largest banks, Banco Santander and BCH.

Finally, the UK banking sector has traditionally been one of the most open, and is characterised by a rapidly increasing foreign bank presence, and by the widespread conversion of building societies into banks. The sector has therefore experienced relatively high levels of entry, exit and merger activity. Concentration levels in the UK retail sector are relatively high. In recent years, there has been a high level of merger and acquisition activity both within banking, and across banking and insurance (Morgan Stanley Dean Witter, 1998d). Consequently, at present there is a tendency for the UK competition authorities to adopt a more interventionist regulatory stance.

CONCLUSION

Using stochastic simulation techniques, this chapter has examined the implications for market structure of various departures from the LPE in its strictest form. The simulations illustrate the effects of variations in the relationship between bank size and growth, and of variations in the levels of entry, exit and merger activity, on the evolution of bank sizes and market concentration, for seven simulated industry types. Using a simulated industry in which the LPE holds as the benchmark, the implications of various alternative assumptions regarding patterns of growth were examined. In simulated industries in which large banks tend to grow faster than small banks, concentration naturally increases faster than under the LPE. If small banks grow faster than large banks, there is no long-term tendency for concentration to increase. The tendencies toward increasing concentration develop more quickly when large banks experience more variable growth than their smaller counterparts, and when there is positive serial correlation or persistence of growth. The same tendencies develop more slowly when small banks have more variable growth than their larger counterparts, and when there is negative serial correlation or persistence of growth.

Superimposition of entry tends to lead to a lower mean bank size and less dispersion of bank sizes, and results in lower levels of concentration in all simulated industries. Entry, even at the lowest rate, moderates quite substantially the effect of LPE on concentration in the benchmark case, and there is a tendency towards deconcentration over time in the cases of medium and high entry rates. In simulated industries in which large banks tend to grow faster than their smaller counterparts, however, concentration continues to increase, even with high rates of entry.

If small banks are more likely to exit than large banks, then exit naturally leads to a higher average bank size and an increased level of concentration among the survivors. As a result of exit, the dispersion of bank sizes increases in simulated industries in which large banks grow faster than smaller banks, or in which there is less interfirm variation in the growth of large banks. The opposite is found in simulated industries where the growth process favours smaller banks. Finally, as expected, mergers lead to increases in mean bank size, in the dispersion of bank sizes, and in levels of concentration in all simulated industries.

Chapter 9

Empirical tests of the law of proportionate effect for European banking

INTRODUCTION

Describing the pattern and modelling the process by which members of a group of economic units increase or decrease in size (on some appropriate measure) over time, both in absolute terms and relative to one another, is a key endeavour in a number of fields of empirical economic enquiry. In international economics, for example, it is of interest to enquire whether the average prosperity of a group of countries, measured by their per capita gross domestic product (GDP), can be expected to converge or diverge over time. Do wealthier countries enjoy faster or slower growth in per capita GDP than their smaller counterparts? If the rich are becoming richer at a faster rate than the poor are becoming richer (or if the poor are actually becoming poorer), then there may be a need for interventionist policies by development agencies and the governments of the richer countries to offset rising inequality. Alternatively, if the poor are becoming richer at a faster rate than the rich, then inequalities between nations may tend to diminish naturally over time without the need for any such intervention (Solow, 1956; Baumol, 1986; Barro, 1991; Temple, 1999).

As we have seen, industrial economists may wish to identify and predict trends in industry concentration. These indicate the extent to which an industry is dominated by a small number of large firms, or in the present context, banks. To model the evolution of a banking sector's structure, it is useful to study the empirical relationship between the relative sizes of the member banks, and their growth performance. Do the larger banks tend to grow faster than the smaller ones? Alternatively, is there no statistical relationship between bank size and growth? In other words, is the probability of growing at a certain rate over any given period the same for a large bank and a small bank? Finally, do the smaller banks tend to grow faster on average than their larger counterparts?

Chapter 9 reports a number of empirical tests of the law of proportionate effect (LPE), using a data set containing annual size and growth measures for a sample of 551 European banks from seven countries, with data covering the period 1990–96. First, we describe a number of standard measures of convergence or divergence in the sizes of a cohort of firms. We then describe our methodology for empirical tests of the LPE, using both cross-sectional and panel techniques. We go on to describe the data set and report a number of descriptive statistics, before finally reporting the results of the empirical tests.

MEASURES OF CONVERGENCE AND DIVERGENCE

This section describes a number of measures of convergence and divergence based on statistical analysis of data sets containing information about the size and growth of a collection of economic units. The first such measure is based on one of the concentration measures already introduced in Chapter 3. It considers movements over time in the standard deviation across banks of a suitably defined logarithmic size measure for bank i at time t, denoted s_{it}. The level and growth of bank size are expressed in logarithmic form in order to focus on the size distribution of firms within the sector. Effectively, the logarithmic transformation eliminates distortions arising from inflation and other influences on the chosen size measure that are common to all banks. There is *sigma convergence* if the standard deviation of logarithmic bank sizes is decreasing over time, and *sigma divergence*, or no sigma convergence, if this standard deviation is constant or increasing over time.

It is also possible to measure convergence using a regression analysis of the relationship between bank size and growth in logarithmic form. As shown below, the regression-based tests of the LPE described in Chapter 7 can be derived from a data-generating process for observations of bank size and growth defined as follows:

$$s_{it} - s_{it-1} = \alpha_i + \delta_t^{(k)} + (\beta - 1)s_{it-1} + u_{it}; \qquad u_{it} = \rho u_{it-1} + \varepsilon_{it} \qquad [9.1]$$

where s_{it} is the natural logarithm of size of bank i at time t, as before, and α_i and $\delta_t^{(k)}$ allow for individual bank and time effects, respectively. If equation 9.1 is taken to refer to banks located in more than one country, separate time effects are specified for the banks in each country, k. The parameter β determines the relationship between size and growth, and ρ captures serial correlation (if any) in u_{it}, the error term in the growth equation. α_i is assumed to be distributed with $E(\alpha_i) = \mu_\alpha$ and $var(\alpha_i) = \sigma_\alpha^2$. The interpretation of α_i depends on the numerical value of β. First, if $\beta \geq 1$, then bank sizes are not mean-reverting. If $\alpha_i = \alpha$ and $\sigma_\alpha^2 = 0$, then all banks grow at the same rate on average. If $\alpha_i \neq \alpha$ and $\sigma_\alpha^2 > 0$, then the average growth rates differ between banks. Second, if $\beta < 1$, then bank sizes are mean-reverting. If $\alpha_i = \alpha$ and $\sigma_\alpha^2 = 0$, then there is a common long-term mean size for all banks. If $\alpha_i \neq \alpha$ and $\sigma_\alpha^2 > 0$, then the long-term values to which individual bank sizes are mean-reverting differ between banks. ε_{it}, a random disturbance, is assumed to be normal, independent and identically distributed (IID) with $E(\varepsilon_{it}) = 0$ and $var(\varepsilon_{it}) = \sigma_\varepsilon^2 > 0$.

As discussed in some detail in Chapter 8, the implications for the evolution of the size distribution of banks over time for various values for the parameter β are as follows:

- If $\beta > 1$, then growth in size over any period tends to be related positively to initial size at the start of the period, so on average the larger banks grow faster than their smaller counterparts. The dispersion of banks by size will tend to widen over time, and there is no sigma convergence. This case corresponds to I3 (Industry 3) in Chapter 8.

- If $\beta = 1$, then there is no relationship between growth in size and initial size. In this case, the distribution of banks by size tends to widen over time, and there is no sigma convergence. If growth is unrelated to size, each bank's growth rate in each period is effectively drawn randomly from a theoretical distribution of all possible growth rates, which is the same for all banks. Over time, however, the cumulative effects of 'good luck' (banks that, by chance, get slightly more than their fair share of high growth) and 'bad luck' (banks that get slightly more than their fair share of low growth) are such that size distribution tends to widen. Again, there is no sigma convergence. This case corresponds to I1 in Chapter 8.

- If $\beta < 1$, $\alpha_i = \alpha$ and $\sigma_\alpha^2 = 0$, then growth over each period tends to be related negatively to initial size at the start of the period, so on average the smaller banks grow faster than the larger banks. In the long term, the revenues of all banks tend to be mean-reverting towards the same average value, and there is no tendency for the size distribution to widen over time. In terms of the parameters of equation 9.1, the expression for the value to which log size is mean-reverting is $\alpha/(1 - \beta)$. If $\rho = 0$, the expression for the standard deviation of the distribution of log size at any given time is $\sigma_\varepsilon/\sqrt{(1 - \beta^2)}$. In the short term, if the current standard deviation of log size is smaller than $\sigma_\varepsilon/\sqrt{(1 - \beta^2)}$, then the log size distribution will tend to widen, so there is no sigma convergence. If the current standard deviation is larger than $\sigma_\varepsilon/\sqrt{(1 - \beta^2)}$, then the log size distribution will tend to narrow, and there is sigma convergence. This case corresponds to I2 in Chapter 8.

- If $\beta < 1$, $\alpha_i \neq \alpha$ and $\sigma_\alpha^2 > 0$ for each bank, then there is an average value towards which size is mean-reverting in the long run. These long-run average values differ between banks. For any individual bank, growth over each period again tends to be related negatively to initial size (relative to that bank's long-run average value). Cross-sectionally, however, across the population of banks as a whole, there is no clear relationship between initial size and growth. This case is a variant of I2 in Chapter 8, in which size is mean-reverting, but the long-run equilibrium size differs between banks.

Figure 9.1 illustrates the four cases described above. In each panel, the diagram on the left shows the scatter plot of the cross-sectional relationship between growth in size and initial size (in logarithmic form), represented by equation 9.1, and the diagram on the right shows the implications of this relationship for the time path of sizes for two representative banks. In Figure 9.1(a), the gulf between the banks that were initially larger and smaller tends to widen over time. In Figure 9.1(b), the sizes of the two banks tend to 'wander' randomly. It is possible by chance for the bank that was initially poor to overtake its richer counterpart. The size distribution again tends to widen over time. In Figure 9.1(c) the sizes of the two banks always tend to revert towards the same long-run average value (represented by the dotted line). The bank that was initially larger does not maintain any long-term advantage over its smaller counterpart, and the width of the size distribution remains the same in the long term. Finally, in Figure 9.1(d), the sizes of the two banks always tend to revert towards their individual long-run average values (represented by the two dotted lines). As in Figure 9.1(c), the width of the size distribution remains the same in the long term.

It is clear that the numerical value of the parameter β in equation 9.1 plays a critical role in determining whether there is convergence or divergence in sizes. An alternative measure of convergence or divergence, based directly on the numerical value of β itself, is *beta convergence*. If $\beta \geq 1$, then there is no beta convergence. If $\beta < 1$ and $\sigma_\alpha^2 = 0$, then there is unconditional beta convergence, and if $\beta < 1$ and $\sigma_\alpha^2 > 0$, then there is conditional beta convergence. From the previous discussion, it is evident that beta convergence is a necessary, but not sufficient, condition for sigma convergence.

EMPIRICAL METHODOLOGY

Later in the chapter, the results of a number of cross-sectional and panel tests of the LPE are reported. Most previous empirical

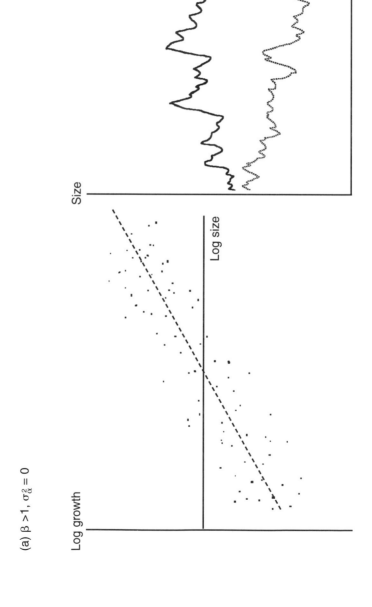

Figure 9.1 Evolution of the size distribution of banks over time for various values of β.

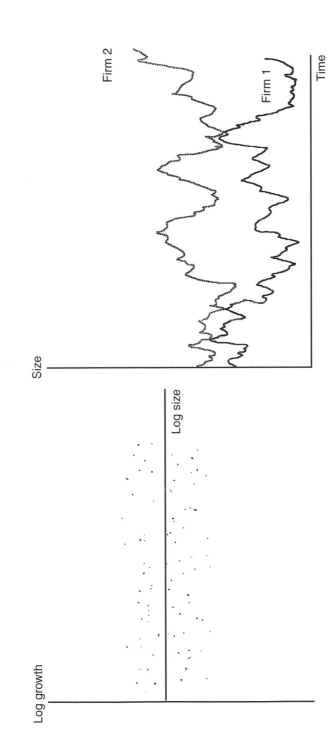

(b) $\beta = 1$, $\sigma_\alpha^2 = 0$

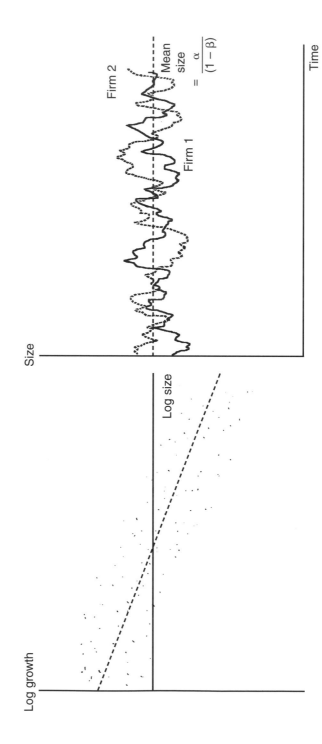

(c) $\beta < 1$, $\sigma_\alpha^2 = 0$

(d) $\beta < 1$, $\sigma_\alpha^2 => 0$

Log growth

Log size

Size

Mean size = $\dfrac{\alpha_1}{(1-\beta)}$

Firm 1

Mean size = $\dfrac{\alpha_2}{(1-\beta)}$

Firm 2

Time

studies are based on cross-sectional estimation of a regression of growth over a certain period on initial size (and in many cases, a lagged growth term). If T, the number of time periods over which growth is observed, exceeds one period in equation 9.1, then the cross-sectional model can be obtained by reparameterising equation 9.1 as follows:

$$s_{iT+1} - s_{i1} = a_i + (b - 1)s_{i1} + r(s_{i1} - s_{i0}) + v_{iT+1} \qquad [9.2]$$

where $b = \beta^T$ and a_i, r and v_{iT+1} are transformations of α_i, $\delta_t^{(k)}$, ρ and $\varepsilon_{i2} \ldots \varepsilon_{iT+1}$. In equation 9.2, t = 1 and t = T + 1 are the two points in time between which the T-period growth rate $s_{iT+1} - s_{i1}$ is calculated.

For equation 9.2 to be estimable, an assumption of homogeneity in α_i (and therefore in a_i) is required, otherwise the number of parameters in equation 9.2, n + 2, exceeds the number of cross-sectional observations, n. If $\sigma_\alpha^2 = 0$, however, we can write $\alpha_i = \alpha$ in equation 9.1 and $a_i = a$ in equation 9.2. If $\sigma_\varepsilon^2 > 0$ but equation 9.2 is estimated assuming $a_i = a$, then the resulting ordinary least squares (OLS) estimator of b is upward biased and inconsistent if the true value of b is less than one. The standard test of the LPE using the t-statistic on $\hat{b} - 1$ loses power, and is therefore loaded towards 'acceptance' of the LPE. Effectively, therefore, cross-sectional estimation of the relationship between size and growth excludes the possibility that bank sizes may tend toward different long-run average values. Recent advances in the econometric analysis of panel data sets, however, permit estimation without the imposition of any such conditions.

For the purposes of panel estimation, equation 9.1 can be re-written as follows:

$$s_{it} - s_{it-i} = \alpha_i(1 - \rho) + (\delta_t^{(k)} - \rho\delta_{t-1}^{(k)}) + (\beta - 1)s_{it-1}$$
$$+ \rho(s_{it-1} - s_{it-2}) + \eta_{it} \qquad [9.3]$$

where $\eta_{it} = \varepsilon_{it} + \rho(1 - \beta)s_{it-2}$.

Note that the presence of s_{it-2} in η_{it} in equation 9.3 does not present any problems for tests of $H_0 : \beta = 1$, because $\eta_{it} = \varepsilon_{it}$ under the null. Three alternative procedures for estimation of equation 9.3 using panel techniques are described below. The methodological issues associated with the use of panel techniques to test the

LPE are discussed in greater detail by Goddard et al. (2001) and Goddard and Wilson (2001).

First, if $\sigma_\alpha^2 = 0$ under $H_1 : \beta < 1$, then $\alpha_i(1 - \rho)$ in equation 9.3 can be replaced with $\alpha(1 - \rho)$. Equation 9.3 can then be estimated by pooling the data across banks and over time, and using OLS with time dummy variables to allow for the (fixed) time effects, $(\delta_t^{(k)} - \rho\delta_{t-1}^{(k)})$. If $\sigma_\alpha^2 > 0$ under $H_1 : \beta < 1$, however, then panel estimation using OLS runs into the same problems as the cross-sectional OLS estimation: the OLS estimator of β is upward biased and inconsistent, and the test of the LPE based on the t-statistic on $\hat{\beta} - 1$ loses power and is loaded towards 'acceptance' of the LPE.

Second, equation 9.3 could be estimated using the fixed effects model. This is equivalent to estimation by OLS including (as well as the time dummy variables) a full set of cross-sectional dummy variables to allow for the individual bank effects, α_i. As is well known, however, the fixed effects estimator of β is downward biased and the sampling distribution of the t-statistic on $\hat{\beta} - 1$ is non-standard. The bias in the fixed effects estimator does not diminish as $N \rightarrow \infty$, but it does diminish as $T \rightarrow \infty$. Table 9.1 shows the critical values for the t-statistic on $\hat{\beta} - 1$, for illustrative values of N with $T = 5$, as in the estimations that are reported later in this chapter. Note that even in the case where $H_0 : \beta = 1$ is tested against $H_1 : \beta > 1$, the critical values are *negative*. In other words, if $\beta > 1$, then the fixed effects estimator still tends to return $\hat{\beta}$ smaller than one. The main advantage of the fixed effects estimator of β, relative to the OLS cross-sectional and panel estimators, is that its properties are unaffected if $\sigma_\alpha^2 > 0$. The t-statistic on $\hat{\beta} - 1$ can therefore be used to test the LPE null hypothesis ($H_0 : \beta = 1$) against an alternative ($H_1 : \beta < 1$) that can accommodate both $\sigma_\alpha^2 = 0$ and $\sigma_\alpha^2 > 0$.

The fixed effects estimator accommodates the case $\sigma_\alpha^2 > 0$ by producing a full set of estimates of the individual effects, α_i. These may not be required, however, if the main objective is to investigate the size–growth relationship, expressed in the value of the parameter β. The third and final panel estimator suggested by Breitung and Meyer (1994) takes an alternative approach to dealing with the individual effects, effectively eliminating them from the model prior to estimation. This is achieved by deducting the

Table 9.1   Critical values for t-statistic on $\hat{\beta} - 1$, fixed effects estimation, various N, T = 5

N	$t^{0.005}$	$t^{0.025}$	$t^{0.975}$	$t^{0.995}$
20	−7.80	−7.12	−2.44	−1.75
30	−8.87	−8.14	−3.55	−2.77
50	−10.65	−9.90	−5.27	−4.54
100	−13.73	−13.02	−8.42	−7.76
200	−18.21	−17.47	−12.82	−12.18
500	−26.89	−26.22	−21.62	−20.91
Standard normal critical values	−2.57	−1.96	+1.96	+2.57

first observation (s_{i0}) for each bank from the right-hand side of equation 9.3, and incorporating the individual effects into the error term. The resulting estimable model is as follows:

$$s_{it} - s_{it-1} = (\delta_t^{(k)} - \rho\delta_{t-1}^{(k)}) + (\beta - 1)(s_{it-1} - s_{i0}) + \rho(s_{it-1} - s_{it-2}) + \xi_{it} \qquad [9.4]$$

where $\xi_{it} = \eta_{it} + \alpha_i(1 - \rho) + (\beta - 1)s_{i0}$.

The Breitung–Meyer panel estimator of β is unbiased under $H_0 : \beta = 1$, while the t-statistic on $\hat{\beta} - 1$ is asymptotically normal. If $\beta < 1$, then the Breitung–Meyer estimator is upward biased because of the presence of $(\beta - 1)s_{i0}$ in ξ_{it}. Breitung and Meyer (1994) show that the magnitude of the bias is $\beta + (1 - \beta)/2$. Unlike the cross-sectional estimator, however, the properties of $\hat{\beta}$ under H_1 are the same under both $\sigma_\alpha^2 = 0$ and $\sigma_\alpha^2 > 0$.

THE DATA SET

The EU banking data set was obtained from the BankScope database, compiled by International Bank Credit Analysis Limited (IBCA). The database contains company accounts data on more than 8000 banks worldwide. The sample selection criteria were as follows:

- banks that were classified as commercial, savings or cooperatives;
- banks for which complete annual data were available for all years between 1990 and 1996, inclusive;
- banks that operated in a country that was an EU member in 1990, and that had a reasonably large banking sector. Complete data had to be available for at least 15 banks per country for that country's banks to be included. On this criterion, banks from the Netherlands, Portugal, Ireland and Greece were excluded.

Banks with operations in one country, but that are centrally located in another country, posed particular problems for the selection of the sample. First, many EU banks have subsidiaries located in other countries. To include these subsidiaries, however, would introduce an element of double counting. Second, subsidiaries of significant numbers of foreign banks from outside the EU are located in many EU countries. The pattern of growth of these types of institutions is perhaps influenced more by the corporate objectives of the parent institution than by the competitive environment of the country in which the subsidiary is located. It was therefore decided to remove all subsidiaries from the sample. In the case of Luxembourg, the removal of foreign subsidiaries left only four domestic banks. Consequently, Luxembourg banks (in common with those from the countries listed above) were excluded altogether. The initial sample therefore consisted of indigenous banks from seven EU countries: Belgium, Denmark, France, Germany, Italy, Spain and the UK.

Three measures of size were used in the empirical analysis: total assets, total equity and off-balance-sheet (OBS) business. Following Tschoegl (1983), total assets and total equity both represent widely accepted measures of bank size. Tschoegl argued that the equity measure circumvents some of the difficulties with the assets measure, which arise from differences in accounting practices between countries. In some countries, banks are permitted to keep hidden reserves, allowing them to smooth performance but biasing empirical tests towards acceptance of the LPE. OBS business, although not a measure of overall bank size, is included because this type of business has become increasingly important for EU banks during the 1990s (European Commission, 1997). It is of interest to assess whether OBS business exhibits growth patterns similar to those for total assets and total equity.

The data were collected in nominal terms in domestic currencies and converted into ECUs using an ECU exchange rate. The effects of inflation were removed by using an ECU GDP deflator, with all values expressed in 1991 prices.

Tables 9.2–9.4 show descriptive statistics for the assets size measure. Tables 9.5–9.7 do the same for the equity size measure, and Tables 9.8–9.10 do the same for OBS business. Tables 9.2 and 9.5 show that total assets and total equity data were available for 551 banks. The largest numbers of banks were from Spain, Germany, Italy, the UK and France, with 109, 105, 105, 102 and 91 banks, respectively. Overall, the sample consists of 355 commercial, 153 savings and 43 cooperative banks. Table 9.8 shows that fewer banks reported OBS business either at the beginning or throughout the sample period. The coverage was especially poor for Belgian banks at the beginning of the sample period, and consequently Belgium was omitted from the OBS estimations. The final sample size for the OBS measure was 412 banks. The largest numbers of banks reporting OBS business were from Spain, Germany and France, with 94, 91 and 86 banks, respectively. The OBS sample consists of 285 commercial, 103 savings and 24 cooperative banks.

Tables 9.2, 9.5 and 9.8 show the mean of each size measure in each of the seven years from 1990 to 1996, inclusive, and the mean annual logarithmic growth rate in each of the six years from 1991 to 1996, inclusive, for all banks and for the banks in each country. It should be noted that the mean growth rate is calculated by averaging the growth rates of each bank, and is therefore not the same as the growth in mean size. It is possible, for example, for the latter to increase but for the former to be negative in the same year. It should also be noted that some of the variations in size and growth between countries are attributable to exchange rate fluctuations. Banks from Italy and the UK, for example, recorded negative growth on both the mean assets and equity size measures in 1992, as the lira and sterling fell sharply against the ECU. In the tests for the LPE reported later in this chapter, these effects are controlled by including suitably defined dummy variables in the

Table 9.2 Assets: mean size and mean growth by country, 1990–96

	No. of banks	1990	1991	1992	1993	1994	1995	1996
All countries	551	8521	8791 *0.040*	8794 *–0.062*	9244 *–0.005*	9211 *0.003*	9754 *0.057*	10 568 *0.035*
Belgium	17	9521	11 803 *0.093*	11 767 *0.037*	12 356 *0.073*	13 139 *0.021*	15 283 *0.082*	16 474 *0.049*
Denmark	22	2785	2766 *0.039*	2509 *–0.036*	2563 *0.046*	2505 *0.006*	2778 *0.071*	3006 *0.013*
France	91	11 635	11 504 *–0.030*	12 317 *–0.014*	12 965 *–0.021*	11 873 *–0.043*	12 228 *0.019*	12 347 *–0.048*
Germany	105	8601	8799 *0.004*	9351 *0.042*	10 595 *0.077*	11 182 *0.038*	12 412 *0.042*	13 395 *–0.003*
Italy	105	8336	8786 *0.056*	7940 *–0.131*	7584 *–0.074*	7305 *–0.042*	7447 *0.015*	8061 *0.107*
Spain	109	4303	4589 *0.055*	4487 *–0.097*	4528 *–0.087*	4718 *0.026*	5153 *0.098*	5291 *–0.015*
UK	102	11 431	11 655 *0.096*	11 421 *–0.126*	12 204 *0.058*	12 363 *0.024*	12 686 *–0.035*	14 935 *0.127*

Mean asset values are in million ECUs, 1991 prices.
Mean annual logarithmic growth rates are shown beneath in italics.

Table 9.3 Assets: other descriptive statistics, 1990 and 1996

			Assets					Log assets	
	Mean	S.D.	Q1	Q2	Q3	Skew	Kurt	Skew	Kurt
1990									
All countries	8521	25 090	424	1249	3951	5.1	32.6	0.5	3.2
Belgium	9521	18 877	293	836	3526	1.8	4.3	0.7	2.4
Denmark	2785	9352	136	259	399	4.2	18.8	1.5	4.9
France	11 635	36 516	249	931	4284	4.5	23.2	0.6	2.9
Germany	8601	27 362	614	1277	3610	4.8	26.8	0.9	4.1
Italy	8336	19 786	619	1203	2960	3.2	12.5	0.5	3.5
Spain	4303	10 478	486	1172	3310	4.5	24.4	0.2	3.0
UK	11 431	28 811	593	2644	6256	4.5	25.5	0.0	3.2
1996									
All countries	10 568	32 687	455	1391	4582	5.2	35.2	0.4	3.2
Belgium	16 474	33 951	559	1529	5426	1.9	5.1	0.6	2.5
Denmark	3006	10 360	200	304	732	4.2	19.2	1.6	5.3
France	12 347	39 047	182	804	4582	4.2	19.8	0.4	3.0
Germany	13 395	47 418	691	1585	4464	5.1	30.2	1.0	4.2
Italy	8061	18 725	636	1230	4025	3.2	13.0	0.8	3.1
Spain	5291	14 208	457	1195	3156	4.8	26.9	–0.2	3.3
UK	14 935	35 739	542	2378	7804	3.6	16.6	0.2	2.6

Mean, standard deviation (S.D.) and first, second and third quartiles (Q1, Q2 and Q3) of asset values are in million ECUs, 1991 prices.
Skew, sample skewness; kurt, sample kurtosis.

Table 9.4   Banks with three largest asset values by country, 1990 and 1996

	Top 3, 1990	Assets	Top 3, 1996	Assets
Belgium	Générale de Banque	55 782	Générale de Banque	111 425
	Banque Bruxelles Lambert	49 959	Kredietbank	72 826
	Kredietbank	39 883	Banque Bruxelles Lambert	72 450
Denmark	Den Danske Bank	43 982	Den Danske Bank	48 888
	Jyske Bank A/S (Group)	7306	Jyske Bank A/S (Group)	6418
	Sydbank A/S	3875	Sydbank A/S	4154
France	BNP Paris	212 534	Société Générale	218 474
	Crédit Lyonnais	209 226	Crédit Lyonnais	199 466
	Société Générale	160 186	BNP Paris	179 000
Germany	Deutsche Bank AG	190 587	Deutsche Bank AG	345 044
	Dresdner Bank AG	135 700	Dresdner Bank AG	227 375
	Commerzbank AG	104 190	Commerzbank AG	180 776
Italy	Gruppo Bancario San Paolo	96 139	Gruppo Bancario San Paolo	99 015
	Banca Nazionale del Lavoro	96 137	Cassa di Risparmio delle Provincie Lombarde	80 994
	Banca di Roma	85 631	Banca commerciale Italiana	74 271
Spain	Banco Central Hispano	66 586	Banco Santander SA	96 038
	Banco Bilbao Vizcaya	63 625	Banco Bilbao Vizcaya	83 919
	Caja de Ahorros y Pensiones de Barcelona	42 595	Banco Central Hispano	57 399
UK	Barclays	190 759	National Westminster Bank	199 547
	National Westminster Bank	171 262	Barclays	196 985
	Midland Bank	84 338	Abbey National	126 875

Asset values are in million ECUs, 1991 prices.

regressions. Growth in OBS business was especially strong between 1990 and 1996, with particularly high average growth rates of 9.1%, 10% and 14.5% recorded for the years 1991, 1992 and 1995, respectively. This can be explained by banks diversifying into new areas of business, as the process of deregulation within the EU gathered momentum (Canals, 1993, 1997). The growth in equity reflects the emphasis on capital growth in banking (Morgan Stanley Dean Witter, 1998c).

Tables 9.3, 9.6 and 9.9 show the mean and standard deviation of each of the three size measures for all banks and for the banks located in each country, at the start and end of the sample period, in 1990 and 1996. Also shown are the first, second and third quartiles and the sample skewness and kurtosis coefficients, which

Table 9.5 Equity: mean size and mean growth by country, 1990–96

	No. of banks	1990	1991	1992	1993	1994	1995	1996
All countries	551	378	414	398	410	420	434	469
			0.077	*–0.020*	*0.015*	*0.018*	*0.048*	*0.053*
Belgium	17	314	363	363	385	405	448	476
			0.027	*0.018*	*0.040*	*0.009*	*0.093*	*0.059*
Denmark	22	180	169	144	150	156	179	192
			–0.048	*–0.076*	*0.024*	*0.022*	*0.133*	*0.067*
France	91	388	409	454	471	442	456	460
			0.038	*0.082*	*–0.019*	*–0.029*	*0.085*	*–0.010*
Germany	105	315	324	336	368	402	427	432
			0.023	*0.051*	*0.092*	*0.077*	*0.044*	*–0.001*
Italy	105	391	508	467	453	443	427	468
			0.226	*–0.045*	*–0.003*	*–0.023*	*0.006*	*0.090*
Spain	109	272	306	292	272	282	296	319
			0.057	*–0.030*	*–0.106*	*0.009*	*0.078*	*0.056*
UK	102	588	588	516	558	602	630	737
			0.072	*–0.140*	*0.107*	*0.052*	*0.005*	*0.120*

Mean equity values are in million ECUs, 1991 prices.
Mean annual logarithmic growth rates are shown beneath in italics.

Table 9.6 Equity: other descriptive statistics, 1990 and 1996

			Equity					Log equity	
	Mean	S.D.	Q1	Q2	Q3	Skew	Kurt	Skew	Kurt
1990									
All countries	378	986	29	73	225	5.0	33.5	0.5	3.1
Belgium	314	596	19	50	111	1.9	4.8	0.5	2.7
Denmark	180	556	13	30	54	4.2	18.8	1.5	5.0
France	388	1081	14	36	170	4.3	21.8	0.7	2.8
Germany	315	989	31	50	145	5.6	38.5	1.0	4.3
Italy	391	809	44	88	228	3.1	12.0	0.4	3.4
Spain	272	619	39	87	179	4.5	24.5	0.4	3.5
UK	588	1403	40	138	428	4.6	26.0	0.2	2.7
1996									
All countries	469	1197	35	96	272	17.8	345.8	0.8	3.9
Belgium	476	950	21	88	133	1.9	5.1	0.7	2.7
Denmark	192	592	21	35	53	4.2	18.8	1.6	5.5
France	460	1296	15	36	217	4.3	21.9	0.7	2.8
Germany	432	1349	41	73	197	5.1	31.0	1.1	4.3
Italy	468	997	52	107	288	3.1	12.0	0.7	3.2
Spain	319	763	36	104	222	4.6	25.5	0.3	3.1
UK	737	1568	40	161	497	3.4	15.2	0.4	2.4

Mean, standard deviation (S.D.) and first, second and third quartiles (Q1, Q2 and Q3) of equity values are in million ECUs, 1991 prices.
Skew, sample skewness; kurt, sample kurtosis.

Table 9.7 Banks with three largest equity values by country, 1990 and 1996

	Top 3, 1990	Equity	Top 3, 1996	Equity
Belgium	Générale de Banque	1934	Générale de Banque	3112
	Banque Bruxelles Lambert	1358	Kredietbank	2267
	Kredietbank	1304	Banque Bruxelles Lambert	1844
Denmark	Den Danske Bank	2629	Den Danske Bank	2801
	Jyske Bank A/S (Group)	439	Jyske Bank A/S (Group)	480
	Sydbank A/S	257	Sydbank A/S	260
France	Crédit Lyonnais	6467	BNP Paris	7500
	BNP Paris	6009	Société Générale	7437
	Société Générale	4366	Crédit Lyonnais	5457
Germany	Deutsche Bank AG	7891	Deutsche Bank AG	10 024
	Dresdner Bank AG	4752	Dresdner Bank AG	6199
	Commerzbank AG	3198	Commerzbank AG	5368
Italy	Cassa di Risparmio delle Provincie Lombarde	4154	Cassa di Risparmio delle Provincie Lombarde	4685
	Gruppo Bancario San Paolo	3826	Gruppo Bancario San Paolo	4589
	Banca Commerciale Italiana	3145	Banca di Roma	4411
Spain	Banco Bilbao Vizcaya	4143	Banco Bilbao Vizcaya	4886
	Banco Central Hispano	3617	Banco Santandar SA	4858
	Banco Santandar SA	2546	Banco Central Hispano	2623
UK	Barclays	9306	National Westminster Bank	8442
	National Westminster Bank	8543	Barclays	8288
	Abbey National	3823	Halifax Building Society	7216

Equity values are in million ECUs, 1991 prices.

perhaps give a more representative indication of the size distribution of the sample as a whole. Tables 9.3, 9.6 and 9.9 show that across all countries, the mean and standard deviation of bank size increased for all size measures between 1990 and 1996. In common with the firm size distributions in most other industries, it is also apparent from these descriptive statistics that the distributions of banks on any of the three size measures are highly skewed. This is evident because the standard deviation of size is invariably much larger than the mean size; the mean size is usually larger (and often much larger) than the third quartile; and the skewness coefficient is invariably large and positive. The final two columns of Tables 9.3, 9.6 and 9.9 suggest, however, that in most cases the size distribution is not too dissimilar to the log-normal distribution. Under the latter, the sample skewness and kurtosis

Table 9.8 OBS business: mean size and mean growth by country, 1990–96

	No. of banks	1990	1991	1992	1993	1994	1995	1996
All countries	412	1184	1218	1548	2112	2029	2265	2458
			0.091	*0.100*	*0.016*	*0.064*	*0.145*	*0.049*
Denmark	22	335	340	339	350	388	454	627
			0.020	*0.000*	*0.222*	*–0.219*	*0.130*	*0.195*
France	86	2755	2784	3219	3628	3347	3710	3865
			0.030	*0.105*	*0.054*	*–0.064*	*–0.047*	*–0.018*
Germany	91	698	728	762	2197	2228	2426	2635
			–0.023	*0.068*	*0.104*	*0.334*	*0.109*	*–0.023*
Italy	55	1129	1390	1827	732	693	1603	1829
			0.440	*0.325*	*–0.700*	*–0.107*	*0.767*	*0.124*
Spain	94	110	120	131	120	153	176	200
			0.115	*–0.047*	*0.002*	*0.090*	*0.139*	*0.107*
UK	50	1817	1680	2998	5387	5122	4941	5458
			0.008	*0.219*	*0.517*	*0.057*	*–0.124*	*0.040*

Mean OBS business values are in million ECUs, 1991 prices.
Mean annual logarithmic growth rates are shown beneath in italics.

Table 9.9 OBS business: other descriptive statistics, 1990 and 1996

	OBS business						Log OBS business	
	Mean	S.D.	Q1	Q2	Q3	Skew	Kurt	Skew	Kurt
1990									
All countries	1184	5011	25	69	284	7.8	79.9	0.5	3.5
Denmark	335	1151	18	37	108	4.2	19.3	1.2	4.5
France	2755	9058	47	190	833	5.4	35.4	0.2	3.0
Germany	698	2440	47	88	205	5.5	35.4	1.2	4.7
Italy	1129	3884	23	62	341	5.4	34.7	0.4	3.3
Spain	110	256	11	30	111	9.1	85.8	0.5	4.3
UK	1817	5020	30	166	1060	3.9	18.0	0.0	2.3
1996									
All countries	2458	9669	41	114	463	5.4	34.5	0.7	3.6
Denmark	627	2363	29	50	104	4.3	19.7	1.3	5.1
France	3865	13 548	51	213	694	4.7	24.9	0.4	3.2
Germany	2635	9499	62	150	451	4.5	22.8	1.2	4.4
Italy	1829	5686	67	141	470	3.7	15.5	0.9	3.9
Spain	200	724	14	56	191	8.8	82.4	0.6	4.0
UK	5458	14 485	72	315	1819	3.3	13.1	0.1	2.5

Mean, standard deviation (S.D.) and first, second and third quartiles (Q1, Q2 and Q3) of OBS business values are in million ECUs, 1991 prices.
Skew, sample skewness; kurt, sample kurtosis.

Table 9.10 Banks with three largest OBS portfolios by country, 1990 and 1996

	Top 3, 1990	OBS business	Top 3, 1996	OBS business
Denmark	Den Danske Bank	5443	Den Danske Bank	11 164
	Jyske Bank A/S (Group)	620	Jyske Bank A/S (Group)	904
	Sydbank A/S	479	Sydbank A/S	510
France	Crédit Lyonnais	67 852	Crédit Lyonnais	85 043
	Société Générale	39 669	Société Générale	70 689
	Banque Paribas	21 870	Banque Paribas	54 205
Germany	Deutsche Bank AG	18 395	Deutsche Bank AG	58 467
	Dresdner Bank AG	9955	Dresdner Bank AG	48 262
	Commerzbank AG	9401	Commerzbank AG	39 764
Italy	Credito Italiano	26 468	Credito Italiano	26 531
	Cassa di Risparmio di Verona Vicenza Belluno e Ancona Banca	9497	Cassa di Risparmio delle Provincie Lombarde	25 608
	Banca Nazionale del Lavoro	6162	Banca Nazionale del Lavoro	21 983
Spain	Banco Santandar SA	1810	Banco Santander SA	6631
	Banco Popular Espanol SA	952	Caja de Ahorros y Pensiones de Barcelona	1697
	Banca March SA	828	Banco Popular Espanol SA	1659
UK	Barclays	25 528	National Westminster Bank	66 711
	National Westminster Bank	23 674	Barclays	63 314
	Midland Bank	9348	Midland Bank	44 311

OBS business values are in million ECUs, 1991 prices.

coefficients for the logarithm of size (on any measure) should approximate to zero and three, respectively. For all three size measures, the relevant coefficients seem to come reasonably close to meeting these criteria.

Finally, Tables 9.4, 9.7 and 9.10 show, for each country, the three banks with the largest values for each of the three size measures in 1990 and in 1996. On all three size measures, it is apparent that there is considerable stability in the rankings at the top end of the size distribution. Using the assets size measure, for example, the same banks occupied the top three positions for Belgium, Denmark, France and Germany in 1990 and 1996. For Spain and the UK, there was only one change each in the top three positions, while for Italy there were two changes. Even with OBS business, for which many portfolios were expanding rapidly during this period, the dominant banks in each country remained mostly unchanged.

EMPIRICAL RESULTS

Sigma convergence and divergence

Tables 9.11, 9.12 and 9.13 show the standard deviation of the natural logarithm of each size measure in each of the seven years from 1990 to 1996, inclusive. These results enable us to assess whether there has been sigma convergence or divergence as defined at the beginning of this chapter. Table 9.11 suggests that there is little evidence of sigma convergence in the assets size measure across all countries, with the standard deviation of logarithmic assets increasing from 1.765 to 1.855 between 1990 and 1996. The pattern is the same in the individual country calculations for Belgium, France, Germany, Spain and the UK. For Denmark and Italy on the other hand, there is some evidence of sigma convergence. For equity, Table 9.12 indicates that there is almost no change in the sigma convergence measure for all countries between 1990 and 1996. Belgium and Spain recorded increases in the standard deviation of logarithmic equity, while Denmark and Italy again recorded reductions. The standard deviation remained approximately constant for France, Germany and the UK. Finally, Table 9.13 shows that there was a moderate increase in the standard deviation of logarithmic OBS business from 2.067 to 2.120 between 1990 and 1996. The standard deviation increased sharply for Germany and the UK, more modestly for Denmark and Spain, remained approximately constant for France, and fell sharply for Italy.

Beta convergence:
the size–growth relationship

Tables 9.14, 9.15 and 9.16 report our estimates of the parameters b in equation 9.2 and β in equations 9.3 and 9.4, which identify the relationship between size and growth for the sample of European banks. Table 9.14 reports the results obtained using assets as the size measure; Table 9.15 does the same for the equity

Table 9.11 Standard deviation of log assets, 1990–96

	1990	1991	1992	1993	1994	1995	1996
All countries	1.765	1.756	1.790	1.818	1.828	1.822	1.855
Belgium	2.051	2.113	2.101	2.093	2.131	2.213	2.184
Denmark	1.605	1.577	1.538	1.512	1.545	1.531	1.547
France	2.016	2.030	2.086	2.119	2.104	2.127	2.175
Germany	1.537	1.541	1.537	1.566	1.585	1.597	1.614
Italy	1.697	1.684	1.699	1.707	1.709	1.614	1.606
Spain	1.544	1.558	1.667	1.701	1.729	1.736	1.769
UK	1.877	1.784	1.820	1.846	1.845	1.871	1.918

Table 9.12 Standard deviation of log equity, 1990–96

	1990	1991	1992	1993	1994	1995	1996
All countries	1.609	1.623	1.606	1.611	1.616	1.593	1.610
Belgium	1.786	1.815	1.810	1.822	1.865	1.886	1.841
Denmark	1.400	1.382	1.286	1.268	1.340	1.341	1.346
France	1.870	1.870	1.890	1.917	1.889	1.868	1.886
Germany	1.408	1.416	1.417	1.393	1.408	1.408	1.413
Italy	1.552	1.569	1.549	1.530	1.526	1.428	1.434
Spain	1.369	1.423	1.409	1.442	1.434	1.454	1.449
UK	1.697	1.643	1.644	1.630	1.650	1.661	1.694

Table 9.13 Standard deviation of log OBS business, 1990–96

	1990	1991	1992	1993	1994	1995	1996
All countries	2.067	2.019	2.066	2.168	2.153	2.119	2.120
Denmark	1.616	1.634	1.658	1.602	1.639	1.671	1.675
France	2.282	2.181	2.223	2.215	2.185	2.235	2.296
Germany	1.518	1.549	1.540	1.912	1.899	1.815	1.857
Italy	2.206	2.131	2.041	1.969	1.911	1.865	1.842
Spain	1.553	1.530	1.561	1.534	1.568	1.582	1.585
UK	2.411	2.373	2.454	2.644	2.584	2.616	2.600

size measure; and Table 9.16 does the same for OBS business. Using the assets size measure (Table 9.14), the evidence as to whether the LPE provides an appropriate description of the relationship between bank size and growth is rather mixed. In the estimations using the data for all countries, $H_0 : b = 1$ is accepted in the cross-sectional estimation, and $H_0 : \beta = 1$ is accepted in the panel OLS estimation. $H_0 : \beta = 1$ is rejected, however, in both the fixed effects and Breitung–Meyer panel estimations. In both of these cases, the estimated coefficients suggest that the true coefficient is greater than one.

Table 9.14 Tests for beta convergence: assets

	Cross-sectional OLS	Panel OLS	Panel fixed effects	Panel Breitung–Meyer
	$\hat{b} - 1$	$\hat{\beta} - 1$	$\hat{\beta} - 1$	$\hat{\beta} - 1$
All countries	0.002 (0.15)	0.001 (0.22)	−0.431* (−19.13)	0.045* (2.98)
Belgium	0.046 (1.37)	0.009 (1.04)	−1.003 (−4.74)	−0.146 (−1.01)
Denmark	−0.037 (−0.77)	−0.007 (0.83)	−0.408 (−5.32)	0.068 (1.44)
France	0.039 (1.56)	0.009** (2.12)	−0.378* (−7.27)	0.100* (3.14)
Germany	0.024 (1.14)	0.005 (1.90)	−0.229* (−6.00)	0.133* (4.88)
Italy	−0.13* (−3.29)	−0.028* (−3.29)	−0.418* (−3.16)	0.053 (0.53)
Spain	0.032 (0.68)	0.008 (0.95)	−0.419 (−9.86)	0.036 (1.09)
UK	0.045 (1.61)	0.008 (1.51)	−0.569 (−12.94)	0.045** (2.25)

t-statistics are shown in parentheses.
* Denotes rejection of $H_0 . b = 1$ or $H_0 . \beta = 1$, two-tail test, 1% significance level.
** As above, 5% significance level.

In the individual country estimations, the cross-sectional and panel OLS methods are both reasonably consistent in producing estimated values of b and β close to one. The main exception is Italy, for which the estimated coefficients produced by both of these methods are significantly smaller than one at the 1% level. For France, the panel OLS method produces an estimated coefficient that is significantly greater than one at the 5% level. The results produced by the fixed effects and Breitung Meyer

Table 9.15   Tests for beta convergence: equity

	Cross-sectional OLS	Panel OLS	Panel fixed effects	Panel Breitung–Meyer
	$\hat{b} - 1$	$\hat{\beta} - 1$	$\hat{\beta} - 1$	$\hat{\beta} - 1$
All countries	−0.043**	−0.011*	−0.492*	−0.006
	(−2.38)	(−2.73)	(−15.63)	(−0.28)
Belgium	0.005	0.002	−0.435	−0.009
	(0.14)	(0.21)	(−2.68)	(−0.08)
Denmark	−0.026	−0.014	−0.699*	−0.038
	(−0.56)	(−1.11)	(−8.87)	(−0.72)
France	−0.016	−0.007	−0.883*	−0.139*
	(−0.66)	(−0.96)	(−15.14)	(−3.00)
Germany	−0.030	−0.006	−0.454	0.048
	(−1.25)	(−1.24)	(−10.41)	(1.28)
Italy	−0.207*	−0.046*	−0.492*	−0.044
	(−4.50)	(−4.45)	(−5.05)	(−0.68)
Spain	−0.034	−0.008	−0.657	−0.008
	(−0.96)	(−1.04)	(−12.95)	(−0.22)
UK	0.005	0.001	−0.646*	0.034*
	(0.22)	(0.19)	(−17.51)	(1.99)

t-statistics are shown in parentheses.
* Denotes rejection of H_0:b = 1 or H_0:β = 1, two-tail test, 1% significance level.
** As above, 5% significance level.

panel estimators are rather different. The estimated coefficients for France, Germany and Italy produced by the former, and those for France, Germany and the UK produced by the latter, all suggest true coefficient values that are greater than one.

In the case of Italy, how can we explain the contrast between the findings of the cross-sectional and panel OLS estimations on the one hand, and those of the panel fixed effects and Breitung–Meyer estimations on the other? As noted previously, the latter two estimation methods make allowance for individual bank effects, which are ignored using the former two methods. If individual effects on growth are present, they will influence the estimates of the parameters b or β under the estimation methods that ignore them. Suppose, for example, the true data-generating process is: $s_{it} - s_{it-1} = \alpha_i + u_{it}$, so β = 1 and each bank's growth has an individual component and a random component.

Table 9.16   Tests for beta convergence: OBS business

	Cross-sectional OLS	Panel OLS	Panel fixed effects	Panel Breitung–Meyer
	$\hat{b} - 1$	$\hat{\beta} - 1$	$\hat{\beta} - 1$	$\hat{\beta} - 1$
All countries	−0.050**	−0.028*	−0.917*	−0.140*
	(−2.28)	(−3.91)	(−32.81)	(−7.05)
Denmark	−0.013	−0.004	−0.719	−0.004
	(−0.21)	(−0.24)	(−6.42)	(−0.06)
France	−0.042	−0.010	−0.580**	0.020
	(−0.83)	(−1.03)	(−12.40)	(0.68)
Germany	0.124**	0.014	−0.749*	−0.096*
	(2.57)	(1.14)	(−14.08)	(−2.28)
Italy	−0.241*	−0.075*	−0.718*	−0.054
	(−4.18)	(−4.08)	(−11.08)	(−1.30)
Spain	−0.077	−0.025**	−0.728*	−0.052**
	(−1.65)	(−2.27)	(−16.33)	(−2.14)
UK	−0.024	−0.008	−0.743*	−0.037
	(−0.33)	(−0.47)	(−11.45)	(−0.94)

t-statistics are shown in parentheses.
* Denotes rejection of H_0:b = 1 or H_0:β = 1, two-tail test, 1% significance level.
** As above, 5% significance level.

Suppose also that cross-sectionally the individual effects, α_i, are related inversely to bank size. In this case, the cross-sectional and panel OLS estimators tend to produce estimates of b and β that are smaller than one and therefore incorrect in terms of the parameterisation of the model, but correct in the sense that they succeed in detecting the inverse cross-sectional relationship between size and growth. The size of any individual bank is non-convergent, however, and follows a random walk (with drift) over time. After controlling for the individual effects, the fixed effects and Breitung–Meyer panel estimators tend to produce the correct results, with estimates suggesting that β is equal to (or in the case of the fixed effects estimator, greater than) one.

In any event, there is some evidence from the cross-sectional and panel OLS estimations that the smaller Italian banks grew faster than their larger counterparts over the sample period. A recent European Commission (1997) report shows that the

Italian banking sector was required to implement more sweeping regulatory changes than was the case in most other EU countries, in order to comply with the requirements of the European Single Market. The necessary adjustments were significantly greater for the larger than for the smaller Italian banks, and may have checked the growth of the former during the early 1990s. In other words, rejection of the LPE for Italy using the cross-sectional and panel OLS methods may reflect the impact of short-term influences, rather than any permanent departure from the LPE.

Using the equity size measure (Table 9.15), the evidence as to whether the LPE provides an appropriate description of the bank size–growth relationship is also mixed. In the estimations using the data for all countries, $H_0 : \beta = 1$ is rejected at the 5% level in the cross-sectional OLS and at the 1% level in the panel OLS estimations, with estimated coefficients significantly smaller than one obtained in each case. In the fixed effects estimation, $H_0 : \beta = 1$ is also rejected, but with an estimated coefficient suggesting that the true value of β is greater than one. In the Breitung–Meyer estimation, $H_0 : \beta = 1$ is accepted. As before, the contrast between the results produced by the cross-sectional and panel OLS methods on the one hand, and the fixed effects and Breitung–Meyer methods on the other, might be explained by individual effects that are related inversely to size.

In the estimations for individual countries using the equity size measure, the cross-sectional OLS and panel OLS estimators reject the LPE for Italy with estimated coefficients significantly smaller than one, but accept the LPE for all other countries. In contrast (but following the same pattern as the results for the assets size measure), the fixed effects panel estimator rejects the LPE with an estimated coefficient that suggests β is greater than one for Italy. It also rejects estimated coefficients that suggest β is smaller than one for Denmark, France and the UK. The Breitung–Meyer estimator produces the same result for France. It accepts the LPE for all other countries at the 1% level (but rejects the LPE at the 5% level in the case of the UK).

Using the OBS size measure (Table 9.16), the balance of evidence seems to weigh against the LPE and in favour of an inverse relationship between size and growth. In the estimations for all countries, $H_0 : \beta = 1$ is rejected at the 1% level using the panel OLS, fixed effects and Breitung–Meyer methods, with estimated coefficients significantly smaller than one obtained in each case. H_0: b = 1 is also rejected at the 5% level in the cross-sectional OLS estimation, again with an estimated coefficient significantly smaller than one. The 24 individual country estimations produce 11 rejections of $H_0 : b = 1$ or $H_0 : \beta = 1$ at the 5% level. Ten of these are associated with coefficient estimates significantly smaller than one, while in only one case (for Germany using cross-sectional OLS estimation) $H_0 : b = 1$ is rejected with an estimated coefficient suggesting a true value of β greater than one.

Overall, the evidence concerning the LPE using the conventional assets and equity bank size measures is rather varied. Certainly, however, there is no consistent Europe-wide evidence of mean-reversion in bank sizes. In most cases, growth is either independent of size or (in a few cases) perhaps related positively to size. The Italian banking sector, for which there is more consistent evidence of mean-reversion, appears to represent an exception to the general pattern. For OBS business, there are stronger grounds for rejecting the LPE in favour of a growth process in which there is mean-reversion. Smaller banks with relatively small OBS portfolios in 1990 tended to expand more rapidly in this area than their larger counterparts during the first half of the 1990s. Since the larger banks were generally faster than their smaller counterparts in establishing OBS portfolios initially during the 1980s, this finding presumably reflects a period of catching up on the part of the smaller banks.

Persistence of growth rates

Tables 9.17, 9.18 and 9.19 report our estimates of the parameters r in equation 9.2 and ρ in equations 9.3 and 9.4, which allow for serial correlation or persistence effects in the growth equation. As before, the three tables report the results for the assets, equity and OBS size definitions, respectively. The parameter r in equation 9.2, which quantifies the relationship between growth

Table 9.17   Tests for persistence of growth: assets

	Cross-sectional OLS	Panel OLS	Panel fixed effects	Panel Breitung–Meyer
	$\hat{r}$	$\hat{\rho}$	$\hat{\rho}$	$\hat{\rho}$
All countries	0.202	0.003	0.030	−0.040
	(1.89)	(0.15)	(1.31)	(−1.52)
Belgium	−0.598	−0.320*	0.284	−0.105
	(−1.29)	(−2.74)	(1.54)	(−0.59)
Denmark	0.514	0.127	−0.037	−0.042
	(1.25)	(1.53)	(−0.44)	(−0.34)
France	0.58**	0.031	−0.073	−0.090
	(2.18)	(0.64)	(−1.31)	(−1.33)
Germany	0.402	0.174*	−0.092	−0.014
	(1.42)	(4.06)	(−1.91)	(0.22)
Italy	0.521	−0.019	0.116	−0.080
	(0.63)	(−0.43)	(0.90)	(−0.73)
Spain	0.065	0.028	0.021	−0.015
	(0.19)	(0.63)	(0.42)	(−0.25)
UK	0.218	−0.026	−0.049	−0.093
	(1.77)	(−0.70)	(−1.37)	(−1.77)

t-statistics are shown in parentheses.
* Denotes rejection of $H_0{:}r = 1$ or $H_0{:}\rho = 1$, two-tail test, 1% significance level.
** As above, 5% significance level.

over the first year of the sample period (1990–91), and growth over the remaining five years (1991–96), does not have a direct interpretation as a measure of persistence of growth from one year to the next, and is therefore not included in the discussion of the results below. In contrast, the parameter ρ in equations 9.3 and 9.4 provides a suitable measure of the strength and direction of persistence in growth from each one-year period to the next. The evidence as to the presence and direction of persistence effects in the estimation results, however, is relatively weak. Using the assets size measure (Table 9.17), none of the three panel estimation methods produces a significant estimate of ρ using the data for all countries. In the individual country estimations, OLS estimation produces one estimate that is positive and significant (Germany) and one that is negative and significant (Belgium). Neither the fixed effects nor the Breitung–

Table 9.18 Tests for persistence of growth: equity

	Cross-sectional OLS	Panel OLS	Panel fixed effects	Panel Breitung–Meyer
	$\hat{\imath}$	$\hat{\rho}$	$\hat{\rho}$	$\hat{\rho}$
All countries	−0.282**	−0.041**	0.115*	−0.026
	(−2.07)	(−2.18)	(3.74)	(−0.88)
Belgium	−0.030	−0.092	0.020	−0.017
	(−0.07)	(−0.82)	(0.13)	(−0.10)
Denmark	2.755*	0.069	0.132	0.050
	(3.06)	(0.72)	(1.53)	(0.49)
France	−0.724*	−0.256*	0.104**	−0.112**
	(−3.76)	(−5.74)	(2.20)	(−2.02)
Germany	−0.237	−0.047	−0.037	−0.094
	(−0.66)	(−1.09)	(0.77)	(−1.51)
Italy	−0.193	−0.007	0.182	0.029
	(−0.56)	(−0.17)	(1.91)	(0.37)
Spain	−0.166	−0.181*	0.011	−0.132**
	(−0.68)	(−4.32)	(0.24)	(−2.55)
UK	0.241	0.038	−0.005	−0.045
	(1.69)	(1.03)	(−0.14)	(−1.03)

t-statistics are shown in parentheses.
* Denotes rejection of H_0:r = 1 or H_0:ρ = 1, two tail test, 1% significance level.
** As above, 5% significance level.

Meyer estimations produce any significant persistence coefficients for individual countries. A small number of rejections of H_0: ρ = 0 could simply reflect a typical dispersion of Type I errors (incorrect rejection of a correct null hypothesis) across a range of similar tests.

Using the equity size measure (Table 9.18), the panel OLS method produces an estimated coefficient for all countries that is negative and significant at the 5% level, while the fixed effects estimate is positive and significant at the 1% level. In the individual country estimations, the OLS and the Breitung–Meyer methods are consistent in producing estimated persistence coefficients that are negative and significant at the 5% level for France and Spain, and insignificant for all other countries. Fixed effects estimation, in contrast, produces a positive and significant estimated coefficient for France. Finally, using the OBS size

Table 9.19   Tests for persistence of growth: OBS business

	Cross-sectional OLS	Panel OLS	Panel fixed effects	Panel Breitung–Meyer
	$\hat{r}$	$\hat{\rho}$	$\hat{\rho}$	$\hat{\rho}$
All countries	−0.082	−0.240*	0.094*	−0.197*
	(−0.89)	(−11.33)	(4.28)	(-7.66)
Denmark	0.067	−0.236**	−0.089	−0.337*
	(0.18)	(−2.47)	(−0.91)	(-2.76)
France	0.295	0.004	0.030	−0.042
	(1.04)	(0.08)	(0.62)	(−0.73)
Germany	−0.401	−0.157*	0.102**	−0.063
	(−1.39)	(−3.28)	(2.13)	(-1.06)
Italy	−0.067	−0.138*	0.040	−0.147**
	(−0.38)	(−2.59)	(0.72)	(−2.15)
Spain	0.566**	0.101**	0.213*	0.061
	(2.56)	(2.25)	(4.99)	(1.27)
UK	−0.390	−0.162*	0.017	−0.148**
	(−1.35)	(−2.63)	(0.29)	(-2.28)

t-statistics are shown in parentheses.
* Denotes rejection of H_0:r = 1 or H_0:ρ = 1, two-tail test, 1% significance level.
** As above, 5% significance level.

measure (Table 9.19), the panel OLS and Breitung–Meyer estimations again produce negative and significant persistence coefficient estimates for all countries, while fixed effects estimation produces a positive and significant estimate. In the individual country estimations, there is also a mix of positive and negative estimates. In general, the OLS and Breitung–Meyer methods tend to return negative persistence estimates, while the fixed effects method has a greater propensity to return positive estimates. Most studies of other industrial or financial sectors have found there to be either no persistence of growth (Acs and Audretsch, 1990; Dunne and Hughes, 1994), or positive persistence (Chesher, 1979; Kumar, 1985; Wagner, 1992). Negative persistence of growth is a relatively unusual finding (Contini and Revelli, 1989).

Heteroscedasticity in growth rates

A final set of tests investigates the relationship between bank sizes and the variability (between banks and over time) of growth rates. In other words, we test a a null hypothesis of homoscedasticity against the alternative that there is heteroscedasticity in the residuals of equations 9.2, 9.3 or 9.4. In each case, a Lagrange multiplier test based on an auxiliary regression of the squared residuals on the square of the initial size measure, s_{i1}^2 in equation 9.2 or s_{it-1}^2 in equations 9.3 or 9.4, produces parameter estimates denoted $\hat{g}$ (in the cross-sectional estimation) and $\hat{\gamma}$ (in the panel estimations). The test statistic is the number of observations multiplied by R^2 from the auxiliary regression, which follows the χ_1^2 distribution under the null hypothesis of homoscedasticity. The test results are reported in Tables 9.20, 9.21 and 9.22.

Using the assets size measure (Table 9.20), the auxiliary regressions from all four estimations using the data for all countries produce negative estimated coefficients for the relationship between squared initial bank size and the variance of the residual. In the three panel estimations, the heteroscedasticity test statistic is significant at the 5% level, and in two cases (the panel OLS and fixed effects estimations) it is significant at the 1% level. In 28 estimations for individual countries, there are 23 negative estimates of g and γ, and five positive estimates. Nine of the negative estimates (and none of the positive estimates) are significantly different from zero at the 5% level. Overall, the evidence from the estimations using the assets size measure is reasonably clear in suggesting an inverse relationship between bank size and the variability of growth.

Using the equity size measure (Table 9.21), the auxiliary regressions from the cross-sectional OLS estimation using the data for all countries produce a heteroscedasticity test statistic that is significant at the 1% level, and a positive estimated coefficient. The same estimator repeats this result in the individual country estimation for Italy. Elsewhere, there is no evidence of heteroscedasticity in the panel OLS, fixed effects and Breitung–Meyer estimations for all countries. In the case of Spain, however, the three panel estimators all produce heteroscedasticity test statistics

Table 9.20   Tests for heteroscedasticity: assets

	Cross-sectional OLS	Panel OLS	Panel fixed effects	Panel Breitung–Meyer
	$\hat{g}$	$\hat{\gamma}$	$\hat{\gamma}$	$\hat{\gamma}$
All countries	−0.302	−0.164*	−0.001*	−0.187**
	(0.79)	(6.65)	(10.98)	(5.63)
Belgium	−0.038	−0.043	−0.024	−0.035
	(0.72)	(1.73)	(2.32)	(0.62)
Denmark	0.135	0.014	0.009	0.018
	(0.13)	(0.54)	(0.80)	(0.44)
France	−0.347**	−0.040*	−0.024**	−0.042**
	(5.44)	(6.84)	(6.44)	(5.82)
Germany	−0.162	−0.016*	−0.008*	−0.012
	(2.45)	(7.00)	(7.69)	(2.26)
Italy	3.563	−0.610	−0.048*	−0.775
	(3.83)	(3.65)	(7.04)	(3.80)
Spain	−3.251*	−0.195	−0.086	−0.157
	(7.23)	(1.42)	(1.57)	(0.66)
UK	−0.442**	−0.040	−0.022	−0.033
	(3.98)	(1.33)	(3.18)	(1.56)

Chi-squared statistics (one degree of freedom) are shown in parentheses.
* Denotes rejection of H_0:g = 1 or H_0:γ = 1, two-tail test, 1% significance level.
** As above, 5% significance level.

that are significant at the 5% level with negative coefficients. The fixed effects estimator also produces a negative and significant estimated coefficient for Italy. Overall, the evidence for heteroscedasticity with the equity size measure is rather weaker than was the case with the assets size measure.

Finally, using the OBS size measure (Table 9.22) there is no evidence of heteroscedasticity in any of the four estimations using the data for all countries. In the individual country estimations, the three panel tests are consistent in identfying significant heteroscedasticity with a negative estimated coefficient for France. In addition, there are negative and significant estimated coefficients for Spain in two cases, and for the UK in one case. For Italy, the cross-sectional OLS estimation again produces a significant heteroscedasticity test statistic, with a positive estimated coefficient. Elsewhere the null of homoscedasticity is accepted in all other tests.

Table 9.21   Tests for heteroscedasticity: equity

	Cross-sectional OLS	Panel OLS	Panel fixed effects	Panel Breitung–Meyer
	$\hat{g}$	$\hat{\gamma}$	$\hat{\gamma}$	$\hat{\gamma}$
All countries	3.580*	–0.083	–0.055	–0.090
	(44.36)	(0.49)	(0.74)	(0.37)
Belgium	–0.055	–0.043	–0.032	–0.054
	(0.10)	(1.66)	(3.18)	(1.66)
Denmark	0.054	–0.032	–0.004	–0.005
	(0.03)	(0.19)	(0.03)	(0.01)
France	–0.038	–0.072	–0.031	–0.090
	(0.05)	(0.81)	(0.69)	(1.10)
Germany	0.395	0.056	0.016	0.055
	(2.26)	(1.21)	(0.67)	(0.76)
Italy	8.074*	0.738	0.624**	1.046
	(7.78)	(1.80)	(4.05)	(2.20)
Spain	–0.428	–0.295**	–0.152**	–0.304**
	(1.83)	(6.16)	(5.97)	(4.80)
UK	–0.138	–0.049	–0.011	–0.013
	(0.96)	(1.39)	(1.45)	(0.40)

Chi-squared statistics (one degree of freedom) are shown in parentheses.
* Denotes rejection of H_0:$g = 1$ or H_0:$\gamma = 1$, two-tail test, 1% significance level.
** As above, 5% significance level.

Overall, where evidence of heteroscedasticity in the residuals of the growth equation is detected, it is usually associated with a negative coefficient estimate in the auxiliary regression, indicating that growth rates tend to be more variable for smaller banks than for their larger counterparts. Similar results for other industries have been reported in a number of previous studies (Singh and Whittington, 1968; Jovanovic, 1982; Dunne and Hughes, 1994). In manufacturing, Singh and Whittington and Dunne and Hughes argue that larger firms are likely to pursue a strategy of diversification, and so can spread risk over a large number of production activities, making them less susceptible to fluctuations in growth. Jovanovic argues that larger firms are likely to be older than smaller firms, and may experience learning economies of scale, which enable them to avoid costly mistakes. Both of these explanations may have some relevance in the case of European banks.

Table 9.22   Tests for heteroscedasticity: OBS business

	Cross-sectional OLS	Panel OLS	Panel fixed effects	Panel Breitung–Meyer
	$\hat{g}$	$\hat{\gamma}$	$\hat{\gamma}$	$\hat{\gamma}$
All countries	0.129 (0.12)	0.149 (0.43)	0.001 (0.41)	0.168 (0.40)
Denmark	0.266 (0.46)	−0.108 (1.69)	−0.044 (1.35)	−0.099 (0.43)
France	−0.538 (0.18)	−0.401** (6.29)	−0.200* (10.67)	−0.309** (5.27)
Germany	−0.610 (2.39)	−0.164 (1.50)	−0.065 (1.37)	−0.061 (0.16)
Italy	8.571* (21.35)	0.478 (2.06)	−0.008 (0.01)	0.526 (2.12)
Spain	0.826 (1.19)	−0.242 (1.31)	−0.163** (6.51)	−0.323** (6.51)
UK	1.964 (2.61)	−0.543** (4.50)	—0.206** (6.28)	−0.276 (1.19)

Chi-square statistics (one degree of freedom) are shown in parentheses.
* Denotes rejection of H_0:$g = 1$ or H_0:$\gamma = 1$, two-tail test, 1% significance level.
** As above, 5% significance level.

CONCLUSION

This chapter has reported tests for the LPE for banks based in seven European countries, using data for the period 1990–96. Conventional tests based on a cross-sectional regression of growth on size, and panel tests that make full use of the time series as well as the cross-sectional dimension of the data set, have been reported. Using both an asset and an equity measure of bank size, we find that for the majority of countries, there is little evidence of mean-reversion. Either the distribution of rates of growth across banks appears to be independent of bank size, or (in the panel tests in particular) there is some evidence of a positive association between bank size and growth. One important exception to this pattern is the Italian banking sector, in which the smaller banks appear to have grown faster than their larger counterparts. It has been suggested that this finding may reflect short-term adjustments following the creation of the European Single Market.

For OBS business, the LPE is rejected rather more frequently, with smaller banks tending to grow faster than their larger counterparts in many countries. It has been suggested that this pattern may reflect a catching-up process. Smaller banks, having initially been slower than larger banks to create portfolios of OBS business in the late 1980s, have sought to expand rapidly in this area during the 1990s.

For the conventional assets and equity size measures, the finding that the LPE holds in the majority of cases, or that larger banks may be growing faster than their smaller counterparts in some cases, suggests that a pattern of increased concentration could develop over time in European banking, even in the absence of factors such as efficiency advantages for large banks or the implementation of entry-deterring strategies by incumbent banks. The policy implications that could follow include recommendations for market share ceilings, and the enforced divestiture of the largest portfolios of banking business.

The aim of this book was to identify the impact of both systematic and non-systematic determinants of recent and current structural changes in the European banking industry. European banking has undergone fundamental transformation over the last decade, and is likely to continue to do so for the forseeable future. National banking markets have become more homogeneous and more open than ever before. The distinctions between the various types of financial services have become blurred as a result of technological change and developments such as deregulation and European integration. In response to these pressures, banks have attempted to improve efficiency, in order to be capable of expanding output and increasing the range of services offered. Many banks have also pursued strategies of diversification and financial innovation. The outcome is that banks now offer a wider range of products and services, and conduct much of their business off balance sheet.

In view of the limited attention that has been paid to the determinants of concentration in banking, and to the relationship between the size and growth of banks, this book has attempted to contribute towards filling the void. The objective has been to examine both systematic and non-systematic influences on bank growth, and therefore on structural change, in the European banking industry. Even if growth is non-systematic and the LPE provides an appropriate description of the pattern of growth in the European banking sector, banking can be expected to become more highly concentrated over time. Systematic factors, including technological change, economies of scale and scope and other efficiency advantages for large banks, and European integration seem likely merely to accelerate this trend towards increased concentration.

References

Aaronovitch, S and Sawyer, MC (1975) 'Mergers, growth and concentration', *Oxford Economic Papers*, **27**, 136–55.

Acs, ZJ and Audretsch, DB (1990) *Innovation and Small Firms*, Cambridge: Cambridge University Press.

Adelman, MA (1955) 'Concept and statistical measurement of vertical integration', in GJ Stigler (ed.), *Business Concentration and Price Policy*, Princeton: Princeton University Press.

Aigner, D, Lovell, CAK and Schmidt, P (1977) 'Formulation and estimation of stochastic frontier production models', *Journal of Econometrics*, **6**, 21–37.

Aitchison, J and Brown, JAC (1966) *The Lognormal Distribution*, Cambridge: Cambridge University Press.

Akhavein, JD, Berger, AN and Humphrey, DB (1997) 'The effects of megamergers on efficiency and prices: evidence from a bank profit function', *Review of Industrial Organisation*, **12**, 95–139.

Alhadeff, DA (1954) *Monopoly and Competition in Banking*, Berkeley: University of California Press.

Alhadeff, DA and Alhadeff, CP (1964) 'Growth of large banks, 1930–1960', *Review of Economics and Statistics*, **46**, 356–63.

Alhadeff, DA and Alhadeff, CP (1976) 'Growth and survival patterns of new banks, 1948–1970', *Journal of Money Credit and Banking*, **8**, 199–208.

Aliber, RZ (1975) 'International banking: growth and regulation', *Columbia Journal of World Business*, **10**, 9–15.

Allen, L and Rai, A (1996) 'Operational efficiency in banking: an international comparison', *Journal of Banking and Finance*, **20**, 655–72.

Allen, F and Santomero, AM (1998) 'The theory of financial intermediation', *Journal of Banking and Finance*, **21**, 1461–85.

Altunbas, Y, Evans, L and Molyneux, P (2001) 'Ownership and efficiency in banking', *Journal of Money, Credit and Banking*, forthcoming.

Altunbas, Y, Gardener, EPM, Molyneux, P and Moore, B (2001) 'Efficiency in European banking', *European Economic Review*, forthcoming.

Altunbas, Y, Goddard, J and Molyneux, P (1999) 'Technical change in banking', *Economics Letters*, **64**, 215–21.

Altunbas, Y, Liu, H, Molyneux, P and Seth, R (2000), 'Efficiency and risk in Japanese banking', *Journal of Banking and Finance*, **24**(10), 1605–28.

Altunbas, Y, Molyneux, P and DiSalvo, R (1994) 'Inefficiency in the Italian credit co-operative bank sector: a stochastic frontier analysis', research paper, Bangor: Institute of European Finance, University of Wales.

Altunbas, Y, Molyneux, P and Thornton, J (1997) 'Big bank mergers in Europe: an analysis of cost implications', *Economica*, **64**, 317–29.

Aly, HY, Grabowsky, R, Pasurka, C and Rangan, N (1990) 'Technical, scale and allocative efficiencies in US banking: an empirical investigation', *Review of Economics and Statistics*, **72**(2), 211–18.

Amel, D and Froeb, L (1991) 'Do firms differ much?', *Journal of Industrial Economics*, **39**, 323–29.

Arrow, KJ (1971) *Essays in the Theory of Risk-Bearing*, Amsterdam: North Holland.

Arthur Andersen (1986) *European Banking and Capital Markets – A Strategic Forecast*, London: Economist Intelligence Unit.

Arthur Andersen (1993) *European Banking and Capital Markets – Research Report*, London: Economist Intelligence Unit.

Athanassopoulos, AD (1997) 'Service quality and operating efficiency synergies for management control in the provision of financial services: evidence from Greek bank branches', *European Journal of Operational Research*, **98**, 300–13.

Axelrod, R (1984) *The Evolution of Cooperation*, New York: Basic Books.

Baer, H and Mote, R (1985) 'The effects on nationwide banking and concentration', *Federal Bank of Chicago Economic Perspectives*, **9**, 3–17.

Bailey, D and Boyle, SE (1971) 'The optimal measure of concentration', *Journal of the American Statistical Association*, **66**, 702–6.

Bain, JS (1951) 'Relation of profit rate to industry concentration: American manufacturing, 1936–1940', *Quarterly Journal of Economics*, **65**, 293–324.

Bain, JS (1956) *Barriers to New Competition*, Cambridge: Harvard University Press.

Bain, JS (1959) *Industrial Organisation*, New York: John Wiley & Sons.

Baldwin, JR and Gorecki, PK (1987) 'Plant creation versus plant acquisition: the entry process in Canadian manufacturing', *International Journal of Industrial Organisation*, **5**, 27–41.

Ballarin, E (1986) *Commercial Banks Amid the Financial Revolution: Developing a Competitive Strategy*, Cambridge: Ballinger.

Baltagi, BH and Griffin, JM (1988), 'A general index of technical change', *Journal of Political Economy*, **96**, 20–41.

Baltensperger, E and Dermine, J (1990) 'European banking: prudential and regulatory issues', in J Dermine (ed.) *European Banking in the 1990s*, London: Blackwell.

Bank for International Settlements (1996) *66th Annual Report*, Basel: Bank for International Settlements.

Bank for International Settlements (1998) *Statistics on Payments Systems in the G10 Countries*, December, Basel: Bank for International Settlements.

Bank for International Settlements (1999), *Payments Systems in Australia*, 2nd edn, June, Basel: Bank for International Settlements.

Barnes, P and Dodds, C (1983) 'The structure and performance of the UK building society industry 1970–78', *Journal of Business, Finance and Accounting*, **10**, 37–56.

Barro, RJ (1991) 'Economic growth in a cross-section of countries', *Quarterly Journal of Economics*, **106**, 407–43.

Bauer PW, Berger AN and Humphrey, DB (1993) 'Efficiency and productivity growth in US banking', in HO Fried, CAK Lovell and SS Schmidt (eds) *The Measurement of Productive Efficiency: Techniques and Applications*, Oxford: Oxford University Press.

Bauer PW, Berger AN, Ferrier GD and Humphrey, DB (1997) 'Consistency conditions for regulatory analysis of financial institutions: a comparison of frontier efficiency methods', *Finance and Economics Discussion Series*, **50**, Federal Reserve Board, Washington, DC.

Baumol, WJ (1982) 'Contestable markets: an uprising in the theory of industry structure', *American Economic Review*, **72**, 1–15.

Baumol, WJ (1986) 'Productivity growth convergence and welfare: what the long run data show', *American Economic Review*, **76**, 1072–85.

Baumol WJ, Panzar, JC and Willig, RD (1982), *Contestable Markets and the Theory of Industry Structure*, New York: Harcourt Brace.

Baumol, WJ, Panzar, TC and Willig RD (1988) *Contestable Markets and the Theory of Industrial Structure*, revised edition, New York: Harcourt Brace Jovanovich.

Bell, FW and Murphy, NB (1968) 'Economies of scale and division of labour in commercial banking', *Southern Economic Journal*, October, 131–9.

Benston, GJ (1965a) 'Economies of scale and marginal costs in banking operations', *National Banking Review*, **2**(4), 507–49.

Benston, GJ (1965b) 'Branch banking and economies of scale', *Journal of Finance*, May, 312–31.

Benston, GJ, Berger, AN, Hanweck, GA and Humphrey, DB (1983) *Economies of Scale and Scope*, proceedings of the Conference on

Bank Structure and Competition, Chicago: Federal Reserve Bank of Chicago.

Benston, GJ, Hanweck, GA and Humphrey, DB (1982a) 'Scale economies in banking: a restructuring and a reassessment', *Journal of Money, Credit and Banking*, **14**(4) part 1, 435–56.

Benston, GJ, Hanweck, GA and Humphrey, DB (1982b) 'Operating costs in commercial banking', *Federal Reserve Bank of Atlanta Economic Review*, **6** , 6–21.

Berg, SA (1992) 'Mergers, efficiency and productivity growth in banking: the Norwegian experience', *Norges Bank Arberds Notat*, 12 June.

Berg, SA, Bukh, PND and Førsund, FR (1995) 'Banking efficiency in the Nordic countries: a four countries Malmquist Index analysis', working paper (September), Aarhus: University of Aarhus, Denmark.

Berg, SA, Claussen, CA and Forsund, FR (1993) 'Bank efficiency in the Nordic countries: a multi-output analysis', *Arbeidsnotat from Norges Bank*.

Berg, SA, Forsund, FR, Hjalmarsson, L and Suominen, M (1993) 'Bank efficiency in the Nordic countries', *Journal of Banking and Finance*, **17**, 371–88.

Bergendahl, G (1995) 'DEA and benchmarks for Nordic banks', working paper, Gothenburg: Gothenburg University, Sweden.

Berger, AN (1991) *The Profit–Concentration Relationship in Banking: Tests of Market Power and Efficient Structure Hypotheses and Implications for the Consequences of Bank Mergers*, Board of Governors of the Federal Reserve System, Washington, DC, no. 176.

Berger, AN (1993), 'Distribution-free estimates of efficiency in the US banking industry and tests of the standard distributional assumptions', *Journal of Productivity Analysis*, **4**, 261–92.

Berger, AN (1995) 'The profit–structure relationship in banking – tests of market power and efficient structure hypotheses', *Journal of Money Credit and Banking*, **27**, 404–31.

Berger, AN and DeYoung, R (1997) 'Problem loans and cost efficiency in commercial banks', *Finance and Economics Discussion Series*, **8**, Federal Reserve Board, USA.

Berger, AN and Hannan, TH (1989) 'The price-concentration relationship in banking', *Review of Economics and Statistics*, **71**, 291–9.

Berger, AN and Hannan, TH (1998) 'The efficiency cost of market power in the banking industry: a test of the quite life and related hypotheses', *Review of Economics and Statistics*, **80**, 454–65.

Berger, AN and Humphrey, DB (1990) 'Measurement and efficiency issues in commercial banking', *Finance and Economics Discussion Series*, **151**, Federal Reserve Board, USA.

Berger, AN and Humphrey, DB (1991) 'The dominance of inefficiencies over scale and product mix economies in banking', *Journal of Monetary Economics*, **20**, 501–20.

Berger, AN and Humphrey, DB (1992) 'Measurement and efficiency issues in commercial banking', in Z Griliches (ed.) *Output Measurement in the Service Sectors*, National Bureau of Economic Research Studies in Income and Wealth, vol. 56, Chicago: University of Chicago Press.

Berger, AN and Humphrey, DB (1997) 'Efficiency of financial institutions: international survey and directions for future research', *European Journal of Operational Research*, **98**, 175–212.

Berger, AN and Mester, LJ (1997) 'Inside the black box: what explains differences in the efficiencies of financial institutions', *Journal of Banking and Finance*, **21**, 895–947.

Berger, AN, Bonime, SD, Goldberg, LG and White, LG (1999) 'The dynamics of market entry: the effects of mergers and acquisitions on de novo entry and small business lending in the banking industry', Federal Reserve working paper.

Berger, A, Demsetz, R and Strahan, P (1999) 'The consolidation of the financial services industry: causes, consequences and implications for the future', *Journal of Banking and Finance*, **23**, 2–4, 135–194.

Berger, AN, Hancock, D and Humphrey, DB (1993) 'Bank efficiency derived from the profit function', *Journal of Banking and Finance*, **17**, 317–47.

Berger, AN, Hanweck, GA and Humphrey, DB (1987) 'Competitive viability in banking. scale, scope and product mix economies', *Journal of Monetary Economics*, **20**, 501–20.

Berger, AN, Hunter, WC and Timme, SG (1993) 'The efficiency of financial institutions: a review and preview of research past, present and future'. *Journal of Banking and Finance*, **17**, 221–49.

Berger, AN, Leusner, JH and Mingo, JJ (1994) 'The efficiency of bank branches', working paper, Philadelphia: Wharton Financial Institution Center.

Berger, AN, Leusner, JH and Mingo, JJ (1997) 'The efficiency of bank branches', *Journal of Monetary Economics*, **40**(1), 141–62.

Berkovitch, E and Narayanan, MP (1998) 'Motives for takeovers: an empirical investigation', *Journal of Financial Economics*, **48**, 347–62.

Bertrand, J (1883) 'Book review of Cournot's work', *Journal des Savants*, **67**, 499–508.

Bhattacharya, S and Thakor, AV (1993) 'Contemporary banking theory', *Journal of Financial Intermediation*, **3**, 2–50.

Bhattacharya, A., Lovell, CAK and Sahay, P (1997) 'The impact of liberalisation on the productive efficiency of Indian commercial banks', *European Journal of Operational Research*, 332–45.

Blair, JM (1972) *Economic Concentration*, New York: Harcourt Brace Jovanovich.

Boot, AWA (1999), 'European lessons on consolidation in banking', *Journal of Banking and Finance*, **23**, 609–13.

Bourke, P (1989) 'Concentration and other determinants of bank profitability in Europe, North America, and Australia', *Journal of Banking and Finance*, **13**, 65–79.

Breitung, J and Meyer, W (1994) 'Testing for unit roots in panel data: are wages on different bargaining levels cointegrated?', *Applied Economics*, **26**, 353–61.

Brockett, PL, Charnes, A, Cooper, WW, Huang, ZM and Sun, DB (1997) 'Data transformations in DEA cone-ratio envelopment approaches for monitoring bank performance', *European Journal of Operational Research*, **98**, 250–68.

Brozen, Y (1971) 'Bain's concentration and rates of return revisited', *Journal of Law and Economics*, **351**, 69.

Business Intelligence Report (1998), *Electronic Banking in Europe*, London: HMSO Stationary Office.

Call, GD and Keeler, TE (1985), 'Airline deregulation, fares and market behaviour: some empirical evidence, in AH Daugherty (ed.) *Analytical Studies in Transport Economics*, Cambridge: Cambridge University Press.

Canals, J (1993) *Competitive Strategies in European Banking*, Oxford: Clarendon Press.

Canals, J (1997) *Universal Banking. International Comparisons and Theoretical Perspectives*, Oxford: Oxford University Press.

Casu, B and Girardone, C (1998) 'A comparative study of the cost efficiency of italian bank conglomerates', research paper 98/3, Bangor: Institute of European Finance, University of Wales.

Caves, RE and Porter, ME (1977) 'From entry barriers to mobility barriers: conjectural decisions and contrived deterrence to new competition', *Quarterly Journal of Economics*, **91**, 241–61.

Cecchini, P (1988) *The European Challenge in 1992: The Benefits of a Single Market*, Aldershot: Gower.

CEPR (1999) *The Future of European Banking*, Centre for Economic Policy Research Series in Monitoring European Integration, 9, January, London: Centre for Economic Policy Research.

CEPS (1998a) *Capital Markets and EMU: Report of a Centre for European Policy Studies Working Party*, Brussels: Centre for European Policy Studies.

CEPS (1998b) *Prudential Supervision in the Context of EMU*, Centre for European Policy Studies memo, Brussels: Centre for European Policy Studies.

Chamberlin, EH (1962) *The Theory of Monopolistic Competition*, 8th edn, Cambridge: Harvard University Press [originally published 1933].

Chandler, AD (1990) *Scale and Scope: The Dynamics of Industrial Capitalism*, Cambridge: Harvard University Press.

Charnes, A, Cooper, WW, Huang, ZM and Sun, DB (1990) 'Polyhedral cone-ratio DEA models with an illustrative application to large commercial banks', *Journal of Econometrics*, **46**, 73–91.

Chesher, A (1979) 'Testing the law of proportionate effect', *Journal of Industrial Economics*, **27**, 403–11.

Clark, JA (1984) 'Estimation of economies of scale in banking using a generalised functional form', *Journal of Money, Credit and Banking*, **16**, 53–68.

Clark, JA (1988) 'Economies of scale and scope at depository financial institutions: a review of the literature' *Federal Reserve Bank of Kansas City, Economic Review*, **73**, 16–33.

Clark, JB (1899) *The Distribution of Wealth*, London: Macmillan.

Clarke, R (1979) 'On the lognormality of firm and plant size distribution: some UK evidence', *Applied Economics*, **11**, 415–33.

Coase, RH (1937), 'The nature of the firm', *Economica*, **4**, 386–405.

Colwell, RJ and Davis, EP (1992) 'Output, productivity and externalities – the case of banking', Bank of England discussion paper 3.

Comanor, WS and Wilson, T (1967) 'Advertising, market structure and performance', *Review of Economics and Statistics*, **49**, 423–40.

Contini, B and Revelli, R (1989) 'The relationship between firm growth and labour demand', *Small Business Economics*, **1**, 309–14.

Cooper, JCB (1980) 'Economies of scale in the UK building society industry', *Investment Analysis*, **55**, 31–6.

Cooper, WW (1997) 'New approaches for analysing and evaluating the performance of financial institutions, *European Journal of Operational Research*, **98**, 170–4.

Cournot, AA (1927) *Researches into the Mathematical Principles of the Theory of Wealth*, New York: Macmillan [originally published 1838].

Cubbin, JS and Geroski, PA (1990) 'The persistence of profits in the United Kingdom', in DC Mueller (ed.) *The Dynamics of Company Profits: An International Comparison*, Cambridge: Cambridge University Press.

Curry, B and George, K (1983) 'Industrial concentration: a survey', *Journal of Industrial Economics*, **31**, 203–55.

Daniel, DL, Longbrake, WA and Murphy, NB (1973) 'The effect of technology on bank economies of scale for demand deposits', *Journal of Finance*, **28**, 131–46.

Datamonitor (1999a) *IT in US Retail Banking*, London: Datamonitor.

Datamonitor (1999b) *IT in European Retail Banking*, London: Datamonitor.

Davies, S (1987) 'Vertical integration', in R Clarke and T McGuiness (eds) *The Economics of the Firm*, Oxford: Blackwell.

Davies, SW (1989) 'Concentration', in S Davies and B Lyons (eds) *The Economics of Industrial Organisation*, London: Longman.

Davies, SW and Lyons, BR (1982) 'Seller concentration: the technological explanation and demand uncertainty', *Economic Journal*, **92**, 903–19.

De Bandt, O (1999) 'EMU and the structure of the European banking system', in BIS conference papers: *The Monetary and Regulatory Implications of Changes in the Banking Industry*, **7**, March, 121–41, Basel: Bank for International Settlements.

De Bandt, O and Davis, EP (1998) 'Competition, contestability and market structure in european banking sectors on the eve of EMU: evidence from France, Germany, and Italy with a perspective on the United States', paper presented at the VII Tor Vegata Financial Conference on Post Euro competition and strategy among financial systems and bank firm relations, Rome, 26–27 November 1998.

De la Fuente, M (1998) 'Spain', in *Banking in the New EU and Switzerland and Norway*, London: Financial Times Publishing, 252–73.

DeBorger, B, Ferrier, G and Kerstens, K (1995) 'The choice of a technical efficiency measure on the free disposal hull reference technology: a comparison using banking data', working paper, Arkansas: University of Arkansas.

Debreu, G (1951) 'The coefficient of resource utilization', *Econometrica*, **19**, 273–92.

Demsetz, H (1973) 'Industry structure, market rivalry and public policy', *Journal of Law and Economics*, **16**, 1–9.

Demsetz, H (1974) 'Two systems of belief about monopoly', in HJ Goldschmid, HM Mann and JF Weston (eds) *Industrial Concentration: The New Learning*, Boston: Little Brown.

Demsetz, H (1982) 'Barriers to entry', *American Economic Review*, **72**, 47–57.

Deprins, D, Simar, L and Tulkens, H (1984) 'Measuring labour-efficiency in post offices', in M Marchand, P Pestiau and H Tulkens (eds) *The Performance of Public Enterprises: Concepts and Measurements*, Amsterdam: North Holland.

Dermine, J (1999) 'The case for a European-wide strategy', *European Investment Bank Papers*, **4**(1), 137–43.

Dietsch, M and Weill, L (1998) 'Banking efficiency and European integration: productivity, cost and profit approaches', presented at the 21st Colloquium of the Société Universitaire Europeenne de Recherches Financieres, Frankfurt, 15–17 October 1998.

Dixit, A (1982) 'Recent developments in oligopoly theory', *American Economic Review, Papers and Proceedings*, **72**, 12–17.

Downie, J (1958) *The Competitive Process*, London: MacMillan.

Drake, L (1995) 'Testing for expense preference behaviour in UK building societies', *Service Industry Journal*, **15**(1), 50–65.

Drake, L and Howcroft, B (1993) 'A study of the relative efficiency of the UK bank branches', economic research paper 93/13, Loughborough: Loughborough University of Technology.

Dunne, P and Hughes, A (1994) 'Age, size, growth and survival: UK companies in the 1980s', *Journal of Industrial Economics*, **42**, 115–40.

Dunne, T, Roberts, MJ and Samuelson, L (1988) 'Patterns of firm entry and exit in US manufacturing industries', *Rand Journal of Economics*, **19**, 495–515.

Dunne, T, Roberts, MJ and Samuelson, L (1989) 'The growth and failure of US manufacturing plants', *Quarterly Journal of Economics*, **104**, 671–98.

Eckard, EW (1995) 'A note on the profit–concentration relation', *Applied Economics*, **27**, 219–23.

Economist (1998) 'The economics of antitrust', *Economist*, 2–8 May, 94–6.

Edgeworth, FY (1932) *Mathematical Psychics*, London: Kegan Paul [originally published 1881].

Eisenbeis, RA, Ferrier, GD and Kwan, SH (1996) 'An empirical analysis of the informativeness of programming and SFA efficiency scores: efficiency and bank performance', working paper, Chapel Hill: University of North Carolina.

Elysiani, E and Mehdian, S (1990a) 'Efficiency in the commercial banking industry: a production frontier approach', *Applied Economics*, **22**, 539–51.

Elysiani, E and Mehdian, S (1990b) 'A non-parametric approach to measurement of efficiency and technological change: the case of large US banks', *Journal of Financial Services Research*, **4**, 157–68.

Engwell, L (1973) *Models of Industrial Structure*, Lexington: Lexington Books.

Euromoney (1999) 'When cutting costs is not enough', *Euromoney*, November, 58–63.

European Central Bank (1999) *The Effects of Technology on the EU Banking Systems*, Frankfurt: European Central Bank.

European Commission (1997) 'Impact on services: credit institutions and banking', *Single Market Review*, subseries II, vol. 4, London: Office for Official Publications of the European Communities and Kogan Page Earthscan.

Evanoff, DD and Fortier, DL (1988) 'Re-evaluation of the structure–conduct–performance paradigm in banking', *Journal of Financial Services Research*, **1**, 277–94.

Evanoff, DD and Israilevich, PR (1991) *Cost Economies and Allocative Efficiency of Large US Commercial Banks*, Federal Reserve Bank of Chicago, 26th Annual Conference on Bank Structure and Competition, May 1991.

Evanoff, DD, Israilevich, PR and Merris, RC (1990) 'Relative price efficiency, technical change and scale economies for large commercial banks', *Journal of Regulatory Economics*, **2**(3), 281–98.

Evans, DS (1987a) 'Tests of alternative theories of firm growth', *Journal of Political Economy*, **95**, 657–74.

Evans, DS (1987b) 'The relationship between firm growth, size and age: estimates for 100 manufacturing industries', *Journal of Industrial Economics*, **35**, 567–81.

Fanjul, O and Maravall, F (1985) 'La eficiencia del sistema bancario Espanol', research paper, Madrid: Alianza University.

Farrell, MJ (1957) 'The measurement of productive efficiency', *Journal of Royal Statistical Society*, **120**(A), 253–81.

Favero, CA and Papi, L (1995) 'Technical efficiency and scale efficiency in the Italian banking sector: a non-parametric approach', *Applied Economics*, **27**, 385–95.

Ferrier, GD. and Lovell, CAK (1990) 'Measuring cost efficiency in banking: econometric and linear programming evidence', *Journal of Econometrics*, **46**, 229–45.

Ferrier, GD, Kerstens, K and Vanden Eeckaut, P (1994) 'Radial and non-radial technical efficiency measures on a DEA reference technology: a comparison using banking data', *Recherches Economiques de Louvain*, **60**, 449–79.

Financial IT (1999) *Special Report: Electronic Delivery*, 9–20, London: Chartered Institute of Bankers.

Financial World (1999) 'Will a computer in every home ruin your channel delivery strategy?', London: Chartered Institute of Bankers.

Forestieri, G (1993), 'Economies of scale and scope in the financial services industry: a review of recent literature', in Organization for Economic Cooperation and Development (ed.) *Financial Conglomerates*, Paris: Organization for Economic Cooperation and Development.

Fox, KJ (1996), 'Specification of functional form and the estimation of technical progress', *Applied Economics*, **28**, 947–56.

Freixas, X and Rochet, JC (1997) *Microeconomics of Banking*, London: MIT Press.

Fudenberg, D and Tirole, J (1989) 'Non co-operative game theory for industrial organisation: an introduction and overview', in R

Schmalensee and RD Willig (eds) *Handbook of Industrial Organisation*, Amsterdam: North Holland.

Gandy, T (1999a) *The Network Bank*, London: Chartered Institute of Bankers.

Gandy, T. (1999b) *Banking Strategies Beyond 2000*, London: Chartered Institute of Bankers.

Gardener, EPM (1992) 'Financial conglomeration: a new challenge for banking', in EPM Gardener (ed.) *The Future of Financial Systems and Services*, London: MacMillan.

Gardener, EPM. and Molyneux, P (1997) 'The too-big-to-fail doctrine revisited', *European Investment Bank Papers*, **2**, 15–32.

Gathon, H and Grosjean, F (1991) 'Efficacité productive et rendement d'échelle dans les banques belges', *Cahiers Économiques de Bruxelles*, **144**, 145–160.

Genetay, N and Molyneux, P (1998) *Bancassurance*, London: MacMillan.

Geroski, PA (1990) 'Modelling persistent profitability', in DC Mueller (ed.) *The Dynamics of Company Profits: An International Comparison*, Cambridge: Cambridge University Press.

Geroski, PA (1991) *Market Dynamics and Entry*, Oxford: Blackwell.

Geroski, PA (1994) *Market Structure, Corporate Performance and Innovative Activity*, Oxford: Clarendon Press.

Geroski, PA, Machin, R and Van Reenan, J (1993) 'The profitability of innovating firms', *Rand Journal of Economics*, **24**, 198–211.

Gibrat, R (1931) *Les Inegalities Economiques*, Paris: Sirey.

Gilbert, R (1984) 'Bank market structure and competition – a survey', *Journal of Money Credit and Banking*, **16**, 617–45.

Gilbert, RJ and Newbury, DMG (1982) 'Pre-emptive patenting and the persistence of monopoly', *American Economic Review*, **72**, 514–26.

Gilbert PL and Steinherr, A (1989) 'The impact of financial market integration on the European banking industry', *Cahiers, European Investment Bank*, March.

Gilligan, T and Smirlock, M (1984) 'An empirical study of joint production and scale economies in commercial banking', *Journal of Banking and Finance*, **8**, 67–77.

Gilligan, T, Smirlock M and Marshall, W (1984) 'Scale and scope economies in the multi-product banking firm', *Journal of Monetary Economics*, **13**, 393–405.

Giokas, D (1991), 'Bank branch operating efficiency: a comparative application of DEA and the loglincar model Omega International', *Journal of Management Science*, **19**, 549–57.

Goddard, JA and Wilson, JOS (1996) 'Persistence of profits for UK manufacturing and service sector firms', *Service Industries Journal*, **16**, 105–17.

Goddard, JA and Wilson, JOS (1999) 'Persistence of profit: a new empirical interpretation' *International Journal of Industrial Organisation*, **17**, 663–87.

Goddard, JA and Wilson, JOS (2001) 'Cross-sectional and panel estimation of convergence', *Economics Letters*, forthcoming.

Goddard, JA, Wilson, JOS and Blandon, P (2001) 'Panel tests of Gibrat's law for Japanese manufacturing firms', *International Journal of Industrial Organisation*, forthcoming.

Gough, TJ (1979) 'Building societies mergers and the size of the efficiency relationship', *Applied Economics*, **11**, 185–94.

Grabowski, R, Mathur, I. and Rangan, N (1995) 'The role of takeovers in increasing efficiency', *Managerial and Decision Economics*, **16**, 211–23.

Graham, DR, Kaplan, DP and Sibley, RS (1983), 'Efficiency and competition in the airline industry', *Bell Journal of Economics*, **14**, 118–38.

Gramley, LE (1962) *A Study of Scale Economies in Banking*, Kansas City: Federal Reserve Bank of Kansas City.

Greenbaum, SI (1967) 'A study of bank cost', *National Banking Review*, June, 415–34.

Greene, WH (1990) 'A gamma-distributed stochastic frontier model', *Journal of Econometrics*, **13**, 141–64.

Grifell-Tatjé, E and Lovell, CAK (1994) 'A generalised Malmquist productivity index', working paper, Athens, GA: University of Georgia.

Grifell-Tatjé, E and Lovell, CAK (1995a) 'A DEA based analysis of productivity change and intertemporal managerial performance', *Annals of Operational Research*, **73**, 177–89.

Grifell-Tatjé, E. and Lovell, CAK (1995b) 'Deregulation and productivity decline: the case of Spanish savings banks', *European Economic Review*, June, 1281–303.

Groeneveld, JM (1998) 'Fusies in het Europese bankwezen: achtergronden en implicaties', *Maandschrift Economie*, **62**, 293–308.

Grosskopf, S (1996) 'Statistical inference and non-parametric efficiency: a selective survey', *Journal of Productivity Analysis*, **7**, 161–76.

Gual, J and Neven, D (1993) 'Banking in social Europe – market services and European integration', *European Economy*, **3**, 153–83.

Hall, B (1987) 'The relationship between firm size and firm growth in the US manufacturing sector', *Journal of Industrial Economics*, **35**, 583–606.

Hancock, D (1985) 'The financial firm: production with monetary and non-monetary goods', *Journal of Political Economy*, **93**, 859–80.

Hannah, L and Kay, JA (1977) *Concentration in Modern Industry*, London: MacMillan.

Hannah, L and Kay, JA (1981) 'The contribution of mergers to concentration growth: a reply to Professor Hart', *Journal of Industrial Economics*, **29**, 305–13.

Hannan, T (1983) 'Price, capacity and the entry decision: a conditional Logit analysis', *Southern Economic Journal*, **50**, 539–50.

Hardwick, P (1989) 'Economies of scale in building societies', *Applied Economics*, **21**, 1291–304.

Hardwick, P (1990) 'Multi-product cost attributes: a study of the UK building societies', *Oxford Economic Papers*, **42**, 446–61.

Hart, PE (1962) 'The size and growth of firms', *Economica*, **29**, 29–39.

Hart, PE (1981) 'The effects of mergers on industrial concentration', *Journal of Industrial Economics*, **29**, 315–20.

Hart, PE and Oulton, N (1996) 'The size and growth of firms', *Economic Journal*, **106**, 1242–52.

Hart, PE and Oulton, N (1999) 'Gibrat, Galton and job creation', *International Journal of the Economics of Business*, **6**, 149–64.

Hart, PE and Prais, SJ (1956) 'The analysis of business concentration: a statistical approach' *Journal of the Royal Statistical Society*, series A, **119**, 150–91.

Heggestad, AA (1984) 'Comment on bank market structure and competition: a survey', *Journal of Money Credit and Banking*, **16**, 645–50.

Helfat, CE (1987) 'Vertical integration and risk reduction', *Journal of Law, Economics and Organisation*, **3**, 47–68.

Herfindahl, OC (1950) 'Concentration in the US steel industry', unpublished PhD thesis, New York: Columbia University.

Herring, RG and Santomero, AM (1990) 'The corporate structure of financial conglomerates', *Journal of Financial Services Research*, **13**(4), 471–97.

Hicks, JR (1935) 'Annual survey of economic theory: the theory of monopoly', *Econometrica*, **3**, 1–20.

Hirschman, AO (1945) *National Power and the Structure of Foreign Trade*, Berkeley: University of California Bureau of Business and Economic Research.

Horovitz, PM (1963) 'Economies of scale in banking' in PM Horovitz et al. (eds) *Private Financial Institutions*, Englewood Cliffs: Prentice-Hall, 1–55.

Humphrey, DB (1985) 'Cost and scale economies in bank intermediation' in R Aspinwall and R Eisenbeis (eds) *Handbook for Banking Strategies*, New York: John Wiley & Sons.

Humphrey, DB (1987) 'Cost dispersion and the measurement of economies in banking', *Federal Reserve Bank of Richmond Economic Review*, May/June, 24–38.

Humphrey, DB (1991) *The Likely Effect of Interstate Branching on Bank Costs and Service Prices*, prepared for the Congressional Budget Office, October.

Humphrey, DB (1993), 'Cost and technical change: effects from bank deregulation', *Journal of Productivity Analysis*, **4**, 9–34.

Humphrey, DB and Pulley, LB (1997) 'Banks' responses to deregulation: profits, technology and efficiency', *Journal of Money, Credit and Banking*, **29**, 73–93.

Hunter, WC and Timme, SG (1986) 'Technical change, organisational form and the structure of bank production', *Journal of Money, Credit and Banking*, **18**, 152–66.

Hunter, WC and Timme, SG (1991) 'Technological change in large US banks', *Journal of Business*, **64**, 339–62.

Hunter, WC and Timme, SG (1995) 'Core deposits and physical capital: a re-examination of bank scale economies and efficiency with quasi-fixed inputs', *Journal of Money, Credit and Banking*, **27**, 165–85.

Hunter, WC, Timme, SJ and Yang, WK (1990) 'An examination of cost subadditivity and multi-product production in large US banks', *Journal of Money, Credit and Banking*, **22**, 504–25.

Hurdle, GJ, Johnson, RL, Joskow, AS, Werden, GJ and Williams, MA (1989) 'Concentration, potential entry, and performance in the airline industry', *Journal of Industrial Economics*, **38**, 119–39.

Ijiri, Y and Simon, HA (1964) 'Business firm growth and size', *American Economic Review*, **54**, 77–89.

Jackson, WE (1992) 'The price–concentration relationship in banking: a comment', *Review of Economics and Statistics*, **74**, 373–76.

Jevons, WS (1970) *The Theory of Political Economy*, Harmondsworth: Penguin [originally published 1871].

Jovanovic, B (1982) 'Selection and evolution of industry', *Econometrica*, **50**, 649–70.

Kalish, L and Gilbert, RA (1973) 'An analysis of efficiency of scale and organisational form in commercial banking', *Journal of Industrial Economics*, **21**, 293–307.

Kamien, MI and Schwartz, NL (1982) *Market Structure and Innovation*, Cambridge: Cambridge University Press.

Kaparakis, EI, Miller, SM and Noulas, AG (1994) 'Short-run cost inefficiency of commercial banks: a flexible stochastic frontier approach', *Journal of Money, Credit and Banking*, **26**, 875–93.

Kay, JA (1993) *Foundations of Corporate Success*, Oxford: Oxford University Press.

Kim, HY (1986) 'Economies of scale and scope in multi-product financial institutions: further evidence from credit unions' *Journal of Banking and Finance*, **18**, 220–6.

Kindleberger, CP (1984) *A Financial History of Western Europe*, London: Allen and Unwin.

Klemperer, P (1987) 'Markets with consumer switching costs', *Quarterly Journal of Economics*, **102**, 375–94.

Klepper, S (1996) 'Entry, exit, growth, and innovation over the product life cycle', *American Economic Review*, **86**, 562–83.

Knight, FH (1921) *Risk, Uncertainty and Profit*, Part 2, Boston: Houghton Mifflin Company.

Kolari, J and Zardkoohi, A (1987) *Bank Cost, Structure and Performance*, Lexington: Lexington Books.

Krickx, (1995) 'Vertical integration in the computer main frame industry: a transaction cost interpretation', *Journal of Economic Behaviour and Organisation*, **26**, 75–91.

Kumar, MS (1985) 'Growth, acquisition activity and firm size: evidence from the United Kingdom', *Journal of Industrial Economics*, **33**, 327–38.

Kwan, SH and Eisenbeis, RA (1995) 'An analysis of inefficiencies in banking', *Journal of Banking and Finance*, **19**, 733–4.

Kwoka, JE (1983) 'Regularity and diversity in firm size distributions in US industries', *Journal of Economics and Business*, **34**, 391–5.

Landi A (1990) *Dimensioni, Costi e Profitti delle Banche Italiane*, Bologna: Il Mulino.

Lang G and Welzel, P (1996) 'Efficiency and technical progress in banking: empirical results for a panel of German banks', *Journal of Banking and Finance*, **20**, 1003–23.

Langlois, RN and Robertson, PL (1989) 'Explaining vertical integration: lessons from the American automobile industry', *Journal of Economic History*, **49**, 361–75.

Leibenstein, H (1966) 'Allocative efficiency vs "X-efficiency"', *American Economic Review*, **56**, 392–415.

Leibenstein, H (1980), *Inflation, Income Distribution and X-Efficiency Theory*, London: Croon Helm.

Lévy-Garboua, L and Lévy-Garboua, V (1975) 'Les coûts opératoires des banques françaises: une étude statistique' *Revue d'Economie Politique*, **80**, 264–81.

Lintner, V, Pokorny, M, Woods, M and Blinkhorn, MR (1987) 'Trade unions and technological change in the UK mechanical engineering industry', *British Journal of Industrial Relations*, **25**, 19–29.

Litan, RE (1987) *What Should Banks do?*, Washington, DC: Brookings Institution.

Llewellyn, DT (1995) 'The future business of banking', *Banking World*, January, 14–19.

Longbrake, WA and Haslem, JA (1975) 'Productive efficiency in commercial banking', *Journal of Money, Credit and Banking*, **7**, 317–30.

Lovell, CAK (1993) 'Production frontiers and productive efficiency' in HO Fried, CAK Lovell and SS Schmidt (eds) *The Measurement of Productive Efficiency: Techniques and Applications*, Oxford: Oxford University Press.

Lovell, CAK and Pastor, J (1997) 'Target setting: an application to a bank branch network', *European Journal of Operational Research*, **98**, 290–99.

Machlup, F (1952) *The Economics of Seller Competition*, New York: John Hopkins Press.

Maes, M (1975) 'Les économies de dimension dans le secteur bancaire belge', *Tijdschruft voor het Bankwezen*, **4**, 62–76.

Mansfield, E (1962) 'Entry, Gibrat's Law, innovation, and the growth of firms', *American Economic Review*, **52**, 1023–51.

Mansfield, E (1969) 'Industrial research and development: characteristics, costs and diffusion results' *American Economic Review, Papers and Proceedings*, **59**, 65–79.

Marris, R (1964) *The Economic Theory of Managerial Capitalism*, London: MacMillan.

Marshall, A (1961) *The Principles of Economics*, 9th edn, with annotations by CW Guillebaud, London: Macmillan [originally published 1890].

Mason, ES (1939) 'Price and production policies of large scale enterprise', *American Economic Review*, **29**, 61–74.

Mason, ES (1949) 'The current state of the monopoly problem in the United States', *Harvard Law Review*, **62**, 1265–85.

Maudos, J, Pastor, JM and Quesada, J (1995) 'A decade of technical change in Spanish savings banks: a summary of different measurement techniques', Istituto Valenciano de Investigaciones Economicas (IVIE) discussion paper 4.

Maudos, J, Pastor, JM and Quesada, J (1996) 'Technical progress in Spanish banking: 1985–1994', Istituto Valenciano de Investigaciones Economicas (IVIE) discussion paper 6.

Maudos, J, Pastor, JM, Pérez, F and Quesada, J (1998) 'Cost and profit efficiency in European banks', presented at the Annual Conference of the European Association of University Teachers in Banking and Finance, Université la Sorbonne, 2–6 September, Paris.

Maudos, J, Pastor, JM, Pérez, F and Quesada, J (1999), 'The Single European Market and bank efficiency: the importance of specialisation', presented at the Annual Conference of the European Association of University Teachers in Banking and Finance, Universidade Nova de Lisboa, Lisbon, 3–4 September.

McAllister, PH and McManus, D (1993) 'Resolving the scale efficiency puzzle in banking', *Journal of Banking and Finance*, **17**, 389–405.

McCauley, RN and White, WR (1997) 'The euro and European financial markets', Bank of International Settlements, working paper 41, May.

McCloughan, P (1995) 'Simulation of industrial concentration', *Journal of Industrial Economics*, **43**, 405–33.

McKillop, DG and Glass, CJ (1994) 'A cost model of building societies as producers of mortgages and other financial products', *Journal of Business Finance and Accounting*, **21**, 1031–46.

McKillop, DG Glass, CJ and Morikawa, Y (1996) 'The composite cost function and efficiency in giant Japanese banks', *Journal of Banking and Finance*, **20**, 1651–71.

Mester, LJ (1987) 'Efficient production of financial services: scale and scope', *Business Review*, (Federal Reserve Bank of Philadelphia), January/February, 15–25.

Mester, LJ (1992), 'Traditional and non-traditional banking: an information–theoretic approach', *Journal of Banking and Finance*, **16**(3), 545–66.

Mester, LJ (1996) 'A study of bank efficiency taking into account risk-preferences', *Journal of Banking and Finance*, **20**, 389–405.

Mitchell, K and Onvural, NM (1996) 'Economies of scale and scope at large commercial banks: evidence from the Fourier-flexible functional form', *Journal of Money, Credit and Banking*, **28**, 178–99.

Molyneux, P (1993) 'Market structure and profitability in European banking', University College of North Wales, Research Papers in Banking and Finance, RP 93/9.

Molyneux, P (1995) 'Cooperation and rivalry in banking markets', in J Doukas and L Lang (eds) *Research in International Business and Finance*, Greenwich, USA: JAI Press.

Molyneux, P and Forbes, W (1995) 'Market structure and performance in European banking', *Applied Economics*, **27**, 155–9.

Molyneux, P and Thornton, J (1992) 'Determinants of European bank profitability: a note,' *Journal of Banking and Finance*, **16**, 1173–8.

Molyneux, P, Altunbas, Y and Gardener, EPM (1996) *Efficiency in European Banking*, Chichester: John Wiley & Sons.

Molyneux, P. Lloyd-Williams, M and Thornton, J (1994) 'Competitive conditions in European banking', *Journal of Banking and Finance*, **18**, 445–59.

Monteverde, K and Teece, DJ (1982) 'Supplier switching costs and vertical integration in the automobile industry', *Bell Journal of Economics*, **13**, 206–13.

Moore, TG (1986), 'US airline deregulation: its effects on passengers, capital and labour', *Journal of Law and Economics*, **29**, 1–28.

Morgan Stanley (1996) *French Banks: Light at the End of the Tunnel*, European financial briefing, 21 June.

Morgan Stanley Dean Witter (1997) 'European banking: the pace of consolidation accelerates', *European Banking Strategy*, 16 December.

Morgan Stanley Dean Witter (1998a) 'German banks: the emergence of value', *UK and Europe Investment Research*, 20 August.

Morgan Stanley Dean Witter (1998b) 'Consolidation and the Eurobanks: survivability and the "selfish gene" ', *UK and Europe Investment Research*, 13 October.

Morgan Stanley Dean Witter (1998c) 'European banks and restructuring potential: know why you own what you own', *UK and Europe Investment Research*, 20 March.

Morgan Stanley Dean Witter (1998d) 'UK banking commentary: resilient in the downturn', *UK and Europe Investment Research*, 23 July.

Morgan Stanley Dean Witter (1999), 'Moving towards the net,' *European and Financial Services Research*, 20 November.

Morrison, SA and Winston, C (1987), 'Empirical implications of the contestability hypothesis', *Journal of Law and Economics*, **30**, 53–66.

Mueller, DC (1990) 'The persistence of profits in the United States', in DC Mueller (ed.) *The Dynamics of Company Profits: An International Comparison*, Cambridge: Cambridge University Press.

Muldur, U. (1990) 'Jalons pour une analyse microéconomique des restructuration bancaires' in M. Humbert (ed.) *'Investissment International et Dynamique de l'Economie Mondiale*, Paris: Economica.

Muldur, U. (1991) 'Echelle et gamme dans les marchés bancaires nationaux et globaux, *Rapport Fast Monitor*, CEE, Brussels.

Mullineaux, DJ (1975) 'Economies of scale of financial institutions', *Journal of Monetary Economics*, **1**, 233–40.

Mullineaux, DJ (1978) 'Economies of scale and organisational efficiency in banking: a profit–function approach', *Journal of Finance*, **33**, 259–80.

Murphy, NB (1972a) 'A reestimation of the Benston–Bell–Murphy cost functions for a larger sample with greater size and geographic dispersion', *Journal of Financial and Quantitative Analysis*, **7**, 2097–105.

Murphy, NB (1972b) 'Cost of banking activities: interaction between risk and operating cost: a comment', *Journal of Money Credit and Banking*, **4**, 614–15.

Murray, JD and White, RW (1983) 'Economies of scope in multiproduct financial institution: a study of British Columbia credit unions', *Journal of Finance*, **38**, 887–901.

Nathan, A and Neave, EH (1989) 'Competition and contestability in Canada's financial system: empirical results', *Canadian Journal of Economics*, **22**, 576–94.

National Economic Development Council (1983) *Innovation in the UK*, London: National Economic Development Council.

Nelson, RR and Winter, S (1982) *An Evolutionary Theory of Economic Change*, Cambridge: Cambridge University Press.

Neuberger, D (1998) 'Industrial organization of banking: a review', *International Journal of the Economics of Business*, **5**, 97–118.

Neven, DJ (1990) 'Structural adjustment in European retail banking: some views from industrial organisation', in J. Dermine (ed.) *European banking in the 1990s*, Oxford: Blackwell.

Noulas, AG, Ray, SC and Miller, SM (1990) 'Returns to scale and input substitution for large US banks', *Journal of Money, Credit and Banking*, **22**, 94–108.

Odagiri, H and Yamawaki, H (1990) 'The persistence of profits in Japan', in DC Mueller (ed.) *The Dynamics of Company Profits: An International Comparison*, Cambridge: Cambridge University Press.

Orr, D (1974a) 'The determinants of entry: a study of the Canadian manufacturing industries', *Review of Economics and Statistics*, **56**, 58–65.

Orr, D (1974b) 'The economic determinants of entry into Canadian banking: 1963–7', *Canadian Journal of Economics*, **8**, 82–99.

Pacolct, J (1986) 'Analyse d'économie sectorielle du marché des banques d'épargne', in Van Put A. (ed.) *Les Banques d'Épargne Belges*, Tielt: Lannoo.

Pallage, SJ (1991) 'An econometric study of the Belgian banking sector in terms of scale and scope economies', *Cahiers Économiques de Bruxelles*, **130**, 126–143.

Parkan, C (1987) 'Measuring the efficiency of service operations: an application to bank branches' *Engineering Costs and Production Economics*, **12**, 237–42.

Pastor, JT, Lozano, A and Pastor, JM (1997) 'Efficiency of European banking systems: a correction by environmental variables', working paper EC 97–12, Valencia: Istituto Valenciano de Investigaciones Economicas.

Pastor, JM, Pérez, F and Quesada, J (1995) 'Efficiency analysis in banking firms: an international comparison', working paper EC 95–18, Valencia: Istituto Valenciano de Investigaciones Economicas.

Patel, P and Pavitt, K (1987) 'The elements of British technological competitiveness', *National Institute Economic Review*, **122**, 72–83.

Penrose, ET (1959) *The Theory of the Growth of the Firm*, Oxford: Blackwell.

Phillips, A (1976) 'A critique of empirical studies of relations between market structure and profitability', *Journal of Industrial Economics*, **24**, 241–9.

Porter, ME (1980) *Competitive Strategy: Techniques for Analysing Industries and Competitors*, New York: Free Press.

Posner, R (1979) ' The Chicago school of anti-trust analysis', *University of Pennsylvania Law Review*, **127**, 925–48.

Prais, SJ (1976) *The Evolution of Giant Firms in Great Britain*, Cambridge: Cambridge University Press.

Quandt, RE (1966) 'On the size distribution of firms', *American Economic Review*, **56**, 416–32.

Radecki, LJ (1998), 'The expanding geographic reach of retail banking markets', *Federal Reserve Bank of New York Economic Policy Review*, **4**, 15–34.

Rangan, N, Grabowski, R, Aly, H and Pasurka, C (1988) 'The technical efficiency of US banks', *Economic Letters*, **28**, 169–75.

Reder, MW (1982) 'Chicago economics: permanence and change', *Journal of Economic Literature*, **20**, 1–38.

Resti, A (1996) 'Cone-ratio DEA with a set of value-based rules: theoretical framework and empirical findings on Italian banks', research paper 96/16, Bangor: Institute of European Finance, University of Wales.

Resti, A (1997) 'Evaluating the cost-efficiency of the Italian banking system: what can be learned from the joined application of parametric and non-parametric techniques, *Journal of Banking and Finance*, **2**, 221–50.

Revell, J. (1987) 'Mergers and the role of large banks', *Institute of European Finance Research Monographs in Banking and Finance*, **2**, Institute of European Finance, University of North Wales.

Rhoades, SA (1980) 'Entry and competition in banking', *Journal of Banking and Finance*, **4**, 143–50.

Rhoades, SA (1983) 'Concentration of world banking and the role of US banks among the 100 largest, 1956–1980', *Journal of Banking and Finance*, **7**, 427–37.

Rhoades, SA (1985) 'Market share as a source of market power: implications and some evidence', *Journal of Economics and Business*, **37**, 343–63.

Rhoades, SA (1986) 'The operating performance of acquired firms in banking before and after acquisition', staff study no. 149, US Federal Reserve Board.

Rhoades, SA (1997) 'Research on IO topics in banking: an introduction and overview', *Review of Industrial Organisation*, **12**, 1–8.

Rhoades, SA (1998) 'The efficiency effects of bank mergers: an overview of case studies of nine mergers', *Journal of Banking and Finance*, **22**, 273–91.

Rhoades, SA and Yeats, AJ (1974) 'Growth, consolidation and mergers in banking', *Journal of Finance*, **29**, 1397–405.

Robinson, J (1933) *Economics of Imperfect Competition*, London: MacMillan.

Rodriguez, JRO, Alvarez, AA, and Gomez, PP (1993) *Scale and Scope Economies in Banking: a Study of Savings banks in Spain*, Tenerife: Universidad De La Laguna.

Romeo, AA (1975) 'Interindustry and interfirm differences in the rate of diffusion of an invention', *Review of Economics and Statistics*, **57**, 311–19.

Rose, PS (1987) *The Changing Structure of American Banking*, New York: Columbia University Press.

Rose, PS and Scott, WL (1978) 'Risk in commercial banking: evidence from post war failures', *Southern Economic Journal*, **45**, 90–106.

Rossi, CV (1991) *Estimating Scale and Scope Economies in the Thrift Industry*, Federal Reserve Board Research Paper 91–01, June.

Rybczynski, TM (1988) 'Financial systems and industrial restructuring', *National Westminster Bank Quarterly Review*, November, 3–13.

Salomon Brothers (1993) 'Cost management in global banking: the lessons of low cost providers', *International Equity Research*, October.

Salop, SC and Scheffman, D (1983) 'Raising rivals' costs', *American Economic Review*, **73**, 263–71.

Samuals, JM (1965) 'Size and growth of firms', *Review of Economic Studies*, **32**, 105–12.

Samuals, JM and Chesher, AD (1972) 'Growth, survival, and size of companies, 1960–69', in K Cowling (ed.) *Market Structure and Corporate Behaviour*, London: Gray-Mills.

Schaffnit, C, Rosen, D and Paradi, JC (1997) 'Best practice analysis of bank branches: an application of DEA in a large Canadian bank', *European Journal of Operational Research*, **98**, 269–89.

Schankerman, M (1998) 'How valuable is patent protection? Estimates by technology field', *Rand Journal of Economics*, **29**, 77–107.

Schelling, T (1960) *The Strategy of Conflict*. Cambridge: Harvard University Press.

Scherer, FM (1980) *Industrial Market Structure and Economic Performance*, 2nd edn, Boston: Houghton Mifflin Company.

Scherer, FM (1992) 'Schumpeter and plausible capitalism', *Journal of Economic Literature*, **30**, 1416–33.

Scherer, FM (2000) 'Professor Sutton's technology and market structure', *Journal of Industrial Economics*, **48**, 215–23.

Scherer, FM and Ross, D (1990) *Industrial Market Structure and Economic Performance*, 3rd edn, Boston: Houghton Mifflin Company.

Schmalensee, RC (1978) 'Entry deterrence in the ready-to-eat cereal industry', *Bell Journal of Economics*, **9**, 305–27.

Schmalensee, RC (1982) 'The new industrial organisation and the economic analysis of modern markets', in A Hildenbrand (ed.) *Advances in Economic Theory*, Cambridge: Cambridge University Press.

Schmalensee, RC (1985) 'Do markets differ much?', *American Economic Review*, **74**, 341-51.

Schmalensee, RC (1988) 'Industrial economics: an overview', *Economic Journal*, **98**, 643–81.

Schmalensee, RC (1990) 'Emprical studies of rivalrous behaviour', in G Bonnanno and D Brandolini (eds) *Industrial Structure in the New Industrial Economics*, Oxford: Clarendon Press.

Scholtens, B. (2000) 'Competition, growth and performance in the banking industry', Department of Finance working paper, University of Groningen, Netherlands.

Schumpeter, JA (1928) 'The instability of capitalism', *Economic Journal*, **30**, 361–88.

Schumpeter, JA (1943) *Capitalism, Socialism and Democracy*, London: Allen and Unwin.

Schumpeter, JA (1950) *Capitalism, Socialism and Democracy*, 3rd edn, New York: Harper and Row [originally published 1942].

Schwed, F (1965) *Where are the Customers' Yachts?*, New York: Simon and Schuster.

Schweiger I and McGee, JS (1961) 'Chicago banking', *Journal of Business*, **34**, 203–366.

Schweitzer, SA (1972) 'Economies of scale and holding company affiliation in banking', *Southern Economic Journal*, **39**, 258–66.

Sealey, CW and Lindley, JT (1977) 'Inputs, outputs and theory of production and costs at depository financial institutions', *The Journal of Finance*, **34**, 1251–66.

Seiford, LM and Thrall, RM (1990) 'Recent developments in DEA: the mathematical programming approach to frontier analysis' *Journal of Econometrics*, **46**, 7–38.

Shaffer, S (1982) 'A non-structural test for competition in financial markets', in Federal Reserve Bank of Chicago, *Bank Structure and Competition*, conference proceedings.

Shaffer, S (1991) 'Potential merger synergies among large commercial banks', working paper, Federal Reserve Bank of Philadelphia.

Shaffer, S. (1992) 'Can mergers reduce bank costs?', Federal Reserve Bank of Philadelphia working paper 92–17R.

Shaffer, S and David, E (1986) 'Economies of superscale and interstate expansion', Federal Reserve Bank of New York, research paper.

Shepherd, WG (1997) *The Economics of Industrial Organization*. Englewood Cliffs: Prentice-Hall.

Sherman, HD and Gold, F (1985) 'Bank branch operating efficiency: evaluation with data envelopment analysis', *Journal of Banking and Finance*, **9**, 297–315.

Short, BK (1979) 'The relation between commercial bank profit rate and banking concentration in Canada, Western Europe, and Japan', *Journal of Banking and Finance*, **3**, 209–19.

Siegfried, J and Evans, L (1994) 'Empirical studies of entry and exit: a survey of the evidence', *Review of Industrial Organisation*, **9**, 121–55.

Silberman, IH (1967) 'On lognormality as a summary measure of concentration', *American Economic Review*, **57**, 807–31.

Simar, L (1996) 'Aspects of statistical analysis in DEA-type frontier models', *Journal of Productivity Analysis*, **7**, 171–203.

Simar, L and Wilson, P (1995) 'Sensitivity analysis of efficiency scores: how to bootstrap in nonparametric frontier models', discussion paper 9503, Université Catholique de Louvain.

Simon, HA and Bonnini, CP (1958) 'The size distribution of business firms', *American Economic Review*, **48**, 607–17.

Singh, A and Whittington, G (1968) *Growth, Profitability and Valuation*, Cambridge: Cambridge University Press.

Singh, A and Whittington, G (1975) 'The size and growth of firms', *Review of Economic Studies*, **42**, 15–26.

Smirlock, M (1985) 'Evidence of the (non) relationship between concentration and profitability in banking', *Journal of Money Credit and Banking*, **17**, 69–83.

Smirlock, M, Gilligan, TW and Marshall, W (1984) 'Tobin's q and the structure performance relationship', *American Economic Review*, **74**, 1051–60.

Smith, C and Walter, I (1998), 'Global patterns of mergers and acquisitions activity in the financial services industry', in Y. Amihud and G Miller (eds) *Bank Mergers and Acquisitions*, New York: Kluwer.

Solow, R (1956) 'A contribution to the theory of economic growth', *Quarterly Journal of Economics*, **70**, 65–94.

Spence, AM (1977) 'Entry, capacity, investment and oligopolistic pricing', *Bell Journal of Economics*, **8**, 534–44.

Spence, AM (1981) 'The learning curve and competition', *Bell Journal of Economics*, **12**, 49–70.

Spiller, PT (1985) 'On vertical mergers', *Journal of Law, Economics and Organisation*, **1**, 285–312.

Spindt, PA and Tarhan, V (1992) 'Are there synergies in bank mergers?', working paper, Tulane University, New Orleans.

Spong, K, Sullivan, RJ and DeYoung, R (1995) 'What makes a bank efficient? A look at financial characteristic and management and ownership structure' *Financial Industry Perspective*, (Federal Reserve Bank of Kansas City), December, 1–20.

Sraffa, P. (1926) 'The laws of returns under competitive conditions', *Economic Journal*, **36**, 535–50. [Reprinted in KE Boulding and GJ Stigler (eds) *Readings in Price Theory*, London: Allen and Unwin.]

Stigler, GJ (1958) 'The economies of scale', *Journal of Law and Economics*, **1**, 54–71.

Stigler, GJ (1968) *The Organisation of Industry*, Illinois: Irwin.

Strassman, DL (1990), 'Potential competition in the deregulated airlines', *Review of Economics and Statistics*, **72**, 696–702.

Sutton, J (1991) *Sunk Costs and Market Structure*, London: MIT Press.

Sutton, J (1997) 'Gibrat's Legacy', *Journal of Economic Literature*, **35**, 40–59.

Sutton, J (1998) *Technology and Market Structure: Theory and History*, Cambridge: MIT Press.

Sylos-Labini, P (1962) *Oligopoly and Technical Progress*, Cambridge: Harvard University Press [originally published 1957].

Taylor, WM, Thompson, RG, Thrall RM and Dharmapala, PS (1997) 'DEA/AR efficiency and profitability of Mexican banks: a total income model', *European Journal of Operational Research*, **98**, 346–63.

TCA Consulting (1999) Unpublished working paper on technology in banking, London: TCA Consulting.

Temple, J (1999) 'The new growth evidence', *Journal of Economic Literature*, **XXXVII**, 112–56.

Thompson, RG, Brinkmann, EJ, Dharmapala, PS, Gonzalez-Lima, MD and Thrall, RM (1997) 'DEA/AR profit-ratios and sensitivity of 100 largest US commercial banks', *European Journal of Operational Research*, **98**, 213–29.

Thornton, J (1991) 'Concentration in world banking and the role of Japanese banks', *Econmia Aziendale*, **10**, 263–72.

Timme, SG and Yang, WK (1991) 'On the use of a direct measure of efficiency in testing structure–performance relationships', working paper, Georgia State University.

Tirole, J (1988) *Theory of Industrial Organization*, Cambridge: Cambridge University Press.

Tirole, J (1994) 'Western prudential regulation: assessment, and reflections on its applications to Central and Eastern Europe', *Economics of Transition*, **2**, 129–50.

Tschoegl, AE (1982) 'Concentration among international banks: a note', *Journal of Banking and Finance*, **6**, 567–78.

Tschoegl, AE (1983) 'Size, growth and transnationality among the world's largest banks', *Journal of Business*, **56**, 187–201.

Tulkens, H (1993) 'On FHD efficiency analysis: some methodological issues and applications to retail banking, courts and urban transit', *Journal of Productivity Analysi*, **4**, 183–210.

Utton, M (1972) 'Mergers and the growth of large firms', *Bulletin of Oxford University Institute of Economics and Statistics*, **34**, 189–97.

Van Dijcke, P (2000) 'Impact of globalisation on efficiency in the European banking industry: what can we learn from the cost-to-income ratio?', presented at the Société Universitaire Europeenne de Recherches Financiers Colloquim Vienna, Commission 1, 27–29 April.

Vander Vennet, R (1995) 'The effects of mergers and acquisitions on the efficiency and profitability of EC credit institutions', University of Ghent Research Papers, no. 95/07.

Vander Vennet, R (1996) 'The effects of mergers and acquisitions on the efficiency and profitability of EC credit institutions', *Journal of Banking and Finance,* **20**, 1531–58.

Vander Vennet, R (1998) 'Cost and profit dynamics in financial conglomerates and universal banks in Europe', presented at the Société Universitaire Europeenne de Recherches Financiers/CFS colloqium, Frankfurt, 15–17 October.

Vander Vennet, R (1999) 'The law of proportionate effect and OECD bank sectors', working paper, University of Ghent, Belgium.

Vassiloglou, M and Giokas, D (1990) 'A study of the relative efficiency of bank branches: an application of data envelopment analysis', *Journal of Operational Research Society,* **41**, 591–7.

Vives, X (1991a) 'Regulatory reform in European banking', *European Economic Review,* **35**, 505–15.

Vives, X (1991b) 'Banking, competition and European integration', in A Giovanni and C Mayer (eds) *European Financial Integration,* Cambridge: Cambridge University Press.

Vives, X (1998) 'Competition and regulation in European banking', working paper.

Von Stackelberg, H (1934) *The Theory of the Market Economy,* (translated by AT Peacock), London: William Hodge.

Wagner, J (1992) 'Firm size, firm growth and the persistence of chance', *Small Business Economics,* **4**, 125–31.

Walter, I (1999), 'Financial services strategies in the euro-zone', *European Investment Bank Papers,* **4**, 145–68.

Waterson, M (1993) 'Are industrial economists still interested in concentration?', in M Casson and J Creedy (eds) *Industrial Concentration and Economic Inequality,* Aldershot: Edward Elgar.

Weiss, LW (1963) 'Factors in changing concentration', *Review of Economics and Statistics,* **45**, 70–77.

Weiss, LW (1965) 'An evaluation of mergers in six industries', *Review of Economics and Statistics,* **47**, 172–81.

Weiss, LW (1974) 'The concentration–profits relationship and antitrust', in H Goldschmid, HM Mann and JF Weston (eds) *Industrial Concentration: The New Learning,* Boston: Little Brown.

Wheelock, DC and Wilson, PW (1994) *Evaluating the Efficiency of Commercial Banks: Does our View of What Banks do Matter?,* Review, Federal Reserve Bank of St Louis.

White, WR (1998) 'The coming transformation of continental European banking?', Bank of International Settlements working papers, no. 54.

Williams, JM (1996) 'Italy', in *Banking in the EU and Switzerland*, London: Financial Times Publishing.

Williams, JM (1998) 'Italy', in *Banking in the New EU and Switzerland and Norway*, London: Financial Times Publishing.

Williamson, OE (1971), 'The vertical integration of production: market failure considerations', *American Economic Review, Papers and Proceedings*, **61**, 112–23.

Williamson, OE (1975) *Markets and Hierarchies: Analysis and Antitrust Implications*, New York: Free Press.

Williamson, OE (1979) 'Transaction cost economics: governance of non-contractual relations', *Journal of Law and Economics*, **22**, 233–61.

Williamson, OE (1985) *Economic Institutions of Capitalism*, New York: Free Press.

Williamson, OE (1990) *Industrial Organization*, London: Edward Elgar Publishing.

Wilson, JOS and Williams, J (2000) 'The size and growth of banks: evidence from four European countries' *Applied Economics*, **32**, 1101–9.

Yeats, AJ, Irons, ED and Rhoades, SA (1975) 'An analysis of new bank growth', *Journal of Business*, **48**, 199–203.

Yue, P (1992) 'Data envelopment analysis and commercial bank performance: a primer with application to Missouri banks', Federal Reserve Bank of St Louis (USA), working paper 99–17, Financial Institution Center, The Wharton School, University of Pennsylvania.

Yuengert, A (1993) 'The measurement of efficiency in life insurance: estimates of a mixed normal-gamma error model', *Journal of Banking and Finance*, **17**, 483–6.

Zhang, W (1995) 'Wealth effects of US bank takeovers', *Applied Financial Economics*, **5**, 329–36.

Index